The War
We Knew

The War We Knew

RESIDENTS OF RIVERWOODS REMEMBER WORLD WAR II

EDITORS

Katherine Southworth

Jack Taylor

Marilyn Wentworth

Published by RiverWoods
in a first printing of 1500 copies.

RiverWoods
7 RiverWoods Drive
Exeter, NH 03833
(603) 658-1587
WWW.RIVERWOODSRC.ORG

ISBN 978-0-615-44213-6

Photographs and text copyright © 2011 RiverWoods

Design and production by
Stinehour Editions,
South Lunenburg, Vermont.
Printed by Capital Offset,
Concord, New Hampshire.
Binding by New Hampshire Bindery,
Concord, New Hampshire.

Contents

The Pacific Theater / Far East

The European Theater / Africa / Atlantic

Stateside Military Service

Medical Service

Home Front

Living Abroad

Post War Service

Preface

GENERATIONS HAVE NAMES. Baby Boomers, preceded by the Silent Generation, preceded by the Greatest Generation... It is a way to group people by age and category and make them all seem the same. Perhaps this works some of the time, but in reality, we are a country of individuals and our most common trait is that we are all different.

The stories in this book, stories of fighting, history, humor, love, and loss reflect the varied viewpoints and experiences of the group of people that we work with and for on a daily basis. A group of Americans who changed the course of history in WW II and then improved it some more in their post war lives, through business, education, philanthropy, and volunteerism.

As a senior living community, RiverWoods provides an opportunity for these great people to get together, live securely, and continue to contribute to the greater good of society. The authors and organizers and editors of this book represent the truly interesting and intelligent people who make up our community. This work is their work, a sample of the fascinating things they have done and continue to do in their lives. Our residents' individual stories, successes and failures, have shaped their world, our RiverWoods community and the world at large. To live and work among them is an honor. Read on and enjoy.

JUSTINE VOGEL
President and CEO
RiverWoods

Introduction

THIS BOOK IS about the United States in World War II from 1941 to 1945 as provided by the memories of some who took part at home or in the war zones.

The authors, residents at RiverWoods at Exeter, New Hampshire, a continuing care retirement community, wrote their own memories, harking back to those times more than six decades ago. It was the largest and most devastating war in human history resulting in millions of deaths. For America it was two wars, one in the Pacific, the other chiefly in Europe.

In Germany, Adolf Hitler, still stinging from surrender in 1918, gained power with the Nazi party and built a huge army that first annexed Austria, and then in 1939 invaded Poland, which brought the British into the war to defend Poland, and brought Russia into the war to invade Poland from the east. The Nazis soon enveloped most of Western Europe, joined by Mussolini and the Italians.

In 1941, while America was seeking to avoid the war, industry was at a full gallop making materiel for the European war. There were strains between the US and Japan over the Japanese efforts to control the Pacific Basin. This came to a head when Japan attacked Pearl Harbor on December 7, 1941. The attack ended the appeals for peace and the US became, in fact, the realization of what Japanese Admiral Yamamoto wrote in his diary, "We have awakened a sleeping giant." We declared war on Japan and at the same time Germany declared war on us. The Germans attacked Russia in 1941.

The war in the Pacific was fought from the sea, which the Japanese thought they controlled. The way to victory was to be an island-by-island campaign that cost thousands of lives including Japanese soldiers who mostly preferred death to surrender. Here, as in Europe, the technique of modern war was the airplane and in this the Americans overcame the famed Zero and other Japanese planes. Overall, the ship versus ship fighting was not extensive largely because of the dominance of the airplane. It was a time when the battleship was no longer the powerhouse. By the end of the Pacific War in September 1945, the US had 115 aircraft carriers. Airplanes from carriers usually led the invasions until the US occupied islands with airfields. The final blow against Japan was the dropping of the world's first atomic bombs on Hiroshima and Nagasaki.

In Europe the struggle was mostly on land—including the D-Day landing in Normandy on June 6, 1944—but also at sea where German submarines sank many ships. This part of the war included the Atlantic, North Africa (where Americans were first involved), and the Mediterranean. The role of the airplane contributed to the dominance of the Allies: the United States, Britain, Canada, Australia, and others. The war in Europe came to an end on May 8, 1945. Hitler's Nazis, it soon was known, had murdered millions of people, mainly Jews.

This is merely a thumbnail sketch of a terrible war, meant to provide some background to the stories in this volume. Mention should be made of the incredible effort by our home front and industries that supplied and supported two gigantic wars at the same time.

The editors have kept the stories in the voice of each storywriter, who often used the language of the time—the language of their memories.

World War II histories, and there are hundreds of them, record how, in effect, the Americans and their Allies saved the world from tyranny. This book helps recall those critical days and we all are grateful to the writers for their role and their memories.

WILLIAM FERGUSON
World War II Veteran
Resident of RiverWoods

Acknowledgements

The idea for this book germinated from the inspiration of my friends Janet and Rud Colter who shared with me a similar volume from their continuing care community, Wake Robin, in Shelburne, Vermont, and one of the editors of that book, Louise Ransom, who generously served as my counselor at many stages.

It takes a village to make a book, and the execution of the book depended on the contributions of scores of RiverWoods community members, starting, of course, with our seventy-five writers each of whom shared a slice of their life that made this whole so moving and personal. Their stories kept the adrenaline flowing and motivated everyone who read them. My two co-editors, Katherine Southworth and Jack Taylor, whose indefatigable toil amazed and inspired, helped to bring the book to fruition. It could not have been done so timely or thoroughly without them.

With no previous publishing experience, each stage was a new adventure for us as we navigated both the expected plus surprising turns. Several guardian angels appeared at just the right points to guide our way. Thanks especially to Helen Lauenstein, Virginia Widmer and the Ridge Library Committee for their early and ongoing encouragement, and to Barbara Boley, who identified all those who served in the war from our Woods Campus, and to Katherine Southworth who identified the Ridge veterans. We are grateful to Margo Harvey for contributing her many talents to the book by copyediting and who enthusiastically interviewed several residents who could not write their own stories.

The co-editors and I are indebted to Carl Irwin, Allan Prince, Bill Smallwood, Alice Kintner, and Frank Tenny for their careful and perceptive copyediting, and again to Alice Kintner who teamed with Nancy Taylor to aid several Ridge residents who could not write their own stories. Carol Bain, Patience Spiers, and Allan Prince graciously surrendered countless hours to proofreading. We are grateful to William Ferguson for setting the stage with his Introduction to the book and his zealous publicity along with John Wicklein, editor of the Reporter, and to Pat Thomas for sharing her marketing insights from her many years as a bookseller. Thanks also to photographer, Robert Jones, for his interest and skill.

The interest, enthusiasm, and assistance of our Front Desk, Resident Services, and Campus Service personnel were indispensable and greatly appreciated.

Thanks also to Stephen Stinehour, whose quiet patience guided us through the unknown waters of design and book production.

For the unwavering support of the editors' spouses, our deepest appreciation, and many, many thanks to our unpaid consultants: Wendy Wentworth and her husband Richard Joslin for sharing their knowledge of publishing and printing, and to Samuel Southworth, Historian.

Last but not least, we are grateful to Justine Vogel, Cathleen Toomey, and all the staff at RiverWoods, for their resolute and enthusiastic support for this project.

MARILYN WENTWORTH

The Pacific Theater / Far East

Timeline and Map of the war in the Pacific,
with names of some of our authors who were there.

December 7, 1941 Japan bombs Pearl Harbor in Hawaiian Islands
February, 1942 Japanese shell US oil refinery in California
March, 1942 US starts internment of Japanese Americans
April, 1942 Bataan Death March
April 18, 1942 US bombs Tokyo from an aircraft carrier
May, 1942 Japanese fleet defeated in battle of Coral Sea
June, 1942 Decisive US naval victory in the Battle of Midway
June, 1942 Japan invades the Aleutian Islands near Alaska
August, 1942 Campaigns for Guadalcanal and Solomon Islands begin
September, 1942 Japan bombs forests in Oregon
February, 1943 Japanese resistance on Guadalcanal ends
May, 1943 US recaptures Attu, Aleutian Islands; **Dunseith, Remien**
November, 1943 US invasions in the Gilbert Islands
1944 Translation of Japanese messages in India; **Tenny**
January, 1944 US invades Kwajalein in Marshall Islands
June, 1944 US Invades Saipan
July, 1944 US invades Guam
October, 1944 US invades Leyte, Philippines; MacArthur returns; **Bingh**
1945 Bataan survivors reach San Francisco; **Sharpe**
January, 1945 US invades Lingayen Gulf, Luzon, Philippines; **Ferguson,**
    Warlick
February, 1945 US invades Iwo Jima and recaptures Bataan, Philippines;
    Blumenthal, Ferguson, Merritt
April, 1945 US invades Okinawa; **Bingham, March, Merritt, Schaeberl**
July, 1945 USS *Indianapolis* delivers atomic bomb components to Tinian
    Fullerton
August, 1945 From Tinian as a base, US drops atomic bombs on Japan
August 14, 1945 Japan surrenders in principal, relief drops to US POWs
    Japan; **Martin**
September 2, 1945 Japan surrenders
September, 1945
    Wrapping up the surrender of Japanese troops in China; **Tenny**
    Collecting Japanese POWs from Marshall and Gilbert Islands; **Spiers**
1945,1946 Development of government in Japan; **Hood**

LST Adventures

ROBERT CAROL BINGHAM

PRIOR TO WORLD WAR II, I was in ROTC at the University of Florida. I was in the Field Artillery playing nursemaid to horses because the cadets were assured that tanks were "just a passing fancy." Threatened by the draft, I enlisted in the Navy V-12 program the day after Pearl Harbor. This kept me in college enabling me to finish my degree in three years, graduating in 1942.

The Navy sent me to an Officer's Training Program at Columbia University where I became a 90 Day Wonder and was commissioned as a "reserve officer and a gentleman" who serves at the pleasure of the president.

As an ensign I was made Executive Officer on LST 313. Officially LST stood for Landing Ship, Tank, but in Navy jargon this was referred to as a Large Slow Target. I was considered incompetent for the job by the Captain and relieved of that duty. The ill-fated LST 313 sailed without me for the invasion of Sicily where it was blown up with loss of all hands on board.

I was then made "Commodore" in charge of a flotilla of landing craft and sent to Solomon's Island, Maryland, on the Chesapeake Bay where we trained Seabees in underwater demolition.

My next assignment was to Evansville, Indiana, to commission LST 246. I was made First Lieutenant and ship's navigator. In this role I was found competent. LST 246 sailed down the Ohio and Mississippi Rivers to New Orleans and from there through the Panama Canal to Hawaii.

As part of Rear Admiral Turner's V Amphibian Corps in the Central Pacific, the ship made combat landings on Kwajalein and Eniwetok in the Marshall Islands. Typically we ran the ship onto the beach at full speed, opened the bow doors, and lowered the ramp to let the troops drive their vehicles onto the beach, ready for battle. We tried to unload and get off the beach in 20 minutes, making room for the next wave of landing craft. It was during the Marshall Island landings that the US Navy mastered the art of amphibious warfare.

Later we made a practice landing on the southwest side of Hawaii. During the landing my ship went aground and damaged one of our propeller shafts. We had to return to Pearl Harbor at slow speed while the other five ships in the flotilla went ahead and arrived at Pearl Harbor before us. When we arrived the next morning we could see a column of fire and smoke and saw our flotilla burning up at the pier. One ship left the pier, on fire, and sailed by us to get out to sea. We were the lucky ones. Four ships were lost with about 200 men. The cause of the fire was never determined.

In June and July of 1944, LST 246 made combat landings on Saipan and Tinian, and was returned once again to the Southwest Pacific Theater for transport duty along the shore of New Guinea. In September the ship was attached to Vice Admiral Wilkinson's III Amphibious Force for the invasion of Peliliu. This battle is said to have cost almost as many American lives as the assault on Omaha Beach in Normandy.

Next was participation in the landings at Leyte Gulf and in January 1945 LST 246 was part of the convoy headed for Lingayen Gulf. The convoy was plagued by Japanese kamikaze planes. After Lingayen Gulf was secured I stood on deck and watched as several small landing craft came in and unloaded numerous cameramen and newsmen on shore. They scurried around and set up equipment while the landing craft backed off the beach. When all was ready, the landing craft once again came in and touched the beach and then deliberately backed off a few feet so that General MacArthur could wade ashore through the surf for his historic "I have returned" photo. We Navy men were not so impressed, but the event was of tremendous political importance among the Philippine people.

After the Philippine invasion LST 246 joined the combat landings on Okinawa. That battle started on April 1, 1945, and was waged for two months, being the most costly naval campaign of the war. My crew watched kamikaze attacks on larger ships all around us, but we remained unharmed. The Japanese did not think that LSTs were worth their trouble, where actually the LSTs were the backbone of the war. A cruiser near us took a suicide attack, which struck the sick bay and killed all the medical personnel on board. We immediately dispatched our doctor and corpsmen to the cruiser. This prevented us from doing casualty evacuations from the shore. Instead we picked up empty ammunition cans from the bombardment ships, and acted as a filling station for other small craft.

The ship was damaged on a reef at Okinawa and had to return to San Francisco for repairs. I flew ahead with the repair orders, from Hawaii to San Francisco on the famous flying boat, the *China Clipper*.

With the end of the war on August 14, 1945, LST 246 was decommissioned and loaned to the Japanese to repatriate Japanese stranded on Pacific Islands.

I served one more year at the Long Beach Separation Center in California, explaining the benefits of the GI Bill to servicemen and signing their discharge papers. I married, was discharged as a Lieutenant, and went on to pursue further education at University of California, Berkeley.

Bob was born in Pensacola, Florida. He earned a BA Degree in Sociology and Economics at the University of Florida and a MA Degree in Anthropology and Economics at the University of California, Berkeley. His professional career was in city planning.

Two Tales From The South Pacific

Mac Blumenthal

Competition for Macy's

EARLY IN THE 1940´S I was attached to the cruise ship *President Polk*. She was a new world-class cruise ship of the American President Lines, called back from the Near East at the beginning of the war and leased to the Navy as a transport.

We were ordered to the South Pacific. No one knew where, as we were given only a code number, not the name, but it turned out to be Noumea, New Caledonia. And we were carrying the first contingent of US Navy nurses to that area. This was all just at Christmas time. The night before we left San Francisco, all the nurses, together with a few of the ship's officers, were assembled around the piano in the ship's lounge, and everyone was singing—and wondering where we were going and what lay in wait for us. The favorite song was *I'll be Home for Christmas*; we promptly changed the words to "I'll be home for Christmas, just you wait and see. I'll be home for Christmas, in 1983!"

Needless to tell, the cruise to Noumea was most pleasant as we traveled at high speed with the cruiser USS *St. Louis* as escort. We arrived in the late evening of New Year's Eve. As we entered the harbor, which was full of Navy vessels of all sizes, the night lit up as if by magic, with hundreds of lights. It seemed as if every ship there was contacting our ship with such messages as "Admiral So-and-so would like six nurses for dinner", "Captain I-don't-know requests four nurses for dinner", "Captain Unknown invites four nurses for dinner", etc. Somehow the word had gotten around that we had nurses aboard, and the result was a display that could have put Macy's to shame.

Fun and Games During the War

The USS *Agenor* was not a pretty ship. As a matter of fact, she was ugly. She was an LST converted to being a repair ship, with a 30-ton crane attached to the port side and shops installed below deck that could repair almost anything. In addition she carried a crew of about 300 men and officers, most of whom were mustangs, meaning that they had come up through the ranks. They were the savviest men I ever met when it came to naval repairs of any kind.

This ship was stationed for about six months in one of the Solomon Islands, off Guadalcanal. There was a sort of river up the island, well hidden in the vegetation, where we took anchorage. From there we serviced small landing craft and PTs that needed repairs.

Recreation was very limited, mostly movies that were shown once or twice a week depending on where and when we could borrow them. So it remained for us to find our own entertainment. We heard that there were alligators up the river, so a few of the officers organized hunting parties. We could take a big rubber lifeboat with three officers paddling on each side, one in the bow with a powerful searchlight and another with a line-throwing gun equipped with a harpoon. We would attach this boat to the ship's motor launch which would tow us up the river to a point where they could tie up and wait for us. I forgot to say that this all took place at night, after the movies were over.

We would paddle up the river a way and watch the water. Soon we would see two red dots, the eyes of an alligator. We would shine the searchlight at the eyes to hypnotize the alligator and paddle rapidly toward it. When we were just about on him, the officer with the gun would fire at it, hoping to score a hit. But we never did get one; evidently the water deflected the harpoon each time. Maybe it was a good thing for us. If we had ever wounded one of those beasts, his thrashing around could have killed us all. So we would paddle back to our launch and get ferried back to our little ship for a good night's sleep. It was fun, and something to do.

Later, we were offshore at the landings on Iwo Jima, and I remember watching an underwater torpedo pass under our keel, without hitting us.

Mac was born in Houston, Texas. He earned a BA Degree at the University of Texas and worked in the textile industry. He served in the US Navy (1941-1945) in both the Atlantic and South Pacific theaters of the war. Mac died in 2010.

"We Need You Here"

HERMAN DUNSEITH

ENLISTED IN Civil Pilot Training ... completed twenty hours of solo flying ... one black mark for getting lost in a snow cloud and losing visual contact with the ground ... expected to enter Air Corps flying program but cadet program was full ... ordered to Biloxi, Mississippi, for basic training ... tried to get into G-2, intelligence, but was told, "No, we need you here."

Transfer to headquarters was welcome, for this is where the action is. Waited for a good assignment and it happened ... Photo School in Denver ... wonderful after southern heat and humidity ... captain asked me to stay, "We need you here."

After less than two weeks, a choice between staying at Photo School or assignment to Officers' Candidate School ... that I chose ... my wife urged me ... and I became a lieutenant in three months.

Cooler Climate

Assignment as commissioned officer ... but stayed in San Antonio, Texas, then moved to Tennessee ... assigned to move men and equipment—the sergeants did all the work ... but I requested a transfer to a cooler climate ... even though the major said, "We need you here" ... stuck by my conviction that I needed a cooler climate and next day...

Ordered to report to Port of Debarkation destination Adak, part of the Aleutian Chain off Alaska ... flew to Seattle while my wife drove to Michigan to stay with family ... on a Liberty ship I took a lower bunk on the fan tail and in heavy weather the propeller would be out of the water and the ship would shake like a dog ...

the fumes were so bad that everyone was seasick. I reflected on my status—true, I had requested a cooler climate.

The trip to Adak was horrible ... high winds and snow, waves fifty feet high ... I was so sick they put me in the infirmary. I reflected on my status—true, I had requested a cooler climate ... after fourteen days finally docked at Adak and met by captain who had assignments. "Lieutenant," he said to me, "You are the Air Transport officer and will coordinate all air traffic out to Amchitka and Attu and back to Alaska."

I didn't train to be a transport officer ... thank heavens for sergeants. I inherited a very good one ... he trained me very well ... in loading cargo planes you load so the plane is balanced ... he trained his crew as well. At Adak, very long summer days and in the winter long nights. And there was snow and more snow and winds.

There was a memorable night when I was Officer of the Day. The snow had started and planes had been tied down. Suddenly, a bright, red and white light was reflected in the snow. The enlisted men's dining hall was ablaze ... an inferno. After going out to the scene, I returned to my office and decided to call the base commander to report the events of the night. It was 3 a.m. The base commander shouted, "Damn it, Lieutenant. Are we being invaded by the Japanese?" I told him "No sir," and started to explain. "Write up a report and have it available in the morning. You know what time it is?" So I promised myself never to inform him again, even if a tsunami was about to carry us out to sea!

The power failure, winds rattling buildings and roofs of Quonset huts, mess hall fire, it was a rough scene. As soon as I could I let my replacement take over. It was a night to remember.

The war was over and we were counting points to determine our eligibility for release from the military. When I applied, the captain said, "Do you really want to go? We need you here." Where had I heard that before? But I was on the first plane to Alaska, then Seattle, and then home after serving for more than four years. I was on my way home to Marjorie.

Born in Toledo, Ohio, Herman earned BS and MS Degrees at the University of Toledo and a PhD in Public School Administration at Cornell University. Most of his career was spent as Superintendent of Schools in Michigan and Massachusetts. In 1969 he held the Lewis Chair in Education at Harvard and in 1968 was named Outstanding Superintendent in Massachusetts.

Near Misses

Bill Ferguson

THE DESTROYER I was on during the Big War was a carry-over from World War I, called a four piper for its four stacks, which were cut down to three in 1940. It was the USS *Hamilton*, a Destroyer Minesweeper (DMS), 314 feet long, 31-foot beam. It was a fast and sleek ship with a tight turning circle.

I joined the ship as a raw ensign just after the big battle of Leyte Gulf, the Philippines, and my first battle was in the invasion of Lingayen Gulf, in northern Philippines. Our job was to go in close to shore and sweep mines so the cruisers and battle-wagons could come in to bombard. We fought off kamikaze attacks and escorted ships like Landing Ship, Tanks (LST), on the way south.

That was January 1945 but the big test was ahead—Iwo Jima, one of the bloodiest battles of the war on land and sea. My ship began sweeping on February 17, and that night we were on night retirement but still at General Quarters. As assistant gunnery officer, my station was what we called the flying bridge because it was on top of the pilothouse (the bridge). About midnight I happened to look to starboard and there was a Japanese bomber bearing down on us, only about a hundred feet above us. I saw a torpedo drop from the plane, sure to hit us. But the pilot released the torpedo too late. The torpedo went probably twenty feet or more before adjusting to its intended depth—two fathoms (twelve feet) which probably would have sunk us. But it went into the water and right under us.

Near-miss two came on the following day when a swarm of kamikazes showed up. One smashed into the USS *Long* and sank her. One of the officers was also named Bill Ferguson and he was killed.

Later it was our turn and we were firing at a plane diving toward us. The Jap plane was so close I could see the pilot. Suddenly he was hit by our 20 mm gun. His head snapped back and the plane dove into the water about fifty feet from us. Saved again.

The reason to mention the death of my friend Bill Ferguson is that when I got home on leave I met the postman in the driveway. He couldn't believe I was alive. He handed me a packet of my wife's letters marked "Deceased"—a Navy error.

Of the ten DMS in my task force, only two survived Iwo Jima intact—the USS *Hamilton* and the USS *Southard* were unscathed. Two others were sunk and six were damaged by kamikaze hits. On the USS *Southard* was a man I later met: Herman Wouk, who wrote *The Caine Mutiny.*

Later the Navy informed me that my ship, the USS *Hamilton*, was the last of that class and was broken up for scrap. The metal went to Ford, and now and then I'd hear a rattle in my Ford pickup truck and imagined it was coming from a part of the long-gone USS *Hamilton.*

Bill was born in Fall River, Massachusetts, and earned a BA Degree in 1941 at Middlebury College in Vermont and married Helen Gilman Rotch the same year. He served in the US Navy from 1943-1946. Bill owned an insurance agency in New Hampshire and wrote a column for a Milford newspaper for fifty years.

With The Seabees

JOHN H. FULLERTON

IN 1941 YALE accepted me as a freshman to start in September. I was eighteen. Three months later the Japanese bombed Pearl Harbor and the War was on.

Yale, like many colleges, accelerated study by operating year round, no summers off. In early 1943 my draft board granted me a six-month deferment from service since I was by then a sophomore studying engineering. Before my deferment ran out the US Navy announced they would open a V-12 unit at Yale, starting in July 1943, the middle of my junior year. I joined the Navy V-12. We wore thirteen-button sailor suits. In June 1944 Yale granted me a BE degree with a major in Civil Engineering.

The Navy then sent me to an eight-week Midshipman School run by the Navy Civil Engineer Corps at its base at Davisville, Rhode Island. On September 4, 1944, I was commissioned an ensign in the Civil Engineer Corps (CEC), assigned to the Seabees, acronym for CBs (Construction Battalions). I was put in Construction Battalion Detachment 1080, then being formed, along with Navy CEC Lt. Norman Klitz and two hundred enlisted men. We were told to mark our gear with the designation LIRP, which the enlisted men guessed stood for Luzon Island, Republic of the Philippines. Lt. Klitz and I knew better since we had been given secret codebooks showing that LIRP stood for the island of Tinian in the Mariana Islands of the Pacific.

Fearing our being shipped out I married my childhood sweetheart, Pat Dennen, a Deaconess Hospital nurse, on January 13, 1944, on a weekend pass. During our weekend honeymoon a telegram told me to change the weekend pass to a ten-day embarkation leave. Pat presented the colors (American flag) to CBD1080 at a formal commissioning ceremony. Then we were off by troop train to California in an old Pullman sleeper car for the two officers and the chief petty officers and "40 and 8" boxcars for the enlisted men, (40 and 8 boxcars had been designed for either 40 men or 8 horses). It took five days. Three officers were added to our unit, Lt. Spizer to be Commanding Officer and two Chief Warrant Officer Carpenters, Johnson and Barnaby.

In early February, with other forces, we went out under the Golden Gate Bridge at San Francisco on the Navy troop transport USS *Calussa* on its first voyage. It went alone to Pearl Harbor, in convoy to Eniwetok Atoll, and in a small convoy to Tinian. Tinian had been "secured" from the Japanese a few months earlier. Ten miles long and five miles wide, it was mostly plateau except for mountains in the south end into which a few Japs had retreated and had hidden out. It was in the temperate zone with a wind rose about 90% northeast (winds primarily from the northeast) at about ten miles per hour, ideal for an air base for bombers to bomb the Japanese home islands. The island had been largely devoted to sugar cane, which was carried by narrow gauge railroad to a single factory that made Japanese whiskey. It had one town at Tinian Harbor.

Our detachment gear was there ahead of us: trucks, two jeeps, two motorcycles, Quonset huts (erected by CB battalions before us), two cranes, galley equipment, etc. The first night we set up a perimeter patrol, as we had been taught in the States. There was much gunfire that night, and in the morning two cows were found at our perimeter riddled with bullets. Island Command, a Marine general, ordered our firearms put in storage, a carbine from each enlisted man and a .45 caliber pistol from each officer.

Our job as Detachment 1080 was to set up and run an Advanced Base Construction Depot (ABCD) to receive construction supplies, replacement equipment, and spare parts for the ten Seabee Battalions of one thousand men each, that had preceded us onto Tinian. Lt. Spizer was Commanding Officer, Lt. Klitz was Executive Officer, and Warrant Officer Barnaby ran the 11-hour, 100-man night shift, Warrant Officer Johnson ran the 11-hour, 100-man day shift, all seven days of the week. As Ens. Fullerton, my job was everything else: Receiving, Inventory, Shipping, Commissary, and Legal.

Lt. Spizer told me my first assignment was to confirm that we had all the Detachment gear that had been shipped to the island ahead of us. I found it all except one of two large-wheeled fire pumps designed to protect our Depot. I found that at Tinian Harbor being used by the 50th Seabees, a waterfront battalion, to pump out a cofferdam that was part of the building of six Liberty ship piers. When I reported to Lt. Spizer that I had found everything, but the Commanding Officer of the 50th said I could not have the fire pump, Lt. Spizer said, "I'm going to give you an Unsatisfactory Fitness Report." I responded, "Sorry, you can't give an ensign an Unsatisfactory Fitness Report during his first year as an ensign." I guess the Navy felt it took a year for an ensign to become proficient.

Island Command discovered we were one of two outfits on the island that had an ice-cream-making machine. Thereafter we were allowed to use it for one six-hour period a week and other outfits came on schedule with their powdered ice cream mix to make their batch.

All food on the island was handled by an Army Commissary Battalion, sometimes pre-packaged individual K Rations, more often canned C Rations of hash and vegetables, and occasionally beef from Australia. Regularly I sent a truck to pick up our allotment. The truck driver took a loading crew, who were expected to purloin extra when the Army checker wasn't looking.

Being a supply depot we had goods for barter or gift. The adjoining Marine Antiaircraft Unit asked for plywood to make a floor for their tent. A week later they returned it saying their marine captain had ordered them to return it, fearing they would become soft.

After I left the States my wife Pat joined the Army Nurse Corps as a Second Lieutenant. She was sent aboard a white-painted, well-lighted Hospital Ship from New York, through the Panama Canal, to Hawaii, and then to Manila in the Philippines. Her group staffed a hospital at Lingayen Gulf designed to receive casualties from the expected forthcoming invasion of the Japanese home islands. Mail between us took a month because it all went back to the States where it was packaged to overseas destinations.

In July we were told to mark our gear. We learned from our codebooks that we were scheduled to load onto an LST for invasion of the Japanese home islands. Our Detachment was to be augmented by an additional 200 men then enroute between the US and Tinian.

One day in late July, or early August, the cruiser USS *Indianapolis,* anchored outside Tinian Harbor. The beach was cleared of people and Navy lighters carried large boxes to waiting trucks that whisked the boxes off to North Field.

On August 6th the first atomic bomb was dropped on Japan at Hiroshima, having been carried from Tinian on the B-29, *Enola Gay.* The plane was flown by a special crew that had brought it from the States. Tinian Island Command thought there might be a Japanese suicide bomber attack on the island and ordered the reissue of our firearms. Soon the second atomic bomb was flown from Tinian and dropped on Japan. Japan then surrendered. It was August 14, 1945.

Born in Boston, Massachusetts, John earned a BE Degree, Magna Cum Laude, in Civil Engineering at Yale University and did graduate study at MIT. He spent forty years as a professional engineer in engineering firms in the Boston area.

The Philippines

BART HARVEY

ON AUGUST 15, 1945, as the news of the Japanese surrender on the deck of the USS *Missouri* came over the radio, I was packing my gear preparatory to shipping out to the Philippines. I had been through officer candidate school, a few weeks of medical administrative training, and three months of training on the maintenance of medical equipment. These, combined with interminable months of waiting for orders, had kept me in the States throughout the war. Now finally I was going to the Philippines.

It was a long, uneventful train ride to San Francisco followed by a few days in a staging area, and then a boatload of us started out on a Liberty ship. We hit stormy seas right away, the lightly loaded ship pitching wildly. Many of the men, who were in five-high bunks in the hold, with all their gear in the narrow aisles, were seasick. Fortunately, the boat developed engine trouble, and we limped back to San Francisco and the staging area.

The next try was on a Matson Line cruise ship, 4,000 of us on a boat designed for 400 passengers. I was lucky and bunked with five other lieutenants in a stateroom for two. Lord knows where the men slept, but the chow line ran pretty continuously 24/7 to give us all two meals a day. The trip took about ten uneventful days. Finally, we coasted down past the jungle-clad hills of northern Luzon, rounded Bataan, and edged our way into Manila harbor avoiding sunken wrecks. We couldn't reach a dock and had to go ashore in landing craft.

Next came a ride in a narrow-gage train of small open cars with waist-high walls (apparently for carrying sugar cane to the mill) through pleasant countryside of rice paddies and bamboo villages to a reception camp of tents and canvas cots. During several days there waiting for orders, we cased the nearby village, were amazed at the ferocity of a cock fight and the loud vehemence of the betting and cheering them on by the village men. Some of the GIs found a local girl who was willing to lie on her back on the bamboo floor of her hut for their pleasure, but I was glad to have some pocket books with me.

Finally, orders came through consigning me to Batangas, a small port city on the southern coast of Luzon. The trip down there skirted Manila and was mostly through forested country. The narrow, two-lane road had been paved before the war but not maintained. It was full of deep, wide potholes that had to be carefully negotiated.

It was a small camp with a few officers and several hundred Japanese POWs and enough American soldiers to guard them. The officers were housed in tents on platforms with springy split bamboo floors—really very pleasant in that climate.

My first contact with the Japs was walking across the small lawn in front of company headquarters through a group of them on their haunches, trimming the grass with machetes. I looked at them, swallowing hard; they looked at me, and we each went on about our business. Soon I got used to being near Jap work gangs, loading trucks or moving heavy crates with smoothly coordinated teamwork, in marked contrast to the disjointed efforts of the Filipino laborers we also had.

The plan had been for the Philippines to be a major staging area for the invasion of Japan. The army units in Europe had packed up their equipment and sent it east through the Suez canal, with the men expecting to pick it up in the Philippines after a home leave in the US. After the Japanese surrender, the men stayed home, but the equipment kept coming, boatload after boatload. Most of it went to Manila, but because the harbor there was clogged with sunken ships, at least one shipload came to Batangas.

My job as a Medical Administrative Officer, with the help of four

GIs and some Filipino laborers, was to sort through everything that came from medical units, and repack for storage in weather-proof wrapping the clean sheets and towels, etc. (not including the occasional German radio, pistol, or bayonet in them). We set up a sorting line on roller tracks for the miscellaneous stuff, much of which was trashed. We also set a couple of Filipino carpenters to make boxes out of the only lumber we had, regular one-inch boards, to replace those damaged in shipment. These they cut to length sitting on the floor, holding the boards with their feet.

The major equipment went into another big tent where I had something of a shop. There the problem was to identify what we had, was it all there, and did it work. Since an X-ray machine for a base hospital would be shipped in a dozen or more crates which did not arrive together and were not well labeled, this posed many difficulties.

Come Christmas Eve, the men put on a party. A couple of tins of medical alcohol had turned up among the medical supplies. The mess sergeant contributed a case or so of fruit juice, and a large trash can served for punch bowl. Before long half the company were under the table, and the rest were off finding solace in town. I was on duty that night, but there was a cot by the sign-out book in the company headquarters. Thankfully, the men did not disturb me when they signed back in.

Shortly, I was reassigned to the main medical depot in Quezon City, a suburb of Manila. This was a much bigger establishment, but still temporary. Our sleeping tents had wooden floors and steel cots with mattresses. Medical equipment was assigned a huge tent with my shop in one corner of it. Again I was tasked with sorting and checking out X-ray machines, cardiology machines, sterilizers, etc., as they poured in from the hundreds of units that had expected to reform here in preparation for the invasion of Japan. Since much of the medical equipment was of civilian design from different companies, reassembling the big complex multi-crate machines was tricky when we had several on the floor, each missing at least one crate. Fortunately, another officer was responsible for the huge flow of sheets, towels, medicines, bandages, etc., in another tent.

Weekends, we would borrow a jeep and head into town. Manila was amazing. MacArthur had fought his way back into town with artillery, and the Japs had dynamited everything they could as they retreated. There had been a number of big stone banks and hotels that were now leaning crazily or partly demolished. No downtown stores were open, but here and there an entrepreneur had set up a board in the shelter of a wreck to peddle beautifully embroidered blouses of parachute cloth. The first big buildings to be functional were movie houses, and then hotels. The streets were jammed with "taxis" which were jeeps or weapons carriers with small truck bodies with benches built on the back by back-street mechanics. Many of the passengers were clerks coming out of the US colonial school system to serve in US army offices.

One weekend we drove out into the countryside to a big park outside the city. The road led up a rise to a circle where there was a view. A truck, its open body full of standing holiday celebrants, had hit the circle too fast and flipped over on its back. When we got there its four wheels in the air were still turning, the pavement was full of screaming Filipinos, and one poor devil had been caught with the edge of the truck body across his chest and the contents of the gas tank pouring down into his face. We raised the truck with the jack from the jeep enough to get him out and gave him a shot of morphine from our military first aid kit, but couldn't do much for him. It must have been the intervention of angels that kept that gasoline from catching fire. A passing truck had agreed to take the worst injured to the hospital. When we heard the siren of an ambulance climbing the hill, we resumed our excursion.

Bart returned from the Philippines to enroll at Harvard, where he earned a Master's in International Relations and a Master of Public Administration. Before completing his doctoral dissertation, he was tempted by a job offer with the Marshall Plan in Paris. With his wife Margo and four kids in tow, he served with the Economic Recovery Program there, in The Hague, and in Rome. After an interval in

Washington, he was posted to Ankara, Turkey, and finally, as Director of the AID mission to Kabul, Afghanistan. Ensuing years were spent working with non-government agencies for economic development in the Third World. In retirement, Bart took up painting. Bart died in 2010.

Influential Experiences

HENRY HOOD, MD

ON PEARL HARBOR DAY in 1941, I was enrolled in my third year in the Cornell University School of Hotel Administration, majoring in accounting. Reserve Officers Training Corps (ROTC) was a required course during the first two years for all male Cornell students. I was among eighty-five students who enrolled in the elective course in ROTC for the third and fourth years. It permitted us to complete four years and graduate with a degree in June 1943. We were then sent to the Army's Field Artillery Officers Candidate School in Fort Sill, Oklahoma, and commissioned as second lieutenants in September.

I was selected for liaison pilot training. I received basic flight training in Pittsburgh, Kansas, and returned to Fort Sill to complete training. Liaison pilots in the Field Artillery flew light aircraft at low altitudes to direct artillery fire from the air. They were more effective than forward observers crawling to elevations overlooking the battlefield.

In May 1945 my battalion arrived in Leyte, in the Philippines, to prepare for the invasion of Japan. The war ended in August after the two atomic bombs were dropped on Japan. We were moved from the jungle where we were training to tented camps on the beaches. Over the next few months, personnel were sorted for either return to the United States for discharge, or reassignment in the Pacific theater for the business of concluding the war, including the occupation of Japan. It was not a busy time for us.

I shared a tent with our battalion surgeon, a young graduate of Johns Hopkins Medical College, whose specialty was pediatrics!

He was not resigned to simply taking sick call for a young, robust group of soldiers, and found ways to be busy as a physician. After learning I had abandoned a desire to be a physician because the cost of a medical education was beyond my means, he invited me to accompany him in his work.

He visited all physicians attached to the adjacent military units and offered to care for the soldiers in their units. He converted a small thatched open-air cottage on the beach into an infirmary. There he did a muscle biopsy on a soldier with generalized pains that had eluded diagnosis or any treatment he had sought in the past. The biopsy proved that he had trichinosis; a diagnosis that could have remained elusive.

He discovered a native hospital in the jungle at the foot of the mountains. It was one room on stilts with a slatted floor. It was staffed by a nurse trained at Santo Tomas in Manila, who proved to be a remarkably competent clinician and possessed the personal qualities attributed to Mother Teresa! During the invasion of Leyte as General Douglas MacArthur executed his promise to return, the army had carved out a small airstrip near the little hospital. Twice a week I flew our doctor there and he conducted pediatric clinics where he performed miracles on Filipino children with acute and often long-neglected illnesses.

In December 1945, the doctor was returned to the United States and separated from the service. I was assigned to the occupation of Japan. By then he knew I had decided to become a physician. He said that when I returned to the United States and was separated from the service, he would introduce me to the dean of the Johns Hopkins Medical College.

I arrived in Yokohama, Japan, on Christmas Eve in 1945, enroute to my assignment to the 97th Division Field Artillery Headquarters stationed in Nagano, in the Japanese Alps. During the occupation, liaison pilots provided courier services and flew personnel between army installations including the headquarters in Tokyo or Yokohama.

Recalling my experiences in Japan during the occupation, I am most impressed by the peacefulness of it, especially as compared to the occupation of Iraq. General Douglas MacArthur was in command of it, and received much well-deserved credit. It was said that his military career before the war permitted him to gain a profound understanding of the native cultures of the Orient. It was deemed important that the Japanese royal family was preserved. There was a full page photo widely published early in the occupation of General MacArthur standing with Emperor Hirohito in the Imperial Palace during an obviously congenial meeting. Tokyo and Yokohama had been severely damaged by American bombing. There was absolutely no damage to the Imperial compound or residence. The Japanese people were in awe of General MacArthur. Silent crowds gathered every morning and evening across the street from his headquarters in the Dai Ichi building just to watch him arrive and later depart, after which they silently just melted away.

The occupation forces were never in situations that would provoke fear. The Japanese people were friendly and many spoke English. The children clustered around us chattering and asking for candy or gum. We traveled publicly, often in pairs or small groups, but even alone, including on their always crowded trains. We skied at their mountain resorts, golfed on their courses, were invited to their homes.

In the spring of 1946, we received calls for volunteers from MacArthur's headquarters in Tokyo to monitor a national election in Japan. We were told that a Japanese constitution had been written, I believe it was in 1926, which included women's suffrage. It called for free elections, but one had never been held. The first was scheduled for the spring of 1946.

Volunteers were recruited throughout the occupation forces to monitor the election in their region. We were given a jeep, a driver, and an interpreter and advised we had carte blanche to visit Japanese people anywhere; police, municipal officers, shop keepers, mill workers, citizens wherever we might meet them. The citizens greeted us warmly everywhere, and with their native hospitality. I never drank so much tea! In a silk mill, I asked a woman working at a machine if she was going to vote. She nodded shyly and after I asked whom she would vote for, she replied. The interpreter laughed and said, "She said she doesn't have to tell you, or anyone! Not even her husband!" The election went uneventfully, as have free elections since.

In August 1947 I returned to the United States, was discharged from the army at Fort Dix, New Jersey, and returned to my home in Laconia, New Hampshire.

My experience in the military influenced the rest of my life. The association I had, and the experiences I shared with the surgeon in my field artillery battalion in Leyte, inspired me to abandon a career in hotel management and pursue my earlier ambition to be a physician. The veterans' education benefit, the GI Bill, made my medical education affordable.

Epilogue

Henry went to Cornell University in Ithaca, New York, and joined the flood of returning veterans wedging themselves into the available space in colleges and universities. He enrolled in the College of Liberal Arts to obtain the prerequisite courses for Medical School, later entering Cornell Medical College.

During WW II, the applicant pool for medical colleges shrank, coincident with the realization that there was a genuine shortage of physicians in this country. Cornell expanded the pool by accepting applications from people who had demonstrated that they were educable, even in disciplines that appeared unrelated to medicine. Eventually they welcomed the diversity it added to the student body. Our class of eighty-five students included an army nurse, a pharmacist, a young man who had been groomed to be a concert violinist, and several engineers.

Dr. Hood received an MD from Cornell Medical College and trained in surgery and neurosurgery at New York Hospital Cornell Medical Center. He had a twenty-seven year career as a neurosurgeon that overlapped by ten years a seventeen year career as president and CEO of a Pennsylvania integrated health care system, the Geisinger Health System.

US Naval Academy To War

ED KINTNER

ON DECEMBER 7, 1941, Pearl Harbor Day, I was studying for final exams at the US Naval Academy at Annapolis. Our class, the class of 1942, was originally scheduled to graduate in June of 1942, but in the summer and fall of 1941 it was abundantly clear to our government that the country would soon be at war. The date of our graduation was bumped up to December 19, 1941, when Christmas leave would begin.

Several weeks before that, I had my orders to report after graduation to the destroyer *Shaw*. It was one of the ships blown up at Pearl Harbor, and so I was reassigned to another ship, the *Trenton*, an old four-pipe cruiser of World War I vintage.

Thus it was that a few days after New Years of 1942, I found myself with two of my classmates as a passenger on a Grace Line ship assigned to accompany three battleships being transferred from the Atlantic to the Pacific Ocean. The US Pacific fleet had been decimated at Pearl Harbor, and those battleships were badly needed in the Pacific.

Just out of Norfolk we three newly minted ensigns were sitting in the ship's lounge when the ship captain, also a newly commissioned active duty officer, accosted us. "Where did you go to school?" he asked me. "The US Naval Academy," I replied. "You've got the watch," he said.

It must have been sometime after midnight, dark, and raining cats and dogs. A real Hatteras winter storm was blowing! Standing on the wing of the bridge, I could hardly see the very dim stern light of the last battleship. Holding up my binoculars, the rain pouring down the sleeves of my brand new uniform, I was most anxious not to run into any of those battleships. A collision at sea on the first watch of a naval career was nothing I wanted. When daylight finally arrived, those battleships were "hull down on the horizon" about twenty miles in front of us.

From Panama my ship, the *Trenton,* was assigned escort duty for US troop and supply ships headed for Australia. On one of the ships was a contingent of thirty or forty nurses who liked to sun themselves on the sundeck of their ship. There was great competition for the single pair of binoculars available to off duty personnel to watch them. It gave our company much pleasure to see those young women a mile or so away through a pair of binoculars.

Bora Bora is an island in the Pacific about 100 miles from Tahiti in French Polynesia. It is known as the epitome of a romantic South Sea Island. About two miles long and one mile wide, it is surrounded by a coral reef enclosing a beautiful peaceful lagoon. The island is covered with palms and other green trees, and towering over it is an extinct volcanic mountain, topped with a wispy vapor-cloud flag.

It had been many years since a US ship had put in at the island. Our ship spent several weeks around Bora Bora to protect it from being overtaken by the Japanese. Though the natives spoke no English, they were very friendly and hospitable. One day a shipmate and I decided to climb the mountain. We were barely on our way when a native boy offered to guide us. As we were descending, he deftly wove a basket of palm leaves and filled it with native fruits for us to take to our ship.

On the island was a middle-aged woman who sold grass skirts for a dollar or a bar of Ivory soap. In short order, however, she raised the price to five dollars. I always thought she must have been the model for Bloody Mary in the musical *South Pacific.* The ship's dentist gave his services to the natives. They had terrible teeth, and many of the young women had already lost theirs.

On the last night of our stay the natives and ship's company decided to have a party. The natives brought tropical fruits and other native delicacies, and we brought staples and oranges, which the natives did not have. The officers were all in "whites"—full dress uniform. The five villages on the island had all sent their drum bands and dancers who were very good to provide entertainment. Surrounding the big open space facing the lagoon where the party was held were Coleman lanterns. They and the moon provided the only light. When the time came to break up and say good-bye, the two groups tried to find a piece of music that everyone could sing. It was the *Notre Dame Victory March.*

The Executive Officer on our ship, second in command to the Captain, was a very competent officer and well respected by his fellow officers. One day, a few days out of Panama on our way to Australia, the ship's Captain summoned all the officers into the wardroom to make a very important announcement. The Exec was under arrest and in the brig, and the ship had been turned around and was steaming back to Panama at full power. Previously, all our pistols had been collected and placed under guard, ostensibly to be cleaned, but actually for security reasons.

The Exec had been arbitrarily assigning young seamen for duty with him on the fantail of the ship at night. Until one of the seamen had the courage to go to the Captain to tell him what was happening, none of the officers knew, but the enlisted men were well aware. The Exec was forcing himself on young enlisted men. The situation was inimical to good morale. In Panama the Exec and several seamen who could serve as witnesses were removed from the ship. The Exec was court-martialed and sent to prison in the United States.

Epilogue
We will never forget when we first heard that the United States had dropped an atomic bomb on Japan. It was early evening and we were just getting on the streetcar at Kendall Square in Boston. The newspaper boys were shouting only one headline. On the spot I explained to my wife that this was BIG and it would change history forever.

At the time I was taking a graduate course at MIT in Naval Construction and Engineering. That week I and another Naval Academy classmate signed up to take a course in nuclear physics, the forerunner of the nuclear engineering department at MIT. It was a class neither of us was well prepared for, but together we managed to pass it. That action and the fact that I was working on submarines at the Portsmouth Naval Shipyard in New Hampshire in 1949, was what motivated Admiral Rickover, then Captain Rickover, to recruit me for his team to develop a nuclear submarine—the program which culminated in the *Nautilus,* the first nuclear submarine in the world. At that time Rickover's team consisted of about a dozen people, half Navy, half civilian personnel. They called themselves a Band of Brothers. They had a common goal—to turn the terrible threat of nuclear fission to a beneficial end.

Born and raised in Paris, Ohio, Ed was a graduate of the US Naval Academy. He earned two Master's degrees from MIT, one in Nuclear Engineering and a second in Naval Architecture and Engineering. He worked with Admiral Hyman Rickover in the design and development of Nautilus, *the first nuclear-powered submarine. Later he was head of the US Fusion program and after the accident at Three Mile Island, he was in charge of the clean up of the damaged reactor. In retirement, he and his wife Alice lived in Norwich, Vermont, and later moved to Exeter, New Hampshire. Ed died in 2010.*

A Tight Spot

Milt Lauenstein

WHAT WAS I TO DO? I was an unarmed naval officer and was surrounded by Japanese wielding machetes. One swipe of one of those ugly weapons could have beheaded me there and then.

This happened in Guam a few months after the war had officially ended. For quite some time, Japanese soldiers in the hills, unaware that their government had surrendered, fought on.

How did I escape this terrifying predicament? I just walked on to get my meal in the officers' mess. The Japanese prisoners just continued to use their machetes to trim the lawn.

Milt was born in Webster Groves, Missouri. Following his Navy service, he graduated from Purdue University with a degree in Chemical Engineering. He also studied economics at Tufts University as well as spending time studying art in Paris. Milt later received an MBA from the University of Chicago in 1960. For the last ten years he has been working to reduce the incidence of war in the world, and serves as a Director of the Alliance for Peacebuilding and the BEFORE Project.

Marine Infantry Gunner

RICHARD P. MARCH

IGREW UP IN Medford, Massachusetts, a suburb of Boston. At home on one of our bookshelves was a big volume entitled *The Great War*. It was a compilation of WW I pictures copied from the Sunday New York Times. Whenever I would mention this subject, it usually caused my grandmother to tell about poor Uncle John, her son who joined the Canadian army in WW I and volunteered as a machine gunner, joining what at the time was called the "suicide squad".

Right after the Japanese attack on Pearl Harbor, I tried to enlist in the Navy but was told to finish college. I passed the exam for Officer Training for the Navy and waited for assignment only to learn I was in the Marines as a machine gunner in the infantry. I went through training camps and by December 1944 I was on a ship to the South Pacific and the Solomon Islands, landing on the small island of Mog Mog, near Guadalcanal, and assigned as a mail orderly for my unit.

We practiced beach landings and heard rumors of where we were going. Japan? On the radio we heard Tokyo Rose, the Japanese woman whose aim was to destroy our morale, saying our invasion force had been spotted. More and more ships began to join us. Finally we were told we were going to invade Okinawa. (I brought home a "secret" map showing locations of Japanese defenses). I was amazed at what I saw…wish I could give a detailed description. There were hundreds and hundreds of ships of all kinds—over 1320 ships participated in this invasion. I was seeing troop ships, cargo ships, white hospital ships, destroyers, and many other kinds. Most of them were bristling with anti-aircraft guns and they were being fired frantically at Japanese kamikaze planes trying to attack. Every fifth round of the anti-aircraft bullets was a tracer so the bullets looked like rain in reverse. The Jap planes persisted through this hail of bullets trying to crash on their targets and they frequently succeeded while none of them survived.

The first wave to hit the beach reported no resistance from ground fire…a miracle to us! Later we heard that the Japanese commanding officer decided to pull his troops from the beach to strengthen an elaborate defense system strung along the southern part of the island, consisting of caves and fortified to the nth degree.

We were the twenty-first wave to go ashore and as I ran up the cream colored coral sand I noticed an Easter lily in full bloom at the edge of a golden winter wheat field ripe for harvest. It was Easter Sunday morning, April 1, 1945. Sixty thousand American troops landed on Okinawa that day. Our company was an infantry replacement draft designated to remain at the beach area to bring in supplies from the ships and deliver them where needed and also to be available for transfer to the front lines as casualties occurred. The first thing we did was dig foxholes and then I helped dig a slit trench for a latrine—eighteen inches wide, six feet deep and six feet long.

The most exciting event on the beach happened when the sirens wailed announcing the approach of enemy planes—I looked up to see a Jap plane coming very low and heading right for me strafing the beach. I dashed for my foxhole but quickly realized that I could not make it in time. Just then I spotted the slit trench and with no hesitation I dove in as the bullets kicked up dirt by the trench. I got out about as fast as I went in. I was a stinking mess for I had sunk down in at least two feet of human waste. A friend nearby was pinching his nose and asked, "What happened to you?" I peeled off everything but my boxer shorts, went to my foxhole to get some soap and headed for the ocean to clean up.

A post office was set up on Yontan Airfield and as mail orderly it was my duty to go there each day. Mail was given high priority because of its important morale factor with the troops. One day I saw an anti-aircraft Marine unit guarding the airfield and found they had lost a man the previous night. I told the officer I was trained on 50 caliber machine guns and he assigned me there. The unit consisted of a 40 mm anti-aircraft gun, a gun director, and a 50 caliber machine gun in three separate pits. The crew lived in wooden shacks. I made myself an upper bunk with a mosquito netting. One night when the Jap planes were dropping bombs and I was in the gun pit a piece of shrapnel went right through our shack, through one wall, through the mosquito netting, over my pillow, and out the other side. I was glad I was in the gun pit then or I would have been decapitated.

One night, five Japanese twin-engine planes, each loaded with twenty-five demolition men, tried to land on Yontan Airfield. One plane succeeded in landing, wheels up, on the runway before we had a chance to fire on it. The first plane we saw bellied onto the runway. The next plane flew a couple of hundred feet from us. We could see our tracer bullets going into the cockpit. The third plane, following close behind, was very low and on fire. It headed straight toward us, but at the last moment the tail broke off and it crashed right beside us. At least one man got out alive and threw a hand grenade that landed on a sand bag on the edge of our gun pit and exploded.

A piece of shrapnel grazed a gunman's cheek, but the rest of us were unhurt. The Jap proceeded to crawl over to a 70,000-gallon supply of aviation gasoline. Before being killed he managed to set one of the 55-gallon drums on fire that in turn exploded all of the other drums. The next morning I learned that ten demolition men from the Japanese plane that had made the belly landing on the runway, managed to destroy seven of our planes and damage twenty-five others before being killed. Yet at least one man must have survived because one of our marines standing guard duty was knifed in the back and killed. For a while after that we stood guard duty back to back.

The battle for Okinawa lasted eighty-two days and resulted in more overall casualties than any other single World War II engagement. Fifty thousand of our troops were wounded or killed. The Japanese lost over one hundred thousand troops and there were more than one hundred thousand civilians either killed, wounded, or committed suicide.

The atomic bomb was dropped on Hiroshima on August 6th and on Nagasaki on the 9th and finally on August 15th the Emperor of Japan announced its surrender to the Allied Powers.

The war was over and, to put it mildly, we were greatly relieved. In retrospect it was ironical that becoming a machine gunner did not result in my death, as I feared it might, but became a factor in helping with my survival.

In 1946 Dick returned from the war to his wife Barbara and to Cornell University, where he received a Master's degree in Dairy Science. He was soon appointed to the Cornell faculty, for a twenty-year career culminating in a Full Professorship. Dick founded and for a time ran the national Dairy Products Council; he also served on the Executive Board of the International Association for Food Protection. An active volunteer, Dick served as Scout Master, driver for the handicapped, Chair of the Church Council and the church fund drive, and general handyman. Dick and Barbara have three grown children. In retirement Dick is famous as the guru of Nantucket Basket making.

A Memorable Experience

SPENCER MARTIN

I CONSIDER MYSELF very fortunate in my World War II military service. The real backbone of the military is the infantry who bore the brunt of the fighting, under abysmal conditions and for whom I have the greatest respect and admiration. I was lucky to join the Army Air Corps, now the Air Force, in February 1943, and be trained as a pilot. After graduation from flight training and being commissioned, I was assigned to the Training Command as a flight instructor. Later I became an Aircraft Commander in B-29 heavy bombers.

As the war wound down, our crew was sent to Saipan Island in the Pacific for the invasion of Japan. It was there that my most memorable experience began. After the ceasefire, but before VJ Day, our 501st Bomb Group was ordered to fly relief missions, carrying food, clothing, and medicines to Prisoner of War (POW) camps in Japan.

These supplies were attached to parachutes and loaded onto platforms, which in turn were loaded into the aircraft's bomb bay where they were attached to bomb release shackles. These missions typically required about fifteen hours in the air with take-offs around two in the morning.

On this particular mission we were to carry supplies to a location well into the mountains on Honshu Island. The weather was poor with a heavy overcast over the target. Immediately after take-off, an oil leak developed and we had to return to the airfield. Problem #1.

Taking off again we were about two hours behind schedule. Arriving at the target area we found solid cloud cover beneath us. The chart of the area showed a railroad running from the shore of the Sea of Japan, east into the mountain to the presumed location of the POW camp. We decided to go for it.

We let down gradually and broke through the overcast over the sea at about 2000 feet altitude. We found the railroad and followed it into the hills. As the land rose, we were becoming squeezed beneath the overcast but getting very close to the camp. The railroad made a blind turn around a mountain; we followed and suddenly found that the railroad went into a tunnel! Problem #2.

I applied emergency power and pulled up into the overcast. We cleared the ridges with about 400 feet to spare. What to do now? We had an alternate POW camp target and headed for it. When we reached the camp coordinates solid clouds were still below us. We decided to drop the supplies and hope that some of them would reach the prisoners.

The bombardier opened the bomb bay doors and hit the bomb release control. The plane shuddered from some kind of impact. A side gunner reported that something had hit and damaged the tail assembly of the plane. Problem #3.

Then the bombardier announced that he was unable to close the bomb bay doors. One of the bomb shackles had failed to release causing the platform to swing up and into the plane. Problem #4.

We turned for home. It became obvious that we would not make it back to Saipan. Fortunately, a few months earlier, the US had captured Iwo Jima, which had an airfield. It was not a relaxed flight but we landed safely on Iwo Jima. After debriefing, we headed for chow and bed—the end of a very eventful and exhausting day.

Spencer went from Philips Exeter Academy to Yale, where his education was interrupted by his three and a half years' service in the Air Corps. He returned to finish at Yale, worked for thirteen years in industrial research at Arthur D. Little in Cambridge, and then returned to Exeter to lead the Academy's three-year capital fund drive. That accomplished, Spence worked in a succession of small businesses, finally running a store of his own. Then, with his wife Caroline and three growing kids, he moved to Sandwich, New Hampshire, for seventeen years of happy, involved country living.

Fate

DICK MERRITT

IN 1943 I WAS a US Navy Aviation Ordinance Man, Second Class, on the aircraft carrier USS *Franklin*, CV13, on a shakedown cruise in the Caribbean. Upon return to Newport I was transferred to the USS *Wake Island*, CV65. We left for submarine patrol in the North Atlantic. Each time our pilots sank a sub a small flag was posted on the conning tower.

Finally in mid 1944 we were sent through the Panama Canal to join our forces in the Pacific. I was initiated from a pollywog to a shellback as we passed over the equator. Incidents in Lingayen Gulf, Iwo Jima, and finally Okinawa followed.

Fate followed our every move as ships were sunk and hit by kamikaze all around us. Finally, in April 1945 we got ours off Okinawa when one splashed off our port bow and another blew a forty-foot hole at the waterline in our starboard bow. Listing and limping along on one engine we made it to Kerama Retto. The Japanese were swimming out from shore, climbing anchor chains and murdering sailors in their bunks. I was put on an uneventful night watch at the anchor chain but didn't have to shoot anyone that night. In the daylight hours all our ships in the harbor lit smoke pots that obscured us from the sky. After putting off our planes and pilots we limped slowly back to Guam for dry-dock. After dry-dock we were sent back to Okinawa. It was not long before Truman made his fateful decision and Japan was atom bombed. We made our way back to Hawaii and the states and I was free at last.

One episode in my wartime experience convinced me of the importance of FATE in our lives.

I was three decks down in the ammunition locker of our ship. A loose five-hundred pound bomb slipped through the hatch and landed almost at my feet, bouncing around hither and yon. It didn't explode. I am still here.

Fate!

After serving nearly four wartime years in the Navy, Dick married Edna and took his degree in Photography from the Rochester, New York, Institute of Technology. For forty ensuing years Dick taught Photography, a Creative Medium, at the University of New Hampshire. Meanwhile his own photographic art matured and was honored in regional and national shows and in one-man shows in several venues. He was founder and president of the University Photographic Association of America. The Merritts have one son.

A Teenage Sailor

WES NICKERSON

M Y STORY starts on Pearl Harbor Day, December 7, 1941. I was fourteen and eager to enlist as friends and relatives, including my brother, had done. But the Navy recruiting officer in Portsmouth, New Hampshire, said I had to be seventeen and have my mother's permission to enlist. She said I had to graduate from high school first. So I promised her the first thing I would do when I came home was finish high school. I went to enlist in November 1944 when I turned seventeen.

We had ten weeks of boot camp in the very cold Finger Lakes region in Geneva, New York, before our company went to Buffalo, New York. Being a New Englander I have seen my share of snow, but nothing like Buffalo. Our company was sent there to shovel out freight cars for the Lehigh Valley Railroad. We had excellent rooms at the Hotel Buffalo plus we were allowed to order anything we wanted from the menu—no liquor allowed. In addition to this we were paid $5 per hour.

From Buffalo we proceeded to Rhode Island and on to Gulfport, Mississippi, (much warmer) for engineer training. Treasure Island, San Francisco, was my next stop before assignment to a ship.

We boarded the USS *Pickaway*, Auxiliary Personnel Attack (APA) and sailed to sea under the Golden Gate Bridge. It was not a pleasure cruise—everyone had a job to do. After two or three days at sea we noticed there was a lot of activity taking place on the fantail. There was a large platform being built along with a circular canvas tub. There was also a feeling of a surprise waiting for us. The ship stopped for "Message from Neptune by way of Davy Jones."

We were crossing the equator. The initiation ceremonies took place as we moved from being lowly pollywogs to being shellbacks with knowledge of the solemn mysteries of the ancient order of the deep!

The ship made several stops to unload supplies and personnel and arrived at Espiritu Santo (New Hebrides, near New Guinea). These many islands are now called the Republic of Vanuatu. We remained there for three months engaged in hard and boring work. I was happy to transfer to an Auxiliary Tug Rescue, ATR 27, where we were a small crew with excellent spirit and good chow.

Months later we arrived back in San Francisco, greeted by their famous fog. Everyone was on the bow of the ship straining for the first glimpse of the Golden Gate Bridge. Suddenly, it was as if someone had lifted a huge curtain and there it was. What a sight! I had a big lump in my throat and I know I was not alone.

We were two weeks in San Francisco unloading munitions and taking on supplies. Then we proceeded down the California coast, through the Panama Canal, and up the east coast to Charleston, South Carolina, where we prepared the ship to join the mothball fleet. We went home on leave by means of hitchhiking, which was easy on account of our uniforms. It was sure great to see Exeter again. Things I had remembered so well had not changed that much, if at all.

I ended my naval career on July 4, 1946, and went back to high school from which I graduated in 1947.

I would not exchange my experiences for anything. I contributed what I could to the war effort and feel very fortunate that I never had to kill anyone and nobody tried to kill me!

Born in Exeter, New Hampshire, Wes attended Exeter High School. His wartime service of two years was in the Navy in the South Pacific. He married Beverly Gillon in 1984 and they have four children. Wes ran an auto parts store and a real estate business and was active in the AARP, Rotary Club, and the Salvation Army.

He Missed Us On Purpose

BOB SCHAEBERLE

IN 1945 I was aboard US Navy APD 91, the USS *Kinzer,* an Attack Personnel Destroyer, off Okinawa. The Japanese kamikazes were attacking. I saw a two engine "Betty" heading directly for our ship. When it was about two hundred feet from our bow it suddenly swerved up, missing our mast by no more than forty feet. It crashed into the water off our stern. I heard a sailor yelling to the captain, "Go ahead back."

Our ship did back down and we picked up the Japanese pilot. His first words, in perfect English, were, "I was a student at the University of Chicago and there was no way I was going to crash into your ship." The pilot was put in the brig and then transferred to shore for interrogation.

Our ship carried the night raider Marines and their Doberman pinscher war dogs. On many nights before the invasion of Okinawa our landing craft would tow rafts near the shore for the Marines to study it and, if possible, capture some of the enemy. At night we would follow their progress on the ship's maps by listening to the radio. It was like the broadcast of a football game. Fortunately, no Marines were lost in this dangerous pre-invasion exercise. I still cross to the other side of the street if I see a Doberman pinscher approaching, remembering how they would lunge for the throat of someone in their path.

I stayed in the Navy Reserve to complete my twenty years of service. To this day I wonder what happened to the Japanese pilot who decided not to kill himself, and possibly many Americans, by crashing into our ship.

Born in Newark, New Jersey, Bob lived primarily in that state for eighty years. He served with the US Navy for three years during WW II seeing action in the South Pacific and retiring with the rank of Lieutenant Commander USNR. In 1946 he began his forty-year career with Nabisco, serving in his later years as President, Chief Operating Officer, and finally as Chairman and Chief Executive Officer until he retired in 1986.

1943 – 1946: Wartime

RON SPIERS

I WAS DOING high school homework at our dining room table in Madison, New Jersey, on the Sunday the radio announced the news from Pearl Harbor. The next day at school a general excitement, even, paradoxically, a sense of liberation prevailed. We sensed that all of yesterday's certainties and assumptions had become obsolete over night, and that yesterday's constraints no longer counted for anything. We practiced air raid drills, boys in the classes ahead of me began to enlist, and the local paper began to report casualties. The first friend I lost went down when the destroyer USS *Reuben James* was torpedoed off the New Jersey coast and this began a lengthening roster of the dead.

In my senior year I assumed I would be following the legions flowing into the Army. However, a Navy recruiter came to school seeking candidates for a new officer-training program called the V-12. I took the written and physical tests and was one of the few who passed and was selected. We were asked to express a preference from a list of colleges that had been selected to participate in the program. Although having barely heard of Dartmouth I listed it as my first choice.

The courses I took were of little interest to me: electrical engineering, thermodynamics, physics, chemistry, naval history, mathematics, mechanical drawing, naval English, and public speaking. However, my performance prospered except in the case of the first two, which I found incomprehensible. A lot of the faculty was equally indifferent to the subject they taught. A professor of German taught us mechanical drawing, and Shakespeare scholars were reduced to instructing us in "Naval English," etc.

My first housing was on the "third deck" of Middle Mass dormitory. We were crowded five into a two-room suite meant for two. We had random "white glove" inspections, beds had to be made hospital-style, the contents of drawers aligned in military fashion, shoes polished and arrayed in marching order under beds. The "bulkheads" had to be free of undergraduate paraphernalia, and spotless. What my children consider my obsessive tidiness certainly had its origins here: a bed on which the quarter did not bounce earned a demerit. Enough demerits and you were out of the program.

Each morning at five a.m. we had a half hour of calisthenics, rain or shine, winter or summer. At the loudspeaker call "Now Hear This! All Hands, Chow Down!" we lined up and marched to mess in College Hall. We were formally addressed as "Seaman" so and so. We had a watch-standing rotation and would periodically be roused at satanic hours to take our turn sitting for four empty hours at a desk by the "gangway." I sympathized with those who had been selected directly from the fleet and reduced in rank to apprentice seaman. Many of them had already seen combat.

Two years of college equivalence were compressed into four consecutive terms. We were rearranged alphabetically and I moved into New Hampshire Hall with all the other S's. Shortly after the move, the Navy, a then highly segregated institution, announced that it was commissioning the first group of black officers, and they were pictured in *Life* magazine. The Southerners in our midst were outraged; nobody would get them to salute a "nigger"! Disturbed, I wrote a letter to *Life* magazine saying that I was an apprentice seaman who would be proud to salute them. *Life* published it in May 1944. My "shipmates" from below the Mason-Dixon were shocked, and I was also deluged with scurrilous—but unsigned—hate mail from all over the country. There was one letter, however, that I answered: it was from a black army captain named Leslie Polk, stationed in France, and it was a moving expression of appreciation for what I had written. After the war, we met and became lifelong friends.

After completing the V-12 program at Dartmouth I was ordered to Midshipman's School at Abbott Hall in Chicago for an intensive four-month program in gunnery, navigation, ordnance, and communications. The tide of war seemed to be turning rapidly and we were all anxious to get out into the action. Upon receiving our commissions as ensigns, I asked to be assigned to submarines. However, we had been given a surreptitious language aptitude test by naval intelligence, and my score was apparently such that I was soon approached by a Navy commander and told that I had been selected to attend the Naval Intelligence Language School at the University of Colorado to study either Russian or Japanese, as would be determined on my arrival. Mine not to reason why, and I soon found myself in the men's dorm in Boulder, equidistant from either the Atlantic or the Pacific, commencing study of Japanese.

I found the language fascinating and did well. We, all Navy or Marine officers, were schooled in groups of five in a total immersion (the nearest I had gotten to immersion in anything since joining the navy) course, and were being prepared, assembly line fashion, for the invasion and occupation of Japan. Our instructors were all ethnic Japanese-Americans, fluent in the language, and culled from the barren internment camps into which they had been interned in a shameful display of wartime hysteria. Some barely spoke English; others were cultured scholars. We spent hours memorizing Kanji and practicing dictation and conversation. All our films, radio reports, and news bulletins were in the language. We were forbidden to speak English at table. If you needed something you had better learn how to ask for it.

After some months the school was moved to Oklahoma A&M in Stillwater, Oklahoma. The surroundings were much less congenial and our teachers, a group I grew very fond of, suffered the hostility of the local population. The climate was hot and dusty and the end of the war was nearer and I was yearning to get to sea. It was at this time that I received the news that my five closest friends from high school had been killed at Bastogne in the Battle of the Bulge. All still teenagers, they had been in an army officers training program, but as the Germans reversed their retreat in Europe they had been pulled out and sent into combat with a minimum of preparation. They left the United States around Thanksgiving and by January 1945 all were dead. The Bulge was a blood bath.

A group of us decided to try to curtail our program. The authorities were unhappy but acceded. The war in Europe ended and we felt time's winged chariot hurrying near. I was given orders to report to the Naval Operating Base at Kwajalein Atoll in the South Pacific to serve as boat pool officer, and began to question the wisdom of my decision.

I hitched a ride from Oklahoma to San Francisco on an army bomber and reported to the navy headquarters at Treasure Island for onward transportation. I was given a berth on an aircraft carrier heading for Pearl Harbor. We sailed under the Golden Gate Bridge as the war with Japan came to an end.

Kwajalein was an unprepossessing place: barren of trees, surrounded by coral reefs, hot and humid with pools of water that seemed impervious to evaporation. Its capture from the Japanese had been costly in American lives. I was assigned quarters in a tented four man cabin and began to learn the ropes of managing a boat pool. This lasted about a week. Officers with longer service were avid to get home and had the service-computed "points" to qualify for discharge. Vacancies began to appear right and left and as a newcomer I was ripe for plucking.

I was soon reassigned as the junior of the five officers on a Landing Craft, Infantry (LCI), one of the many that had been mobilized for invasion of the Japanese mainland. An LCI is a 155-foot, flat-bottomed ship, with bow doors designed to approach a beach, spew out about 70 troops, pull itself off by its rear anchor and return to the bigger troop ships waiting off shore for another load. It had a crew of about forty. Within weeks I was the fourth, third, and then second ranking officer. Our job was to sail to outlying islands of the Marshall and Gilberts to round up Japanese prisoners of war and bring them to central collection points. Finally my Japanese was serving a function, to the wonderment of my fellow crewmembers.

Before long we received orders to return with the ship to the amphibious base at Norfolk, Virginia. This is quite a trip for a small vessel like an LCI. In the open ocean when the wind is up and the waves high the ship's flat bottom slaps the water with a loud smack that produces kidney shuddering jolts with the regularity of a metronome. This went on day and night until we reached the San Pedro naval station in Los Angeles. We were in a convoy of five LCI's. The captain of the ship was a dour and laconic navy lieutenant from Texas, and teenagers who played the same maudlin country songs over and over on an aged gramophone, dominated the crew.

As we neared land, the sea calmed and gave off a scent of land approaching that was like perfume. When I had the con I could now switch on California radio music stations. I almost broke into tears when I heard the Rienzi Overture, clouded by static, rising and fading in volume.

In San Pedro we had more crew changes and I now became the senior officer responsible for the rest of the journey. It was a relief to get rid of the captain, but I was anxious because with each change, the crew became less and less experienced and vacancies were occurring in key slots. Nevertheless we proceeded south along Baja California, transited the Panama Canal, and sailed north to Virginia. The log recorded an uneventful trip with the simple, archaic entry repeated at the end of every four-hour watch, "Steaming as before." At Norfolk, we were assigned to the Little Creek Amphibious Base and became a water-carrier to the other amphibious ships tied up on Craney Island Flats preparatory to mothballing or other disposition. Threading through the heavy ship traffic in the busy harbor improved my seamanship but the glamour of my war had been reduced to that of a water-borne taxi driver.

Soon I found demobilization was proceeding at such a pace that I would qualify before long. Our squadron commander tried to persuade me to make the Navy my career. However, I applied for discharge and finally, on July 1, 1946, three years after joining the Navy and nine days before my 21st birthday, I was discharged. I was and am still full of gratitude for the time I had spent: it qualified me for the GI Bill, taught me to become a competent ship handler, gave me insight into another language, let me experience the spectacularly shifting palette and awesome silences of horizon-to-horizon South Pacific sunsets, and, most important, had given me responsibilities which, as a teen-ager, I could never have otherwise had.

The most moving moment I experienced came when I told the crew I had my discharge orders and the crusty old chief who had held the crew together said, simply and quietly, "The Navy is losing a really good officer." The crew applauded. Higher praise would have been inconceivable.

I went home, and submitted my application to return to Dartmouth as a Junior, looking forward to two years of the study of history, economics, and philosophy—subjects that really gripped me and would prepare me for the career I had wanted since the age of twelve: diplomacy. During the past three years I had read and thought long and hard about the mistakes of world statecraft after World War I. The loss of practically all the friends of my youth in this second conflict reinforced my conviction that this was the choice I wanted to stay with.

Epilogue

Ron returned to Dartmouth on the GI Bill graduating with a major in International Relations, immediately followed by a Woodrow Wilson Fellowship for a two-year graduate program at Princeton where he earned a Masters Degree in Public Affairs.

Stymied by a hiring freeze at the Foreign Service, he was hired by a new agency, the Atomic Energy Commission, where he wrote a paper proposing an international agency for the peaceful use of atomic energy. This became the progenitor of the International Atomic Energy Agency (IAEA).

Four years later he joined the State Department, now more valuable to the institution than if he had entered on a more conventional path. Nuclear problems were gaining visibility in international affairs at a time when there were no Foreign Service officers who had experience in these issues.

He spent the next thirty-four years in the Foreign Service. An early highlight was helping to set up the first UN operation that came to be known as "peacekeeping" which occurred after the 1956 ill-starred invasion of Egypt by the British, French, and Israelis. Later, in negotiations for a nuclear test ban treaty in 1958, he became aware of how technical judgments of world-renowned scientists were influenced by their political orientations. Scientists might offer valuable assistance but could not be asked to solve problems that were, at bottom, political.

After assignments of ever increasing responsibilities, he became Assistant Secretary of State followed by ambassadorships to Turkey, Pakistan, and the Bahamas, where he established the first US Embassy to that country.

Ronald Spiers was born in Orange, New Jersey, the son of an American businessman. His early youth was spent in Peru, England, France, and Belgium. Ron and Patience were married prior to his graduate study at Princeton. His career appointments were made by four presidents: Nixon, Carter, Reagan, and G.H.W. Bush. He is a member of the Council on Foreign Relations, a Fellow of the National Academy of Public Administration, and of the American Academy of Diplomacy.

A Memoir Of War

FRANK TENNY

$\mathbf{B}$Y JUNE 1942 my draft number had not yet come up. I signed up for an intensive Japanese summer course that Columbia University had set up, and I commuted there daily from my sister's home in suburban New Jersey. Columbia tested me and because I had lived in Japan they put me in their most advanced class. My draft board number did come up at the end of July. I applied to the local board for a one-month extension, and at a hearing I told them that I had orders from the Navy to report September 1. In the meantime I was studying Japanese at Columbia at my own expense to better prepare me for service. The draft board chairman's reply: "What the hell are you studying Japanese for? We ain't talking to them bastards. We're shooting at 'em. You might as well be studying ancient Hungarian."

The next day I was on the bus to Petersburg, Virginia, for induction. My previous contacts must have caught up with me, because in only a couple of weeks I was assigned to the Signal Corps and ordered to report to Arlington, Virginia.

The Arlington Hall School for Girls had gone out of business and the Signal Corps had taken over the property and was constructing office space and barracks. A group of us, new army privates as Japanese language trainees, had arrived together and were put to work moving the furniture out of the former girls' dormitories. About thirty of us were housed in the newly built barracks 311. It was an amazing group that the army had recruited: graduate students with advanced studies in ancient near eastern languages, classical Greek, or what have you. I believe I was the only one with a Japan background, although the army had recruited some older civilians, former missionaries, etc., to work with us on coded message translation. As civilians, they lived off base.

Because my Japanese was more advanced I was soon taken out of the school and assigned as head of the language task force translating Japanese naval code messages from the South Pacific. The brilliant cryptanalysts had solved the problem of unscrambling the machine-scrambled four digit numbers and our job was to match up the new numbers, often garbled in radio transmission and interception, with such incomplete code books as had been rounded up somewhere, and make Japanese language messages of sense, which we then translated.

Fortunately, Japanese naval language was stereotyped, direct, and rather simple, and we had textbook examples. A message might say, for example: "Destroyer Kamikaze at 0700 hours 29 October proceed north 18 degrees east to such and such a point." We never heard what happened to our messages when we passed them in to our superiors, but we assumed that they should be quite helpful to our commanders in the South Pacific battles and should have resulted in the sinking of ships.

I was working for two different American armies in those days. It seemed rather strange and wasteful, but I was young and energetic and we win wars even when we are inefficient. My normal workday might start around 10 p.m. when I reported for overnight translation duty. It was daytime in the South Pacific but I don't know whether our intercepts were really transmitted and processed that fast. Anyway, there were a lot of messages and I got back to the barracks around 4 or 5 a.m. Then around 6 a.m. we were all called out for reveille, barracks inspection, and a full day of basic military training. "Get them books out of the barracks. Don't look good to have books around a barracks." We would have a couple of hours of close order drill marching, then jog a couple of miles in formation down Arlington Boulevard, then perhaps in the afternoon head over to Ft. Belvoir to fire on the rifle range. My vision with glasses wasn't all that good, and after I missed the whole target sheet eighteen out of twenty shots, the corporal tore up the sheet in disgust and said, "OK you pass." Another day we would all go over to Fort Meade to swing over the obstacle course and crawl along the ground under fixed but live machine gun fire. I'd get back to the barracks in time to eat and nap a couple of hours before reporting to my nighttime translation army.

In retrospect I understand what the daytime army was doing in insisting we have basic military training in case we ever got near a battlefront. Since we were needed immediately in our active war duties, they couldn't spare us to go to a basic training camp, or later to officers' training. It had to be done within the same available twenty-four hours.

Almost immediately after commissioning, I was ordered to proceed as fast as possible to New Delhi, India. The Air Transport Command had opened a route from the US via Brazil, Central Africa, and Arabia to India. The small plane carried a number of generals and White House type civilians, but I, as the only company-grade officer, was ordered to be the armed-guard escort to a wooden box some three feet square "said to contain five million dollars in US currency." The US was financing the war in China with US cash because Chinese currency became less valuable every day. The chore turned out to be easy, because every time the plane landed, which was every seven hours, the plane was met by an armed guard who took over the protection while I visited the mess hall and bathroom.

On arrival in New Delhi I was put to work immediately translating Japanese messages with two of my Arlington Hall colleagues, Bernie and Guy, who had come much earlier by ship around the south of Australia. The reason Bernie and Guy were so busy was that the post had come into possession of a Japanese army codebook reportedly retrieved by US Marines from the latrine of a Japanese camp they had overrun in New Guinea. In any case, the book was still in active use by the Japanese army in Burma.

At that time General Stillwell, US theater commander for China-Burma-India, had launched an assault by a small American unit, named Merrill's Marauders, and some Chinese army allies. They were fighting their way from Assam, India, through the jungles of North Burma to Kunming, China, to open a road for the delivery of supplies, especially airplane fuel. The US had begun the bombing of the Japanese home islands from air bases in west China before we could reach Japan by air from Pacific Islands farther away. The fighting was very bitter down the Hukawn Valley.

In New Delhi the three of us were reading and translating dozens, maybe many dozens, of situation report messages a day from the Japanese. This went on for most of 1944, I believe. A few years ago I read a book called *Merrill's Marauders* by Charlton Ogburn. I felt I had been there in every situation, every battle from the other side of the jungle lines with the Japanese. I remember in the end the Marauders captured a key target, the Myitkyna airport, but then the Chinese panicked and lost it again. After a few more weeks of fighting, the Japanese were driven out of the area. I translated the last message of the Japanese commanding general in Myitkyna reporting that the battle was over and he was departing down the Irrawadi River "on a barge with the Korean comfort women."

We also received and translated messages from other fronts in Burma. I remember one night about 1 a.m. I read a message saying: "we have just crossed the river into Imphal province and the invasion of India has begun." I immediately went and awoke my boss, Lt. Col. Bickwit, who got out of bed, jumped in his jeep and drove over to British intelligence headquarters to awaken his counterpart, the British intelligence colonel. When Col. Bickwit returned, he told me with some disgust that his British counterpart had only rolled over, saying "Harrumph, those are our forces entering Burma." Actually, of course, he knew that the British had no forces in the area and could do nothing before daybreak anyway. It was some months before the British were able to muster the mostly Indian Army forces and drive the Japanese back into Burma. The British after all were fighting their big war back home to save the British Isles.

Our liaison and cooperation with British Intelligence in New Delhi were very close. We told each other everything, unlike the US

Navy, which never told us anything. I became very close, lifetime friends with the three British officers who were very well trained in Japanese, and I went on a skiing vacation with them in Kashmir in the spring of 1945. One of them, Wildred Noyce, later died on Mt. Everest, where he was blazing the glacier trail later used by Hillary's party to the summit.

By this time the war in Europe had ended. We in China knew we were the last priority in the US war effort and there were still a million and a half or more Japanese troops in China fully equipped but hardly touched by the Pacific war. We expected those now freed American troops would be coming from Europe, but surely it would still be two or three years before the Japanese troops in China could be defeated. Judging by the cost of the Okinawa battle, the invasion of the Japanese homeland would be long and terrible, and we would still be left in China.

Listening to the British and American short wave radio broadcasts we heard, in early August, that a new and bigger bomb had been dropped. That sounded good. Then we heard the Russians had entered the war in Manchuria against the Japanese, and that would help, we thought. On August 13 it was reported that Japan had surrendered. We cheered and had a big party all night, while Bernie dutifully went back to the code room. The next morning the surrender report was denied as false. We all sobered up glumly and went back to our jobs. Finally on August 15 came the confirmed report that Japan had accepted surrender.

Two weeks later at the beginning of September General MacArthur accepted the Japanese surrender on the USS *Missouri* and his forces went ashore in Tokyo-Yokohama. Bernie, who had by then received a direct commission in China, and I were told by our signal intelligence chief in Kunming to proceed as rapidly as possible to Shanghai. Three of our colleagues were sent individually to Hankou (now Wuhan), Canton, and Hanoi.

Our orders were to find out what the Japanese were doing in signal intelligence, codebooks, intercepts, cryptanalysis, etc. We were told that by allied agreement the Chinese were to accept the Japanese surrender in China, as the Americans were to do in Japan and South Korea and the British in all of Southeast Asia. We were to give no orders to the Japanese. We would be attached to Chinese Nationalist army officers and would ask them to tell the Japanese what we wanted done. We were given no instructions about saluting or any other behavior in meeting Japanese.

Bernie and I caught the first plane we could, which happened to be going to Nanking, with a small number of American and Chinese troops. Shortly after we left Kunming a gun battle broke out between the local Chinese warlord and the nationalist forces, with shooting directly over our Kunming office building. On landing in Nanking the two of us went to the largest hotel. They were completely full of Japanese officers and had no room for us. Japanese troops and vehicles and artillery were everywhere. There was one first class compartment car with one vacant compartment and a sign reading "reserved for the Japanese General." I bought two tickets for 380,000 Chinese Central Reserve Bank dollars, the Japanese puppet bank. Later when I came to prepare a voucher for reimbursement, I discovered they had cost me 15 cents each, so I dropped the claim.

Bernie and I entered the compartment and sat down. Shortly a Japanese Military Police (MP) appeared and ordered us out. The compartment was reserved for the Japanese General. No, I said, Japan had just surrendered and we would stay in the compartment. However there was plenty of room and if the general wanted to ride with us, he was welcome to. That was the last we heard from the MP and no general came.

The next morning the train arrived in Shanghai and we got ourselves somehow to the Park Hotel. It was beautiful. From the rice paddies of west China we were back in New York, modern, twelve stories or so, with lacquered elevators and a glassed-in cocktail lounge on the top floor. The hotel was full of Japanese officers and had no room for us. Bernie and I went next door to the YMCA, which was full of lower ranking Japanese. The YMCA put us on cots in the hall. We decided to go back to the Park Hotel and try the cocktail lounge. We were politely escorted into an elevator already nearly full of Japanese officers in uniform, swords and all. We were in our uniforms with our .45 automatics. No one said anything and each side shrank back and avoided looking at the other. When we reached the top floor, we found the cocktail lounge full of Japanese officers, but the Chinese maitre d' escorted us to an empty table where we sat and gazed at our new world of not war but not yet peace, or what was it.

The next month or more was the strangest interregnum of my lifetime. Japanese troops were everywhere, uniformed and fully armed. Japanese had all the vehicles, all the hotel rooms. Bernie and I did get moved to something better than the corridors of the YMCA. I don't remember what, but after a month or so we ended up in a fairly nice apartment building, the Broadway Mansions, which became company-grade officers' billets for Americans.

A handful of Chinese nationalist and American troops would arrive each day by plane from west China, a thousand miles away. Still no vehicles. The Japanese behaved properly while awaiting orders from the Chinese to get out of their hotels and field camps and vehicles and proceed to internment sites. On the streets they saluted me, an American officer. As I had received no instructions, I did not return the salutes. On the streets the Japanese had stopped policing traffic, so the Chinese began mobbing the streetcars to crowd on, instead of forming lines as the Japanese had made them do. After years of Japanese domination, the Chinese were scared of confronting the Japanese. We, Chinese and Americans together on one side, and fully armed Japanese on the other, rubbed shoulders but passed by with as little contact as required.

For at least a month we all knew that the Japanese could, if they so decided, retake control of east China in five minutes with their million-man army. They did not do so. They waited patiently to be told what to do. They followed the Emperor's orders. There were no incidents, not even scuffles, although the Chinese clearly hated and feared their former masters. Shanghai had a substantial European refugee population: White Russian refugees, German refugees

(Jewish and otherwise), Italians, and others. British and American civilians had been rounded up and put in camps by the Japanese, but the other Europeans were left on their own. The jazz night-clubs, staffed by Russian musicians in the former French town, were booming. Restaurant food of all nationalities was available and delicious, quite a contrast to the rice and cabbage we had been living on in southwest China.

Bernie and I wasted no time in getting started on our intelligence assignment. My orders attached me as advisor to a Chinese Nationalist Army Colonel Liu. He was a wonderful guy, whom I came to respect and admire, though he was reluctant to take much initiative with the Japanese. I think he was more afraid of them than I was. Perhaps, as an American I was ready to bluff my way, assuming everything would work out as it did, and that "surrender" really meant, "surrender." I don't know what happened to Col. Liu later, but I suppose he retreated to Taiwan with the subsequent Nationalist defeat by the Communists.

Anyway, Col. Liu set up all the Japanese appointments, and he always accompanied me with several of his staff, especially a Chinese-Japanese interpreter and a Chinese-English interpreter, though he himself spoke English. Bernie and I usually had one of the American Nisei US Army sergeants with us and I often let them do the introductory talking at least. I had the greatest admiration for these American Nisei who fought, as the Americans they were, with us in Burma and China while their parents were interned in the Utah desert. Although I have lost touch with all of them, I happily contributed recently to the new Nisei War Memorial dedicated in 2001 on the mall in Washington.

So we ended up with quite a party to call on the Japanese offices. A real sleuth might have done better on his own, but these were our orders—do it through the Chinese. Despite the surrender we came and we were treated more as negotiators. We were certainly not captors, as I had been when interviewing POWs in New Delhi. POWs in New Delhi did not expect to live or ever go back to Japan. Japanese officers in Shanghai had not been "captured." In their own theater of war they had not even been defeated. They were accommodating to the changed position and policies of Japan and in the process were even trying to insinuate themselves into the position of cooperators and allies.

We visited and conducted interviews in quite a number of Japanese military offices, which we had identified as possible sources of military communication or intelligence. I can't remember what they all were, but we were always received politely and had some discussion. Without exception they said they had no knowledge of codes, interceptions, cryptanalysis, and such.

Since everybody said they knew nothing, I decided we had to go to the top where somebody must know something. I asked Col. Liu to set up a meeting in town with the Japanese commanding general for the entire east China region. Col. Liu forwarded the request through his channels and after a few days the reply came back that the general could not come into town because he had no vehicle, an obvious lie because he had all the vehicles in east China, but he would be happy to receive us at his base some twenty miles out of town. "What do we do now?" Col Liu said. "We have no vehicle to get out there. Tell him to come in on a bicycle," I replied.

More days passed, and eventually Col. Liu liberated an old 1920s open touring car, one of those big ones, from somewhere. After more roundabout negotiations, a date and hour was set for us to call on the general at his out-of-town headquarters. All eight of us piled into the touring car and drove to the gate of the base, where we were met and escorted in.

The base was huge: hundreds of trucks, tanks, and field artillery pieces. We were escorted to a two-floor office building and into a long conference room with table and chairs on both sides. A Japanese orderly served tea and snacks and in a little while an officer entered to inform Col. Liu that the general was about to come in and it would be very nice if we would all stand up when he did. Col. Liu asked me "What shall we do?" I said, "You do what you want, but they have surrendered and I am not going stand up." Col. Liu decided he wouldn't stand up either, and so informed the Japanese.

There was a delay. More tea and snacks. Then the Japanese officer came back, apologized for the delay, and said the general was very happy to meet us if we would step down the hall this way. We all rose, filed out the door, down the hall, and went into the door of a similar room. Again, long table, tea and snacks waiting, and as we walked in one door, the general walked in the door at the opposite end. Rank was preserved, even in surrender.

The general was very courteous and friendly. We asked all our questions. The general kept saying: Oh, he didn't know anything about that. They didn't do anything like that. We left in our different directions, as politely as we had come from each way, and I saw my intelligence mission with the Japanese at an end.

In 1986 after I had retired from the US Government, I was decorated by the Emperor and Government of Japan with the Order of the Rising Sun, Class Three. I was pleased by this, in part because of the irony that I had spent four years trying to sink the Rising Sun. The war was long since over.

Raised in Japan, Frank studied Chinese at Harvard. He joined the State Department and was assigned to posts in Indonesia, Thailand, and Japan. When Congress appropriated funds for cultural exchange with Japan, he was appointed executive director. He has translated modern Japanese novels into English, publishing several volumes. He was awarded the Order of the Rising Star, Class Three, by the Japanese Government.

A Narrow Escape

Louis Warlick

I SERVED IN THE Pacific on a small destroyer, the USS *Breese*, DM18, brought back from World War I and re-commissioned. Lacking the firepower of modern larger versions, it performed in a quiet defensive role until late in 1944. She patrolled as a screen against Japanese submarines for relatively fast transports such as hospital evacuation ships bringing wounded from Guadalcanal to major facilities in the New Hebrides. The Pacific war at the time was characterized by major naval battles, notably Midway and Coral Sea, which clearly had no place for our ship.

The situation then changed radically for the *Breese*. A navy yard overhaul modernized the ship with new anti-aircraft capability, along with updated radar. We were then assigned to operational attachment to the offensive Third Fleet. This main US naval force was at that time making plans for successive island landings leading toward Japan. Examples were Leyte and Luzon in the Philippines and Iwo Jima and Okinawa. The main threat to the ships was kamikazes, Japanese suicide bombers.

After a rather uneventful landing at Leyte, we found real trouble at Lingayen Gulf on western Luzon. Here, after completing our job on January 4, 1945, of planting buoys off the landing area, to organize the landing craft coming four days later, we protectively screened with others for possible submarines while ships of the line bombarded shore installations. At dusk all vessels were to exit the gulf, retire into the South China Sea, and return at dawn.

The Zimbales Mountains reaching into the sea on each side formed this rather narrow gulf, just a few miles wide and thirty-five miles long. As we were steaming down the gulf toward the sea after the second day of bombardment, kamikazes swooped over the mountains late in the day and suddenly attacked, bombing the USS *Hovey*, a destroyer of our vintage, about 100 yards on our bow. She inclined to 90 degrees and sank within two or three minutes. With our whaleboat soon in the water, we were picking up survivors IN THE DARK. We rescued eighty-seven in total while some otherwise made it to safety. Only about twenty-four of 140 were lost.

Suddenly, we realized that the main battle force was heading directly toward us—in particular the battleship USS *North Carolina*. Our ship could not move without abandoning the survivors so our only choice was to persuade the battleship to change course. Otherwise, we would be run down. Without naval experience one may find it hard to imagine the difficulty in persuading the skipper of a battleship to change course, all in a matter of minutes. It may also be difficult to imagine the size of a battleship standing down on you in a far smaller vessel—something like the Empire State Building coming at you is not much of an exaggeration. I can still remember watching what seemed like approaching disaster, and the RELIEF when the bow of that giant ship began to swing at the last minute.

There were many other losses in that operation, including a sister ship torpedoed during one of the nights in the South China Sea and other problems at Iwo Jima and Okinawa, but none for me were so vivid.

Born in North Carolina, his return to civilian life in 1946 brought marriage that happily lasted sixty years. His wife, formerly Dorothy Garry, supported his two years at Harvard Business School in preparation for a career in investment management. The latter encompassed thirty-eight years almost equally divided between Loomis Sayles and State Street Research and Management, all in Boston. At that time they lived in Andover, Massachusetts, with their three children. Retirement years brought them to Rye Beach, New Hampshire. Once alone, he came to RiverWoods—as close to home as he could happily be.

The European Theater / Africa / Atlantic

Timeline and Map of the war in Europe,

with names of some of our authors who were there.

1939 Hitler invades Poland
1940 France surrenders; Battle of Britain and bombing of London
May, 1940 Germany occupies Belgium; **I. Hyland**
June, 1940 Russian then German occupations of Lithuania; **Baksys**
September, 1940 British children sent overseas; **Hull**
1941 US declares war on Germany and Italy
November, 1942 Operation Torch in North Africa; **R. Southworth**
1943 – 1945 US bombs Europe from England;
Alling, Boyle, Scharff, Willits
May, 1943 Boyle shot down; **Boyle** as POW
July, 1943 Invasion of Sicily; **R. Southworth**
September, 1943 Italy surrenders and declares war on Germany
January – May, 1944 Anzio, Battle of Monte Cassino;
R. Bates, Remien, Smallwood, Prince
February, 1944 Smallwood shot down; **Smallwood** as POW
February, 1944 Submarine danger continues in the Atlantic;
Richardson
June, 1944 Rome occupied by the Allies; **Remien**
June 6, 1944 D-Day: the invasion of Normandy begins at
Sainte Mere-Eglise; **G. Bates**
June – September, 1944 Campaign in France; **Adams, Murray**
August, 1944 Invasion of Southern France; **Remien, McCarthy**
December – February, 1944 Battle of the Bulge and aftermath;
Alexander, Dixon, Jervis
March, 1945 Allies cross the Rhine River
April, 1945 Allies meet the Soviet Union at the Elbe River; **Warner**
May 1, 3, 1945 Emergency food drops in Holland; **Alling**
May 8, 1945 VE Day
Postwar Administration, POWs, DPs, Economy, Marshall Plan;
Adams, Dixon, Hampton, Harvey

A Glimpse Of Combat

Brad Adams

I WAS INDUCTED into the Army on 19 March 1942. The Millbury, Massachusetts representative on the draft board was Harold E. Swenson whose daughter, Charlotte, I married in August 1943.

Embarkation

After two years of training, instruction, and Officers Candidate School, on 5 June we were placed on orders and moved to Camp Shanks, New York, on the west shore of the Hudson River, about twenty miles north of New York City. We moved at night in a train of coaches with a red boxcar for baggage. When we arrived at daylight the public address system was announcing the Normandy invasion.

The letter I wrote to Charlotte from Camp Shanks, after we were on orders to move, was censored. The censor cut out the date on the letter. Of all the letters I wrote from overseas, ten or twelve were opened by the censor but nothing was censored. An interesting item regarding several of my letters, which I read in 1992 while writing these notes, was that they had a stamp of the Millbury Post Office on them. It seems that in order for Charlotte to send me a package, she had to show the Post Office my letter requesting the items she was mailing to me.

Many trains were used to load a convoy and they came from camps in New Jersey, New York, and Long Island. Our train took us to Jersey City, where we boarded ferries that took us around the tip of Manhattan and over to the Brooklyn Navy Yard. Here we unloaded onto the end of the dock. In this way the public was not aware of what was going on. This loading took place at midday so as not to interfere with the commuting hours. Once on the dock we received a donut and coffee from the Red Cross and then boarded the ship.

Convoy to Britain

Our ship was the *Le Jeune*, a new German ship that had been interned in Brazil. The United States had swapped it for military equipment for the Brazilian First Division, which eventually went to Italy. We departed New York after dark on 15 June 1944. About sundown, some Destroyer Escorts (DEs) that were to go with us left the dock and moved out of the harbor to line up other convoy ships as they came out. We were part of a thirty-five-ship convoy that would travel at 8 knots in a zigzag course for fourteen days to cross the Atlantic.

The ship was filled with replacements. Fourteen percent of all US troops sent overseas were infantry. Seventy percent of all US troops killed or wounded were from the infantry. One officer had been wounded with the 9th Division in North Africa, had been six months in hospital, and was returning to duty. Since this officer had been in combat, his opinions were much sought by the others. Some of the officers on this ship were also assigned to the 29th Division.

Our ship moved up the Firth of Clyde past the Isle of Arran and anchored in midstream, opposite Greenoch, Scotland. A British Major General came on board to welcome us to the UK. He told us that Britain had no color line; he also announced that buzz bombs were hitting London. This information had not been released to the newspapers in the US. All anti-aircraft (AA) units arriving in the UK were dispatched to the Thames estuary while awaiting deployment to Europe. The buzz bombs flew in at a relatively low level and the AA units were able to shoot down 20% of them. Two Canadian Pacific liners were anchored in the Firth of Clyde loading German prisoners of war captured since June 6th. They were being sent to Canada for the duration of the war.

Travel to Normandy

We were eventually transported to Plymouth. This city was jammed with men and equipment. We were trucked to a beach on the eastern edge of the harbor. The men had to stand in the trucks and one-ton trailers. British landing craft took us to our ship, which was anchored in the harbor. The ship was very old and had been used in India. The crew was Lascar (East Indian) seamen. It was an iron ship with wooden decks and a clipper stern. None of the staterooms had running water; stewards brought warm water for shaving in the morning.

Our ship consisted entirely of replacements. The return trip would bring wounded back to hospitals in the UK. The first twenty-four hours on board were for processing. We were issued invasion francs that cost us ten cents each, five times what they were worth. But we didn't really need them anyway. We also received a thirty-day supply of PX rations. British cadre for handling troops consisted of a Lieutenant Colonel in charge, a Captain, Adjutant, and Warrant Officers. Our own personnel had to man the twin 40 mm anti-aircraft guns. With no training and no one knowing anyone else, you can imagine how effective our fire would have been if it were needed. Food on board was British; hardly anyone would eat it. We had canned peas and boiled fish for breakfast. US troops hated being fed foreign rations, but there were never any complaints if foreign troops were fed American rations.

In the late evening of the second day on board we left Plymouth for France, in convoy. Plymouth harbor and dock area had hundreds of barrage balloons overhead to prevent low level attacks by enemy aircraft. As an officer I was allowed to eat in the Mess with British Navy and Army officers. It was here that I saw Royal Navy Midshipmen who looked as though they were fifteen-years-old or less. It was also the only place in my nearly four years of active duty that I was served loin lamb chops. At noon the next day while traveling in fog we could hear General Bradley's 1st Army artillery firing as the battle for St. Lo was in progress. In the early afternoon we sailed out of the fog into bright sunlight opposite Omaha Beach. We could see Air Base Number One where our fighter planes were landing in the fields just above the beach. There were hundreds of ships unloading ammunition and supplies, especially equipment for Patton's 3rd Army soon to be activated. Barrage balloons protected all of these ships and the beach area. This would have been about 15 July 1944.

We moved over to Utah Beach and prepared to disembark. A wooden gangway (stairway) was suspended from a boom. We descended to a landing craft and then crossed over to a second landing craft that was lashed to the first one. We wore our seventy-pound packs and were packed into the landing craft so tightly that if anyone fainted he couldn't fall down. As I was crossing from the first landing craft to the second, a sailor stationed between the two ships held my carbine so I would have two free hands to make the crossover. When I took my carbine back I said, "I wouldn't like to have your job, sailor." He answered, "I wouldn't want your job either, Lieutenant. I feel for you." The landing craft dropped the ramp in the surf, and we hardly got our feet wet as we stepped ashore on Utah Beach. As we were landing, one of the barrage balloons broke loose. As soon as it reached about 3,000 feet the anti-aircraft guns shot it down.

Preparation for Battle

The backside of the beach was a very marshy area with many signs saying *Achtung Minen*. We had to stay on cleared paths. As we left the beach we could see tracer ammunition lighting up the sky as it was starting to get dark. Soon we heard German planes overhead. They only came out at dusk and after dark. Ahead of us we had a ten-mile hike with our seventy-pound packs. Most of the dark had passed before we reached our bivouac area.

In the morning we were picked up by trucks and transported to a replacement center. I had an interview with a clerk who had my records. His office was a lean-to shed at the rear of a barn in a Norman apple orchard. At this center I met many officers who had received light wounds and were being returned to duty. All enlisted men in our group were assigned immediately as riflemen, regardless of their advanced training. I was assigned to 29th Division, 116th Infantry, H Company, 81 mm Mortar Platoon. About twelve other lieutenants and I were taken by truck to Regimental Headquarters, where we reported to the Adjutant in the Headquarters tent. As he was busy, he said for us to go across the road to where a wheat field had just been cut and he would join us as soon as he was free to explain our assignments. As we entered the field a German fighter plane strafed it. I did not see the plane but I certainly heard it. In a few minutes a two and a half ton truck came down the road with bullet holes in the windshield. The driver was not hurt.

At H Company the captain was newly assigned. Our mortar platoon leader had served about one month; another lieutenant, about two weeks; another lieutenant and I were newly assigned. The Company was living in pup tents in an apple orchard on a Norman farm in the village of St. Clair sur Elle. The 2nd Battalion had fought through this village five weeks before. We could listen to the British Broadcasting Company (BBC) music and news on our sound-powered telephones in our pup tents, relayed from the Battalion radio. BBC news was extremely biased. Whenever the Royal Air Force or Royal Navy was in the news, it was so designated. If the US Air Force or Army were in the news it would be referred to as "allied forces." Movies were shown in the hayloft of the barn, but they were terrible grade B and C movies.

The Battalion would be formed up in a large field every morning. Colonel Bingham had all the new officers conduct the physical exercises so that all of the men could get to know who we were.

Our mortar platoon leader asked me if I had a woolen (winter) undershirt. I did, and he suggested that I put it on and keep it on all of the time. It was good advice as we were sleeping outside every night and were frequently wet. Our uniform consisted of a woolen shirt and twill pants, which were very tough. After being wet and covered with mud, you could pick off chunks of dried mud and the clothes looked like new. In addition, we were issued a field jacket. I received a second one at Brest after the first one was all torn when a grenade hit me. Our boots were regular issue high shoes with canvas leggings. We cut four inches off the leggings so they weren't so high. Combat boots did not reach us until the fall of 1944 in Holland. Also while in Holland, we received full-length woolen overcoats. It was because of all this wool that we could survive in the cold and rain. I never spent a night inside until mid November 1944.

An Assistant Plans and Training Officer, a G-3 from XIX Corps, came to each company to explain what our next operation was to be. At the start, there was to be a 1,000-plane bombing raid on the German lines. This was to be the first 1,000-plane raid in support of infantry.

While in this area we were given instructions in hedgerow fighting. This subject was never addressed before the invasion, so thousands were killed and wounded because of these obstacles. Some of our tanks had metal cones welded on the front so that the tank could make a hole in the hedgerow two feet deep and ten inches in diameter. After these holes were made, the tank moved back a few yards and engineers put TNT in the holes, packed dirt in them, and then blew the hedgerow up. Another tank equipped with a bulldozer blade cleared soil away so infantry could pass through without going over the top. This operation allowed jeeps with ammunition and also tanks to pass through without exposing themselves to excessive enemy fire. All of these techniques had to be developed after the invasion. The Assistant Division CO told us never to attempt anything alone; you should always have a team to work with.

The 1,000-plane raid was delayed a day for bad weather. We watched from a small hill in the orchard and could see that some of the bombs were very close, too close in fact. General McNair, Commander of Army Ground Forces in the United States, was among those killed. The 30th Division got hit and was so mixed up that we were delayed in making our attack.

After VE Day

Our duties in Germany, in May 1945, were to act as police for the local authorities. I had to investigate all complaints, as locals were not allowed to exercise police duties. One Displaced Person (DP) complained of having too much work to do and of being abused. I went to the farm and met the farmer's wife, who was forty-plus years of age, and spoke perfect English. She had lived in Brooklyn for four years. She told me that the DP was a chronic complainer and did not want to work. I had a meeting with Burgomeister Herman Apst about this. While I explained the nature of the complaint, Herman's wife served us the first strawberries of the season. Herman listened to my explanation of this complaint for a while and finally blurted out that it was a "Goddamn lie," and that was the end of that.

The British cooperated with the Russians by sending DPs home. It was announced that on a certain date trucks would be sent to the town center to take all DPs back to Poland or Russia. The trucks came and only three or four DPs went back. A few days later a civilian arrived with a paper saying he was a representative of the Russian government. He wanted to know why we had not sent our DPs home. He knew exactly how many there were. I told him the US interpretation of the treaty was that DPs would be sent back only if they wanted to go. This Russian, who was carrying a pistol in his pocket, told me he was sending more trucks on a certain day and we had better send them back. I let him know that when the trucks arrived I would be there with my machine guns. No one was going unless he or she wanted to go.

Comments about the War

A mention is made here to explain the status of Negroes in the Army. All trains in the south carried "Jim Crow" coaches for Negroes. All Negroes in the Army were in segregated units. Some units had white officers. Others had all Negroes, enlisted and officers. At Ft. Devens there was a National Guard Regiment from Harlem (NYC) that was 100% Negro. Initially the Navy had zero Negroes and during the war it acquired some Negro mess men. There was a Negro infantry division that fought in Italy. It was made up of

Negro enlisted men and white officers. It was not a successful unit. Until the Negroes were fully integrated into all types of units, their potential could not be reached. Anything less than full integration left them feeling that they didn't have a fair deal.

At this point I would like to make some comments regarding the weapons and equipment that we used or that were used to support the infantry. First consider the trucks. The ten-wheel trucks with four-wheel drives were superior to anything that the enemy or friendly forces had. Also, we had a jeep that relieved the infantry of carrying a lot of heavy equipment and ammunition, except when we were close enough to engage the enemy. As for weapons, the M1 rifle was superior to any rifle in any army. The Browning Automatic Rifle (BAR) was too heavy and very hard to handle.

The heavy water-cooled machine gun was left over from World War I and was too heavy. The German machine gun was superior to either of ours. Ammunition for all these weapons was not smokeless, which was a definite disadvantage. Communications were as good, or better than any other, once we got rid of the sound-powered phones for fire control. Our artillery had no equal, but our tanks were inferior to the German tanks. The light tank with the 31mm gun was worthless. The Sherman tank was not the equal of the German tank, but prevailed because we had more of them. Perhaps if we had not been so stingy with defense appropriations between WW I and WW II we might have had a new machine gun and adequate anti-tank guns.

The US fielded one hundred divisions in WW II, which was quite a feat since in 1938, before the defense build up, not one division existed.

Brad was born in Worcester, Massachusetts, and graduated from Boston University in 1938. He entered the Army in 1942, serving on active duty until 1945, earning a Silver Star, a Bronze Star, and Purple Heart with cluster. He and his wife, Charlotte, had four children. They traveled often, enabling them to visit many of the places his extensive library and interest in history led them. In later years they enjoyed their annual visit to Mexico's west coast. Brad died in 2006.

Three Days In February

JUDD ALEXANDER

Prologue

I GRADUATED FROM high school on May 28, 1943. Ten days later I was drafted. After induction at Ft. Snelling in Minnesota, I was sent off to Georgia for basic training in the infantry and after that to a university to study engineering. In March of 1944, the Army suddenly decided that its need for infantrymen would soon be far greater that its need for engineers. The engineer-training program was closed. Over the next two weeks, one hundred seventy-five thousand scholars in uniform, studying in colleges all over the country, were sent off to infantry divisions. Some of those men had names you may find familiar: Gore Vidal, Ed Koch, Bob Dole, Henry Kissinger, Judd Alexander, and his brother McIndoe. All of us were privates, not privates first class, privates.

Many of my classmates and I were sent to the 8th Armored Division, then on Louisiana maneuvers. I became a mortar gunner in the third platoon of a rifle company in the division's 58th Armored Infantry Battalion. After a summer of training in Louisiana's heat, the 8th left in October 1944, for Europe's cold—its worst winter in forty years.

Armored divisions were different from regular infantry divisions. We had less manpower, but more firepower, mobility, and armor. Our three rifle battalions, three thousand men, made up thirty percent of our division's personnel, and fifty percent of the division's casualties. In addition to infantry, every armored division had three battalions of tanks, three of self-propelled artillery, and three more for reconnaissance, quartermaster, and ordinance. Unlike the foot soldiers in the infantry divisions, all of us rode. Each of our infantry squads had its own halftrack-armored car mounting a heavy machine gun.

We were also different from the other services. Pilots and airmen fight often and intensely but seldom for more than an hour or so at a time. The Navy comes under fire for a few days. But, for the Army and the Marines, battles can rage for a month or more. My older brother, an infantryman in Europe, was once on the frontline and in touch with the enemy for ninety straight days. That is three months without a bed, a shower, a proper toilet, a roof, or heat.

My story begins in late January after The Battle of the Bulge had come to an end. Our division was transferred from General Patton's 3rd Army in Northern France to Holland, 250 miles up the line. There, we joined General Simpson's 9th Army on the extreme left of American forces. Forty-seven American divisions, in four armies, stretched from our position all the way to the Swiss border. To our left lay the British Second Army, the Canadian First Army, and the North Sea. By this time, most of France and all of Belgium had been liberated. Holland, however, was still eighty percent German-occupied and the German homeland had been barely penetrated. For this little essay on my war, I have chosen to cover three days of action for my platoon, February 25-27, as representative of the combat experiences of infantry soldiers.

Day #1, February 25, 1945: The Night Patrol

Ten days earlier, we had relieved a troop of British Royal Marine Commandos. They had taken their front line position three weeks before. We took over their foxholes and trenches as well as their battered billets. My platoon was spread out in and around the tiny Dutch village of Linne. It bordered a huge oxbow bend in the Maas River in Limburg Province. The enemy held the island created by the oxbow, the other side of the river, and the woods two miles to the north. Farmland lay between our position and the woods.

Platoons like mine were populated with a second lieutenant,

ten sergeants, five technicians (drivers for the half-tracks), forty privates, and a medic. About a third of the soldiers in our five squads were teenagers. I had trained with most of these men for ten months. Every one of them was my friend.

Our piece of "the front" had been quiet, except for a few exchanges of artillery and mortar fire, since our arrival. That was about to change. In the early afternoon, our lieutenant visited each squad. He told us that at dawn our battalion would attack along a three thousand yard front. Our objective would be the small city of Roermond located at the juncture of the Maas and Roer rivers. It lay seven miles to our north and three miles from the German frontier. In a preliminary action, my platoon would send out a forty-man combat patrol to test the enemy's defenses. We would leave at midnight. Preparations began at once. Night fighting is different. In the dark, rifles, mortars, and machine guns are not as useful as carbines, pistols, submachine guns, trench knives, and hatchets. The forty of us, two-thirds of the platoon, had assembled on the departure line when the patrol was suddenly aborted. British intelligence warned Battalion that the German position was too strong, too well dug-in for a combat patrol to succeed. They recommended a reconnaissance patrol instead. Battalion agreed. Our young lieutenant, Walter Dahlin, was assigned to lead the new patrol.

Combat patrols fight, recon patrols are much smaller and avoid fights. Their mission is to gather intelligence by stealth. Dahlin hurriedly gathered his team. He selected a sergeant from his half-track and a German-speaking private. Then, he asked for three volunteers. My boisterous friends Greenberg and Maienza were quick to respond, but the third volunteer, the taciturn Kwacz, was a surprise. He was a half-track driver. Normally, drivers stay with their vehicles, but, since volunteering was encouraged, he was welcomed to the patrol.

The six men set out an hour after midnight on the clear and frosty night. The small group made good time to the abandoned farmstead, half way to the wood. From there on, the going was slower and more cautious. As they entered the wood, the lieutenant, leading the way, signaled his men to take to the ground and proceed by crawling. Even in the dark, they could see ahead the outline of the large house that was presumed to be the German headquarters. As they were moving forward, Dahlin realized that he was advancing up a slight rise. Assuming that he was on the parapet of a trench, he rolled on to his left side and reached for a hand grenade with his right hand. At that moment, an enemy sentry popped up, shouted, "Halt!" and fired his rifle at the figure on the ground five yards away. Kwacz, next in line, leaped to his feet, took out the sentry with a burst from his sub-machine gun and dropped a grenade into the trench to finish off a second sentry.

The German's bullet, fired at point-blank range, entered Dahlin's right shoulder at the base of his neck. It passed through the organs on the right side of his body (lung, liver, pancreas, and intestines) before lodging itself in the pelvic bone. The lieutenant went into immediate shock. The rest of the patrol was in panic mode. They could hear shouts and gunfire coming from the house. The sergeant and Greenburg grabbed the stricken officer by his harness and dragging him they set off running laterally through the woods. After a few minutes, they paused for breath. When Kwacz caught up, he announced that he would get help and ran off. The others assumed that the driver was abandoning the patrol; they were wrong. Kwacz ran through the woods and across the fields for nearly two miles until he reached our lines. Without stopping to explain his mission, he commandeered an idle jeep and headed back across the fields at full throttle and with headlights on.

In the meantime, the patrol was struggling to rig a crude litter from tree branches and jackets. Germans were firing machine guns and pyrotechnic flares (similar to Fourth-of-July sky rockets, the flares illuminate a battlefield for a few seconds at a time) and their troops were beating the woods in search of the patrol. Back in Linne, we all knew that our patrol was in trouble, but we had no way of helping it. Miraculously, as the careening jeep neared the woods, Maienza flagged it down. Within moments, the four soldiers and their comatose leader were piled into the little jeep and it was off again racing, weaving, headlights blazing—across the bullet-swept fields to the safety of our lines.

Corporal Henry Kwacz saved the lives of his lieutenant and four of his fellow soldiers that night. The initiative, courage, and audacity exhibited by the corporal in this action reflect the finest traditions in the long history of the United States Army.

The four paragraphs above are my memory of the commendation I wrote up a few days after VE Day. It recommended a Silver Star for Kwacz. I submitted it to our new Captain. He passed it up through channels to Division Headquarters. There, the commendation was not only approved, the award was elevated to a Distinguished Service Cross, the valor award second only to The Congressional Medal of Honor. Then, since the event occurred while our 9th Army was a part of General Montgomery's Army Group, Kwacz was awarded a British medal as well: The Order of Distinguished Service, a sterling silver medal second only to the Brits' Victoria Cross. In later actions, Kwacz was to earn two Bronze Stars and a Purple Heart. The quiet half-track driver became the most decorated soldier in the ten thousand-man 8th Armored Division.

Day #2, February 26, 1945: The Attack

Sleep was impossible for our platoon while our patrol was out and in danger. It was nearing 3:30 a.m. when it finally made it home and the excitement died down. In another two hours we would be moving out to the assembly point for the dawn attack. Since it was to be dismounted (on foot) our half-tracks and our anti-tank platoon would not participate. Four hundred men from three companies would be advancing over open fields. Spread out over the three thousand yards, we were bordered by the Maas River on our left and the Roer River on the right. Our platoon was in the center of the formation. Our initial objective was Heidi Woods. As we were assembling on the starting line, word came down that Battalion was sending us a replacement for the fallen Dahlin.

It was about 7:00 a.m. and still dark when the preliminary barrage from our artillery and tanks began. After about fifteen minutes, we infantry rose from the ditches and headed forward under the umbrella of the screaming shells. We were in a line of skirmishers, shoulder to shoulder, five yards apart, a formation reminiscent of the Civil War. After the troops had advanced a few hundred yards, our barrage lifted. A few minutes later, the enemy in the woods answered with a fusillade of rifle and machine gun fire and airbursts from their artillery. The initial volley brought down a dozen of the men in our long line. Our new lieutenant was one of the wounded. He had been our leader for about an hour. Our initial casualties were relatively light, considering the number of targets we presented, because we were near the limit of the range of their rifles and machine guns. There were a number of close calls in our platoon during that first salvo. One man came away with a two-inch-long bullet crease in his steel helmet. John Finn, later a sheriff and state senator in Vermont, had a bullet pierce the front of his helmet at an odd angle, race around the inner surface of the helmet, and exit after it had traveled three-quarters of the way around. Finn was surprised but not injured. (Would you like to see the helmet? It is on display in the military museum at Norwich University.) As I was diving to the ground, I took a burst from a burp gun (a German machine gun with a rate of fire twice that of our guns). It felt like I was being attacked by a swarm of bees, that everything was happening in slow motion, and I was thinking, "these guys are trying to kill me." I reached the ground safely. Ten minutes later I noticed that the wood stock atop the barrel of my carbine had been shot away. Several splinters had pierced the left sleeve of my field jacket and drew a few drops of blood from my forearm. I had never felt a thing.

When the Krauts started firing, we needed no officer's order to get us to the ground. That comes naturally. After a few minutes of lying flat out, we began to move forward, slowly and painfully, by crawling and by a maneuver called "fire and advance." Two soldiers, both on the ground, pair up. One of them fires off a clip of ammunition (eight rounds) at enemy positions. In the eight seconds it takes to fire off the clip, his partner rises and runs forward for ten zigzag yards before diving back to earth. The partners exchange roles and repeat the maneuver. Sergeant Weller and Greenberg were the first to partner up. Weller made the first dash forward. Then, as he rose up on his elbows to give fire for his partner's dash, a sniper's bullet struck him between the eyes. He became the first man in our platoon to die that day.

The platoon continued to move forward at a slow, slow pace. We were under fire in the flat, treeless fields for more than four hours. Occasionally, we were able to take cover behind some large piles of harvested turnips. Around noon, we reached a farmstead, halfway to the woods. Its buildings offered needed protection. The lieutenant of the second platoon and some of his men were there ahead of us. The lieutenant had taken a bullet through the wrist. An hour later, when the medics evacuated him, he became the fourth lieutenant our company had lost in the last twelve hours: three wounded, one killed. After our captain was relieved late that evening, our two-hundred-man company had no officers left. The three rifle platoons were taken over by their platoon sergeants. They performed well. Six weeks later, all three were given battlefield commissions and second-lieutenant bars.

Back at the farmstead, our day was far from done. We held the farm for about two hours as the firing gradually faded down. Then, orders were received for us to move out to a new position that would allow an attack on the woods from a different direction. Sergeant Mailley, our new leader, marched us around to the right, skirting the woods. We reached a large farmyard about two hundred yards beyond the woods. A medical aid station was being established in the farm's courtyard, and a few civilians, including a small baby, were sheltering in the cellar of the house.

We learned that our sister platoon, the second, joined by a platoon of tanks, would lead the attack. Our platoon would be held in reserve, waiting about half way between the farmhouse and the woods. Infantrymen like tanks because of their firepower. Tankers love infantry because they need our eyes. When a tank comes under fire the hatches are closed. The visibility for drivers and tank commanders now becomes seriously limited. They see the world through narrow slits and periscopes. This makes them vulnerable to attacks by individual enemy soldiers who could reach the tank unseen by the occupants. For this attack, the five squads of infantry would ride on the backs of five Sherman tanks.

Soon, the tanks and their passengers fanned out and headed into the woods. Almost immediately we could hear heavy firing. When a medical jeep hit a land mine on the edge of the woods, its two medics were seriously injured. Mailley sent three soldiers and me to help the fallen medics. When we reached them they were conscious but seriously wounded. They were able to tell us what to do for them with bandages and sulfa powders. Although a handle had broken off each of their two stretchers, we were able to load the medics onto the stretchers and carry them to the aid station, two hundred yards away. By then the wounded, Americans and Germans, had begun to come out of the woods. The aid station doctors asked us for help in recovering the wounded. The first soldier we rescued was a friend from the second platoon. It was obvious that he had lost an eye, but he was alert and angry. He kept shouting that he was not going to ride in any ambulance with any blank, blank German. After brief treatment from the doctors, he was loaded into an ambulance with a wounded German for the trip to a field hospital. Our friend was still shouting his protests.

When we returned to the edge of the woods a third time, a wounded German came running and stumbling toward us. His face was as gray as his gray uniform and he seemed to be carrying something gray grasped in his two hands. As he came closer, I realized that he was carrying his own intestines spilling from a gaping stomach wound. We carried him to the aid station, but I doubt that he survived.

We were still in the courtyard when I heard Sergeant Mailley, one hundred yards away, calling to my platoon to assemble and prepare to mount up. For just a moment, a thought flashed through my mind, "Maybe I didn't hear that. Maybe I could just stay here instead of going into the woods on a tank." Just as quickly I had second thoughts, "What would my parents think? How can I abandon my friends in the platoon right now when they will need me?" The answer came easily.

We scrambled onto the tanks and waited for the order to move out. We waited and we waited on the back of the idling tanks in the looming early darkness of a Dutch winter. Finally, the attack order was countermanded. We marched back on foot the way we had come. We were to spend the night in foxholes in the field near the first farmstead. After digging our holes (every combat soldier carries an entrenching tool, a combination folding shovel, hoe, and axe), we settled down for supper, a box of K-Rations, our first meal since dawn. Our orders were to remain on the alert for the night, appropriate since the enemy often launched strong counter attacks after giving ground. I shared a foxhole with my pal Greenberg that long night. I remember that we talked about the patrol, Weller's death, restaurants in Minneapolis, and what we wanted to do after the war. The casualty list of that afternoon's attack totaled eleven with four dead.

Day #3, February 27, 1945: Sleeping on the March

A bit after sunrise, a platoon of tanks moved up to join us on the line. They came bearing gifts: water, bandoleers of ammunition, fresh first aid packs, and more K-Rations. We were to ride the tanks this morning and, for the third time, attack the Heidi Woods. On the sunny and pleasant day, we set off riding on our steel chariots. The noisy clattering of our tracked vehicles brought no response from the woods ahead. Soon, two explosions reminded us that we were still at war. The blasts from the mines were not large but they were enough to disable two tanks, the one I was riding and another on our left. There were no injuries.

The order to dismount was called out immediately. We jumped to the ground before we realized that we were in a minefield. A few dozen of the little anti-personnel mines that the Germans called *schue minen* (shoe mines) were scattered about. The mines consisted of a quarter-pound block of TNT and a striker in a wooden box the size of two packs of cigarettes. They were designed to blow off a soldier's shoe...and the foot inside it. The fact that the mines had not been buried, signaled that they had been laid in haste.

The undamaged tanks had already begun to back away, carefully. We footsloggers were being pretty careful ourselves. We would stare at the ground, studying it carefully before taking a step. The minefield proved to be no more than fifty yards deep. After that, we could stop worrying about the ground and start worrying about the woods ahead. When we reached the fringe of the woods and entered it cautiously we found that the enemy had abandoned the position during the night. Once again warned about the danger of a counterattack, we posted sentries before setting out to examine the large house and its system of trenches.

Those alertness warnings were not frivolous. About the same time that we were exploring the woods, a sister platoon was moving through some sparse woods about a mile away from us. As our troops advanced, they came across several wounded German soldiers who had spent the night in the place where they had fallen. A little further on they came to a patch of apparently abandoned foxholes. When the platoon passed the last hole, an enemy soldier hiding there fired at the sergeant's back. The sergeant was killed instantly. The German marksman was gunned down before he could get off a second shot. What a waste. If that German had surrendered, he would have saved two lives, one American and one German.

Back in the Heidi Woods, we received a visitor. A runner from the Company Command Post (CP) had been sent to us with two messages. A few of us gathered around the sergeant to hear the news. First, he announced that we had a new Company Commander. The Battalion Commander had selected a lieutenant from Company A, for this promotion. The second part of the runner's message was more intriguing. Late the day before, American forces had captured the two huge dams on the Rohr River that had been holding up the 9th Army's advance. If the Germans had blown up the dams, they would have flooded the flat land favorable to our attack. Now that the way was open for a rapid advance to the Rhine River, the Army needed our division's armor and mobility to exploit the opportunity. Our orders to take Roermond were voided. The new orders called for us, as soon as we could be replaced, to join the powerful drive to the Rhine. We were to be relieved by the 1st Cavalry. It would arrive, possibly, within a few hours.

It did not. We fussed around in the woods preparing the defenses for our successors. Although there were several reports that the relief "would be arriving any time now," the relievers did not show up until dark. After an hour spent indoctrinating the new arrivals, we were ready for the march back to Linne.

We set out in a tight formation for the two-mile hike. Remember, none of us had had more than an hour of sleep at a time in the last ninety hours. We were about to acquire a new talent. We found that we could doze off while marching and still keep on walking. After ten or more yards we would bump into a fellow soldier, wake up for a minute or so, and then go back to sleep.

We reached the company CP just after midnight. It was in a large windmill attached to a large barn. Our cooks, drivers, and vehicles were waiting for us and our bedrolls were laid out on straw in the barn. The new order called for us to move out, mounted, at dawn. First, we were offered a choice: Did we want to sleep or did we want to eat? Every one of us selected "sleep." About half of the platoon was already in their sacks and asleep. I was about to join them when an officer from battalion came into the barn and announced in a loud voice that the "depart at dawn" order was countermanded. We would now be moving out for the drive to the Rhine in ten minutes.

You know, if you are tired enough, you can sleep pretty darn well while sitting up on steel seats and bouncing along in a noisy and springless half-track.

Born in Owatonna, Minnesota, Judd graduated from Carlton College after the war, followed by additional studies at the University of Illinois and Harvard. His working career in the paper and packaging industry led to Executive Vice President positions at the American Can

Company and the James River Corporation. Judd, with assistance from his wife, Theo, served as National Chair of Keep America Beautiful Inc. He has kept busy as a writer and speaker as well as serving in a variety of public service and civic organizations.

Many Thanks, Yanks

CHARLES ALLING

Prologue

CHARLES ALLING joined the Army Air Corps several days after the Japanese attack on Pearl Harbor. It was 1943 before he was called to begin basic training, followed by pilot training. Between his enlistment and his first bombing run over Europe, Charles suffered two losses: his very dear sister, Prudy, and a best friend.

He was sent to eastern England to join the Eighth Air Force. Charles and his crew flew a B-17 bomber in twenty-seven missions over Europe. Many times they were the lead bomber and most of the missions were in a plane he named for his sister, the *Miss Prudy*.

Charles Alling is sharing two chapters from his book, *A Mighty Fortress: Lead Bomber Over Europe*. The book is a story of the last ten months of the war in Europe as experienced by a group of brave men who flew bombing missions that aided in ending the war in Europe.

The air strike over Aussig, Czechoslovakia, was our twenty-seventh mission, and it was also the last aerial engagement in World War II between the Eighth Air Force and the Luftwaffe.

On April 29, 1945, the fascist dictator Mussolini was captured and killed by partisans near Lake Como, a picture-perfect little town in northern Italy. To the south, sloping hills descend gracefully to the lake's edge with cone-shaped cypress trees trailing the landscape. To the north, peaks rise from the water, and fishing villages and harbors are nestled into the hills. To the east, the Swiss Alps rise above the lake with snow-covered crests. Mussolini and his mistress were hanged from their heels at a filling station.

The next day, April 30, Adolf Hitler gave his new wife and long-time mistress, Eva Braun, a poison pill and then he shot himself. Russian troops were by then closing in on his bunker in a Berlin that had been blasted beyond recognition by Allied bombers. Hitler had ordered his body to be burned and buried so that it would not become a Russian trophy.

At the time, word was coming by underground wireless from Holland that Dutch civilians were starving to death at the rate of a thousand a day in the German-occupied areas. Germany had held the major cities and had confiscated the food. The Dutch had to resort to eating their cats and dogs. They begged the Germans for grain to no avail and resorted to eating tulip bulbs for nourishment. The winter had been terribly cold, and without blankets and coal they had wrapped themselves in rugs at night to keep warm. Help was desperately needed and the Dutch could not possibly wait for hostilities to end. Until now, the Allies had avoided civilian areas occupied by German troops, because of the intense concentration of artillery and antiaircraft guns. By the end of April, however, the Allies and Germans had entered into negotiations to set up food drops for the Dutch. These negotiations were documented by Dutch historian Walter Maass and they progressed as follows:

> For several weeks, the International Red Cross had worked to broker a deal with the Germans, British, and Americans. The relief negotiations were held at a school at Achterveld [a village just within the Allied front line near Amersfoort]. General Eisenhower was represented by General Walter Bedell Smith, Montgomery by General De Guingaud. Also present were Prince Bernhard and a Russian officer. The German negotiators arrived by car, were stopped at some distance from the meeting place, and proceeded on foot under a white flag. Both parties had brought their experts for organizing the relief work. [Nazi commissioner for the Netherlands] Seyss-Inquart was accompanied by the Dutch Food Commissioner, Louwes . . .
>
> Discussions started, with the participants facing each other at a large table. Again, Seyss-Inquart rejected unconditional surrender,

because such a step would hurt him in the final judgment of history. An argument began between him and Bedell Smith and the latter impatiently exclaimed: "Come on, speak up! You know you'll be shot anyway!"

Seyss-Inquart replied, "That leaves me cold."

Whereupon the American scoffed, "It certainly will!"

At the close of the negotiations, six food drops were scheduled to take place in early May. The parties agreed to a five-hour truce during which the Eighth Air Force was allowed to fly over Holland without being shot at by the Germans. The American planes would carry a full crew, without ammunition, fly on a predetermined route, and drop cartons of food at designated drop zones. It was agreed that if a bomber strayed out of the safe corridor, the Germans would shoot blanks as a warning.

May 1, 1945 We were briefed for the first mercy mission, known by some as a "chow haul," to Rotterdam, Holland. We were told the Dutch were starving to death; every dog, cat, and vermin had been eaten. The Dutch had even stripped and burned the wood inside their homes to stay warm. The underground radio reported that relief planes would be coming but the message was met with doubt. Who had ever heard of planes dropping food parcels in a territory occupied by the enemy? No one imagined the Germans would permit it.

John K. Gerhart, commanding general of the 93rd Bomb Wing (which included four bomb groups), was to fly with Captain Delmar Dunham. Dunham led four hundred planes of the Eighth Air Force. We were assigned to fly deputy lead, with Colonel Creer as our command pilot.

We were to fly into Rotterdam at three to four hundred feet and drop "ten-in-one" rations of canned meat, butter, bread, jam, and sacks of flour wrapped in heavy burlap secured by thin steel straps. The drop zones were marked by large red crosses in open fields, parks, race tracks, and an airfield.

The Supreme Headquarters Allied Expeditionary Forces (SHAEF) had given the go-ahead to begin the food drops, and we did not know that the final agreement for the delivery of food was not signed until May 2. That meant the first mercy mission began a day before the agreement was official. If we had known, we would have been far more concerned flying into Rotterdam without ammunition, even though we understood the Germans were not to fire at us.

We assembled at one thousand feet and left England, passing over Felixstowe on the way, and a hundred miles from the coast of Britain we reached Holland. We descended to four hundred feet as we approached Rotterdam. As we flew over the city, I looked down for only a few seconds. We were in tight formation off the general's right wing, and there were hundreds of planes behind us. In those moments, I captured a glimpse of the unfolding drama that will rest in my mind forever.

As we approached the drop zone, I realized there were thousands of people lining the streets, leaning out of their windows, and watching from the roof tops. I saw a sea of white; everything was white except for an occasional splash of color. The Dutch were waving anything white they could get their hands on—sheets, handkerchiefs, scarves, towels, and some waved the American flag. Men, women, and children were full of excitement and joy, cheering, clapping, and dancing while German gunners leaned against the barrels of their 88 mm cannons. If a German had dared to shoot, I believe he would have been trampled to death by the Dutch.

Up ahead I could see the drop zone in a field, and as we approached there was a surging mass of people. We had to drop our food quickly and expeditiously to avoid any accidental casualties. There were brave, elderly citizens trying to hold back an exultant crowd.

"Bombs away!" called Bill, and *Miss Prudy* bounced up as cartons of food were released. We gradually gained altitude and slowly banked to the left, heading toward the English Channel as I flew off Dunham's right wing in close formation. As we left Rotterdam, other groups in the fleet of B-17s were still making their way in, each one a part of this mercy mission.

Not far from the coast of England, I was conscious that I was tiring. My left wrist was numb—I had been flying in tight formation for hours without relief. Suddenly, Dunham's plane swerved to the right unexpectedly. Colonel Creer, alert and nimble, grabbed the wheel, turning away just in time to avoid a mid-air collision. Dunham straightened out and we quickly returned to our formation. "Thank you, Colonel Creer, my hands are numb. I can't feel the steering wheel—I can't grip it anymore."

"Alling, why don't you let me fly the plane to the base? I'm sorry I didn't spell you sooner. I got so carried away with the sight below us that I forgot to share the load with you."

May 3, 1945 We were briefed for our second mercy mission, the third launched by the Eighth Air Force in that first week of May. This flight would take us over Amsterdam. We were the lead plane of the Eighth Air Force with Lieutenant Colonel Ed Freeman, 18th Squadron commander as our command pilot. We received instructions to fly single file over the city to ensure the accuracy of the food drop on the designated red cross zones.

As we approached the continent, the weather turned sour and it began to rain. I knew the poor visibility would make the accuracy of this drop challenging. As we were the first to approach Amsterdam, I flew in at three hundred feet off the ground with the 34th Bomb Group behind me. Over the city I dipped my wings to alert the Germans not to shoot. I wondered if every German soldier would heed this armistice; if one fired, we would be the first to go. For a few moments it was tense, but once I believed the Germans would keep their commitment, we searched for the drop zone. Without a break in the clouds and continued poor visibility, we had to circle the city and make another pass. As we approached, Bill called in, "Chuck, I can't see the target!"

"Okay, we're going to do a 360," I replied.

As Colonel Freeman informed the rest of the command pilots,

I knew he was becoming anxious. This assignment was turning out to be more difficult than expected with poor visibility, limited time, limited gas supply, and hundreds more planes of the Eighth Air Force coming up behind us. With each and every minute that we were unable to drop the food, this mission became increasingly complex.

Eight minutes later, we approached the city for another pass. Bill called, "Bomb bay doors open! Flaps down!" I felt a sense of relief knowing the food drop would take place any moment. With the flaps down, it gave *Miss Prudy* the lift she needed as our true ground speed was 140 miles per hour, and we couldn't go any slower or we'd stall out. We were now three hundred feet off the ground. Just moments before the drop, Bill called on the intercom, "Chuck, I still can't see anything!"

Now we were in real trouble. "All right," I said, "Let's circle and we'll try again." I gave Freeman the signal. Thirty-eight planes followed us around the city once more. I took a deep breath.

As we circled Amsterdam, Bill said, "Chuck, we've got to try this one more time, and this time we have to fly as low as we possibly can without stalling out!" Bill was agitated.

"How much lower do you think we can go?" I asked, wondering if this food drop was possible.

"Drop to two hundred feet," Bill called, "But for God's sake don't go any lower!"

This would have to be our final attempt, and I certainly could not fly any lower unless we wanted to wrap ourselves around a tree or a windmill. I was exasperated and worried. As we flew back over Amsterdam, I thought of all the Dutch who were starving and desperate for relief. If we could not find the drop zone, there would be chaos in the streets.

"There it is!" Bill yelled, unleashing all his pent-up tension. "I can see the cross! Bombs away!" Bill pulled the switch and cartons of food fell to the earth.

For those watching from below, I can only imagine the sight of hundreds of B-17s flying into the city at a dangerously low level. The noise of the engines must have been deafening as five hundred bombers flew over Amsterdam, one after the next, every thirty seconds, for three and a half hours, dropping thousands of cartons of food.

I looked down for a few seconds. There were thousands of people running in the streets with their white handkerchiefs, white cloth, white flags, anything white. And then I focused on something I will never forget. There was a gray-haired gentleman with a wooden peg-leg, swinging a cane, and hobbling in the direction of the food. A little girl with long blonde hair, who must have been his granddaughter, was restraining him with all her might. She leaned back, her heels dug into the soil, pulling on his coattails to keep him from moving forward into the falling cartons of food.

Ray saw people standing behind glass doors waving, a cow tumble and fall as it was hit by a carton of food, and a funeral cortege of horses that pulled a caisson with the casket on it, the mourners walking behind clutching flowers. Sometimes it's the odd things that remain fixed in our memory.

During the first three days in May alone, eight hundred tons of food were dropped over Holland, enough to provide 1,080,000 meals. The mercy missions were a massive undertaking and unprecedented in wartime history.

Seven years later, I was invited to join a group of marketing executives on a European trip organized by the Departments of State and Commerce and the U.S. Sales Executive Association. I was one of eight executives traveling to ten European countries. We flew to Scandinavia, Holland, France, England, Scotland, and Ireland.

When we arrived in Amsterdam, I went for a walk with my wife, Gail. I was delighted to see so many Dutch living life to its fullest. During our first night in Amsterdam, the American businessmen and their spouses were guests at a black-tie dinner for fifty at the Grand Amstel Hotel. We were all seated at one large elliptical table, and the American ambassador sat next to us.

In Holland, it is the custom that toasts follow dinner. The burgomaster of Amsterdam was the first to rise to his feet. A stout man with white hair and a ruddy complexion, he began the first toast of the evening. "This is a night in my life I will cherish." He enjoyed holding the floor and continued, "By the spring of 1945, our cities were occupied by the Germans. My fellow citizens were faced with another foe—starvation. We had no food. German soldiers had confiscated our dairy and vegetable products. There was hardly a cow, horse, goat, or chicken within hundreds of miles."

I quickly realized that someone in our group had leaked the story of our food drop. The burgomaster continued. "On May 3, 1945, I remember this day so well," and he paused with a deep breath. "My sister wrote to me, 'Unless a gift comes from Heaven, we will soon die. All we can do is hope and pray.' And then, as if to answer her prayers, I heard a noise outside that sounded like thunder. Looking out the window I could see, off in the distance, a line of bombers approaching Amsterdam. I saw the first plane flying in just above the treetops with a fleet of ships behind. She dipped her wings in her approach. I knew the significance of that friendly gesture. The Germans didn't shoot. They leaned on their cannons and watched.

"A number of B-17s circled the city a few times in a broad sweep, searching for the drop zone. The roar of the engines was thunderous, almost deafening, as the stream of bombers approached the city. Everyone ran outside to see. Then my wife and I, and many others, watched in total amazement, almost disbelief, as an armada of ships—these 'angels of mercy'—came across the horizon and flew into Amsterdam. The ground seemed to shake as they flew over us. We waived to the American pilots and their crews. And then I couldn't believe what I saw. Each plane dropped cartons of food onto a field just up the road. We were crying with joy. I put both arms around my wife and I hugged her and kissed her. We hugged and squeezed our neighbors. We, and thousands of others, were dancing in the streets. Everyone was delirious with joy! We were euphoric! We were, and are, forever grateful!"

I looked around the table nervously. Once again, I saw white—white handkerchiefs, white linen napkins—all reminders of that memorable sight, seven years earlier, as we flew over Amsterdam.

The dinner guests were listening intently, their eyes filled with tears. Even my American colleagues wiped their eyes with their white linen napkins. And then with all the emotion he could muster, the burgomaster continued, "And, my friends, Charles Alling, the young American who led the mighty armada, is with us tonight!"

As if by command, the dinner guests rose to their feet in applause. It was time for me to speak. I rose to my feet slowly, frantically thinking about what I would say. Clearing my throat, I took a very deep breath. "Thank you Mr. Burgomaster. I'm so glad to see you're eating better today." Everyone laughed, which helped. I paused, and this time took a more relaxed breath. "Now, I have a story to tell you." Again I paused, and read the anticipation in their faces, noticing the chefs with their tall, white hats, the waiters, waitresses, and the entire kitchen staff had entered the room to listen. "After the food drop, we flew over your beautiful country toward the sea. As we passed over fields of beautiful, yellow tulips, we saw the most extraordinary sight. You wonderful people had clipped the heads of the tulips to spell, 'MANY THANKS, YANKS.'"

I sat down to a hush as if all the oxygen had evaporated from the room. Stunned by the warm silence, I picked my white napkin off the table and placed it carefully on my lap. No one moved. I looked around and felt as though embraced by the emotion on all their faces and their expressions of sincere gratitude for what the Americans had done for their country.

Sensing the need for another kind of relief, the burgomaster rose to his feet just in time. "Thank you, Captain Alling! Thank you!" he said joyfully. "And now we have a token of our appreciation for you!" And with that, a waiter handed a large box to the burgomaster, who walked around the table and presented it to me. I carefully untied the red, white, and blue striped ribbon. The white tissue crumbled and fell to the table, revealing a suspended parachute on top of the largest bottle I had ever seen. It had six compartments, each with a different liqueur. I shook hands with the burgomaster and those around me, and asked one of the taller waiters if he would serve each guest with the liqueur of their choice.

When I think of the Dutch and what they endured during the war, I feel nothing but respect. They are a people with great spirit. They are survivors. They love life, and even when their families lay starving and dying, their spirit remained intact. The Germans could not tear apart the soul of this ravished country.

I still marvel at their task of clipping hundreds of tulips to create a message clearly visible to our planes hundreds of feet above the ground. This was not a small task for a nation of starving people, and it was a brave one for people fearing possible retribution. When I think about the mission over Amsterdam, I have a single, dramatic image in my mind of fields of yellow tulips, blossoming on the edge of devastation and war.

"Many Thanks, Yanks," is from Charles Alling's book, *A Mighty Fortress: Lead Bomber Over Europe,* published by CASEMATE of Havertown, Pennsylvania, in 2002.

Flying Home On A Wing And A Prayer

WORD WAS out that we would be leaving soon to train in B-29s for service in the Pacific. Days before leaving, we learned that we would not be flying *Miss Prudy* home. She was to be flown to Allied Headquarters in Berlin, where she would be used to fly VIPs around Europe. Somehow that seemed fitting for a plane that I thought deserved recognition. Meanwhile, Glen and I were given orders to fly to an RAF field nearby to collect a B-17 that we would fly home.

When we saw our plane, we were downcast. It was painted black, unlike the sleek silver Flying Fortress we expected to see. This was a ghost ship. No one flew a black ship; that was bad luck. Clearly this plane had been used for covert operations and flown only at night. "Glen," I said, "we're never going to get anyone to fly this home with us, and I'm not sure I want to anyway!" When we returned to the base, we ran into Bill. "Come with us, we've got a terrible problem."

When Bill saw the plane, he said, "I'll tell you what we are going to do. I'll get some white paint and paint *Ole Black Magic* on the side. That'll take the curse off it!"

Glen and I took *Ole Black* up a number of times, checking out each motor with great care, cutting engines and re-starting them, feathering all of them individually. Everything checked out beautifully, particularly the number four engine that had just been broken in with only thirty-four hours of flying time. We were ready for our flight home.

June 18, 1945   We received orders for our departure for the States. I was to fly back with my crew and ten non-commissioned officers. *Ole Black* would be carrying a plane of airmen and passengers with high expectations and hopes.

We shook hands with our friends in the 34th who were still at the base waiting for their departure. Before we gathered to leave, I needed time for one more goodbye. I walked over to *Miss Prudy,* climbed into my familiar cockpit, and sat down in a pilot's seat that was worn with memories. I placed my hand on the instrument panel and dropped my head forward, leaning gently on the steering wheel. I remembered so many times she had brought us back safely. I whispered to her, keeping my voice low, though no one was near. "How did you do this? How did you bring us through?"

I marveled at her simplicity—I looked in the back of the plane where my crew had lived in this shell of steel. I marveled at her toughness and her durability. She was a mighty fortress, all right! I jumped out of the escape hatch for the final time. I walked on the tarmac along her side, stopped and looked up at *Miss Prudy.* She was tall and she was stately. I stood there for a moment, deep in thought, and looked down the runway that we had traveled together so many times. I turned to *Miss Prudy,* saluted her, and paused to take one last look that I will keep with me forever. Then I walked away with a pain that tugged me inside, feeling that I had left a part of me behind. I never looked back; I couldn't do that. I could only look ahead to our return home.

It was time to leave. I climbed into *Ole Black*, battened down the hatches, and revved the engines. The hum of B-17's engines, all so familiar, was soon going to be a sound of the past. I was actually feeling a little nostalgic. I looked out my window where I was accustomed to seeing our ground crew. For this final departure, though, there was no ground crew in sight, no thumbs up. Mendlesham was closing down and crews had been flying home. As my crew never did have their chance to buzz the base, I asked if we could just take *Ole Black* for one last circle over Mendlesham.

As we flew over the airbase, I looked down at the control tower where I had often seen Colonel Creer standing on the open porch, keeping watch over his flock. Creer had left Mendlesham for the States a month earlier. I didn't imagine our paths would cross again. But I was comforted to know that if Creer were here today, he'd be watching us closely in his binoculars, and this time he wouldn't have to sweat it out. Every man who survived was his personal victory. I knew Creer had a lot of pride in the 34th Bomb Group. They were his men, and he had molded them into great pilots and crews.

We circled the Mendlesham airfield and made one final pass directly over the base before heading home. *Ole Black* dipped her wings gracefully and playfully in a final, simple farewell, packed with emotion and memory. I took one last look, said goodbye to Mendlesham, and carrying home a wealth of memories, westward we flew.

Our trip to the States was estimated to be a twenty-three-hour flight. We would cover thirty-four hundred miles from Mendlesham to the States; fifteen hundred of those miles were over the Atlantic. Our first stop was Prestwick, Scotland. After a brief rest in Prestwick, we left for Meek's Field at Reykjavik, Iceland, where the sun sets in the west and half an hour later rises in the east. Shortly after take off, a weather front moved in from the east; but as expected, *Ole Black* sailed through without a hitch. We flew over the southeast tip of Iceland, and during our approach to Reykjavik, I couldn't help but notice the barren, windswept landscape and the small fishing boats that hugged the rugged coastline.

June 19, 1945   Ray, Bill, Glen, and I attended a briefing for our flight pattern and weather for the final leg of our trip. We were informed that due to the large number of planes flying from England to the States, the Navy would maintain a bridge of ships in the northern Atlantic in case a plane had to ditch. This was unimaginable to me, and after all we had been through I could not understand why they were preparing for that possibility.

Our next stop was Goose Bay, Labrador—a fourteen-hundred-mile trip. Six hours later, we saw Greenland off our right wing and we anticipated making Goose Bay in four hours. Bill marveled at the blue pools of water at the tips of icebergs along the way. Greenland, the largest island in the world, seemed vast and desolate.

As part of my routine check, I monitored the designated high-frequency radio station and checked all systems. Everything was fine. I settled into my seat. I felt calm, yet full of anticipation with the thought of returning home. I imagined walking up to the front door and greeting my family.

We were all in good spirits and I could hear Bill telling his jokes, followed by peels of laughter. I knew Ray was sitting beside Bill with a broad grin, and Willie too. I had never seen these guys so relaxed. We were each privately counting down the hours to our return home. Glen, Bill, Mort, Jack, and Willie each carried photographs of their wives, carefully tucked away in their coat pockets. I had Prudy's handwritten copy of the 23rd Psalm in my breast pocket. Our families knew we were flying back although they did not know our exact date of arrival. It was now at least ten days, if not more, since they had heard from us and I imagine they suspected we were en route.

Suddenly, a thunderous explosion shook *Ole Black.* I looked at all my instrument panels and I could feel the engines straining. I realized that number four engine, just broken in, had partially blown up and was virtually useless. Two piston rods had exploded, destroying the cylinders, and the cowling had blown off. One piece of the cowling had hit the exhaust of number three engine, which never functioned adequately from that moment on. Another part of the cowling hit the rudder, and the rudder pedals were vibrating so rapidly that I could not keep my feet on them. I had no rudder control, and could no longer make precise turns. I would now have to make slow turns using the ailerons.

I pressed the feathering button, keeping my thumb on it as hard as I could push. Slowly, thankfully, the prop of number four engine began slicing the air rather than acting as a brake. We started stalling and were losing altitude. To regain speed and altitude, I had to apply pressure on the remaining engines. I eased the throttles forward until the manifold pressure read thirty-eight inches—the pressure setting used for climbing only. I had no idea how long the remaining three engines could maintain that pressure.

I needed to redistribute weight toward the front of the plane. It was critically important to keep the nose down so that *Ole Black* would not stall out, so I asked all ground personnel to move as far forward as possible. They sat in the radio room, the bomb bay, the nose, and the pilot's compartment. Meanwhile, the crew went through the plane, tossing excess and heavy equipment. Guns and the auxiliary starter engine were the first to go. Even our luggage was thrown overboard with some of our mementos from the war, including our Eisenhower jackets with our decorations. The crew used a rifle butt to keep the escape hatch door open to throw out the gear. One piece of heavy equipment got entangled in the door hinge and nearly disengaged the door.

Eddie searched for the string of navy ships that we had expected to see, but couldn't locate any. He tried to reach Goose Bay by radio, but the signal was too weak to continue a dialogue, although Eddie gathered that the base was closed due to inclement weather. I had two choices: either we try to reach Goose Bay or turn north to the Blue West Airstrip in Greenland, a hazardous strip, surrounded by mountains on three sides. Both were equidistant from our current location, but Labrador was on our route. I decided to try and reach Labrador.

Minutes later, we spotted a B-24 Liberator flying at the same altitude just a few miles away. I called on the radio frequency, "B-24, B-24. Do you see a B-17, color black, flying off your left wing?"

"Roger, we see you B-17. Looks like you're about to stall out."

"Our number four engine is gone and we're now just above stalling speed. Who are you B-24?"

The pilot replied, "This is Captain Armentrout, B-17. If you're heading to Goose Bay, why don't we fly along with you as long as we can. We'll keep circling around you, as we cannot travel so slowly. If anything happens, the least we can do is give a radio fix to other planes and ships. I'll do whatever I can, B-17. By the way, B-17, who are you?"

"Captain Alling," I replied. "Thanks for keeping an eye on us."

We were four hundred miles from the Goose Bay airfield and flying against headwinds at a ground speed of only 108 miles per hour. We were three and a half hours from landing. I checked and rechecked the engines for power settings, overheating, and oil pressure. Willie never took his eyes off them. The Wright Cyclone engines were not designed to withstand such pressure and now they would have to stay with us far beyond their specification. We were also running the risk of damaging the remaining engines in the process, and I knew that we would be burning more fuel on three engines than four.

Once more, Eddie made it through to the radio station at Goose Bay, and this time the connection was clear. They suggested we go on to Gander, Newfoundland, because of poor visibility. Eddie relayed the news to me. "Eddie," I said, "we need to inform Goose Bay to get out all their equipment. We're coming in, and we have no choice."

Eddie called in again, "This is an emergency, Goose Bay. We only have three engines running. We're coming in."

"Okay B-17. Stay in touch. We wish you the best of luck," Goose Bay replied.

The minutes seemed interminable. Our passengers were having a tough time and some, who had rarely flown, were nearly frantic. Glen reported in: "Bill's having trouble with a passenger who is desperate and trying to escape through the hatch. It looks like Bill's trying to calm him down."

"Pilot to bombardier. Pilot to bombardier," I called. No answer.

"Pilot to bombardier," I called again, and still no answer. Time seemed to stand still with impending chaos on board.

"Chuck," Bill finally called in. "I've got him pinned down. We're under control. Don't worry."

Ray was soon able to get weak signals from the Cape Harrison radio at the closest point of land in Labrador. By averaging several bearings, he got an acceptable one that provided him with a direct course over the water. The sun was in a perfect position for him to get a Line of Position reading that cut the course line at about ninety degrees. This provided him with a fairly accurate fix and accurate ground speed, which was about one hundred knots most of the time. Bill assisted Ray in taking readings based on their interpretation of the drift from the white caps.

As we flew along, the silence was frightening. The only noise in the plane was the sound of the engines and the vibration of the rudder pedals. There wasn't anything anyone could do but hope and pray. The passengers sat on the floor in the cockpit. No one looked up. No one moved. They stared at the floor, their thoughts miles away. Some held good luck charms in their fingers, some whispering an occasional Hail Mary. Others clasped photos of loved ones in their hands.

I looked down at the icebergs; this was an impossible place to try to land or ditch a plane. I wondered about death. What would it be like? Was it painful? Was this the way it was meant to end? Was our time up? My heart was pounding.

I looked at the engine instruments, most of which were on the co-pilot's side. The oil pressure on engine one and two were fine, but number three engine was low, although slightly above the red mark. While Glen was in charge of the intercom, I monitored the high frequency station, which all pilots checked as closely as they could. It was alarmingly still until Armentrout checked in, "Alling," he called, "I didn't get permission to land at Goose Bay either, but I told them I had to because I was flying as your escort. I can see it's getting dark ahead, and if the weather is bad, I may not be able to stay with you all the way, but I'll do what I can."

"Thanks Captain. When it's time, you'll have to keep going and I understand," I replied.

"OK, we have just under two hours to go," I explained to the passengers and crew. "We're doing as well as we can. Have faith. I believe we'll get there." I was trying to convince my crew and passengers of something that I was privately trying to believe myself.

It was impossible to fly this plane without adjustments and I continually worked the throttles back to reduce the manifold pressure. It had been an hour since we had lost engine four. Now we were carrying a lighter load after we had burned up several hundred gallons of gas and thrown out most of our heavy gear, so I was able to bring down the manifold pressure.

Looking down at the ocean, I noticed that the icebergs were beginning to thin out. That was a good sign. Ray reminded me that the airfield was a twenty-five minute flight from the coast. Once over land, we could bail out if we had to, although that would still be horrendous and rescuers would have a tough time finding us. Even still, I knew it was virtually impossible to ditch safely. We could not find a clear path between the icebergs, and even if we could, we would not survive in the ice-cold water.

My mind raced. I looked over at Glen and then at Willie seated on the jump seat between us. Neither took their eyes off the instruments. I looked at the engines, and somehow they were still running smoothly. If one of the three engines cut out, *Ole Black* would stall against those headwinds and drop from the sky.

We flew into puffs of cumulus, and Armentrout's plane was lost for several seconds in the clouds. I knew we couldn't keep him with us much longer and I called him on the radio. "I think you better go on ahead. You're probably getting low on fuel."

"I was just going to call you. I think that makes sense. Good luck," he said, "I know I'll see you at the base. I'll be there waiting for you."

I hoped that he was right. We were in the clouds flying on instruments. I knew that I would have to make a landing on our first attempt, regardless of the weather and poor visibility. We were now an hour and a half from the airfield. Our number three engine had become more erratic and I could feel the strain of numbers one and two. I could not apply any more manifold pressure or the engines would blow up.

Time was now interminable. Finally Ray called in, "By my calculations, we should be going over Indian Harbor, the closest point of land, in five minutes. We'll follow the Hamilton Inlet west until we come to Lake Melville and then we'll see the airfield."

"Alright, Ray. Great job! Just let me know when we have ten minutes to go," I said, feeling slightly relieved.

Fifteen minutes from the airstrip, we began a slow descent of three hundred feet per minute. If our calculations were correct, that would put us on the runway and also give us enough altitude in case we had to parachute and suddenly ditch the plane.

"Glen, how much gas do we have?" I asked, not really wanting to know the answer.

"I didn't want to tell you," he replied, "I've been trying to keep the tanks evenly distributed in each wing, and they register empty."

I felt sick, but somehow *Ole Black* kept flying. The cloud cover remained thick, and still there was no sign of life below, no sign of land.

Ray called in: "ETA is ten minutes, Chuck."

"Okay guys. We're getting close," I said, hoping everyone would feel encouraged.

I started our descent, knowing full well we were now over a deep lake at the eastern approach to the landing strip, and that we would continue to fly over water until we touched down. I knew Bill and Ray were searching for land, searching for a small airstrip in a vast stretch of wilderness. We were now five minutes from the Goose Bay airfield and there was no sign of land. I wanted to descend faster to find a break in the clouds. "Ray," I called, "I'm hitting the deck. I'm going down to 100 feet."

"Go for it!" he called back with confidence.

We couldn't fly much lower. We had no choice but to be dead on target. There was no room for a mistake or minor error in our calculation. A slight variance from our course would put us belly up on the river or we would crash in the forest that bordered the water's edge. We descended slowly and cautiously, and with each second I wondered whether we were approaching the airfield or the water. I waited and waited, listening to the strain of the engines and the intense vibration of the rudder. And then, to our complete disbelief, we saw land.

"There it is! There it is!" Glen shouted. In a momentary break in the clouds, we saw the airstrip about five miles ahead. We were in a perfect line with the strip. Ray had done it again! He was always on target and never let us down. Even under extreme duress, Ray had charted a brilliant course!

"Ray, you did it! You did it!" I called into the intercom. I was not amazed, because I believed in Ray; I just felt an overwhelming sense of gratitude to him and *Ole Black*. The crew and passengers took a deep breath and quietly sighed their relief. We still had a way to go, but now I believed that we would make it after all.

I waited a minute and then called in, "Flaps, one third," and I paused for a few seconds. "Slowly…" I held my breath, wondering if the flaps had been damaged by metal from the engine cowling when it blew off. I knew that if a piece of number four engine had hit the rudder, other pieces could have hit and damaged the flaps on the right wing, potentially leaving them unusable as well. Flaps were critical in the landing process; they served as a lift to compensate for the reduced engine power and cutting airspeed for a safe landing. If the flaps were to lower on one side only, the drag created on that side could flip the plane over. But quite miraculously, the flaps moved in unison on both wings, and I could feel the plane lift just as the airspeed slightly reduced, just as I had hoped.

"Flaps down! Wheels down!" I called to Glen, and I waited for a few terrifying moments filled with anxiety.

"Full flaps! Wheels down!" Glen responded, his voice sounding assured and confident. That was music to my ears. *Ole Black* was a great workhorse and she was plowing steadily through the very last few minutes of this harrowing journey.

Focusing on a spot three hundred feet short of the runway, I aimed there for the touchdown. Most pilots go beyond the start of the runway, if for no other reason than apprehension. I only had one chance to make it; we could never take a second pass.

We were now a mile away, still flying over the dark lake, and number three engine started to sputter. At last, we approached the edge of the shore. I pulled back the engine throttles and we continued our gradual descent. The end of the runway was still forty or fifty feet away. I couldn't haul back anymore. We were slowing down, but even still, *Ole Black* was eating up runway. Then we heard the screech of the tires on the tarmac. We greased it—rubber to tar! I waited for the tail wheel to touch. It touched. I pressed on the brakes. We were going to stop in time with even a little room to spare. Then we came to a grinding halt just as number three engine sputtered out.

Absurdly, out of habit, I called to Glen, "Taxi instructions."

"Chuck, cut the engines," Glen replied. "We're not taxiing—we can't. We don't have a drop of gas left. The tower says bail out and leave the plane at the end of the runway." I looked over to acknowledge his reply. Glen's face was pale and he seemed dazed.

As the props wheezed and stopped, nineteen guys jumped out of the exits and kissed the ground. Glen was the last of my crew to make his way toward the escape hatch. Speechless, we couldn't say anything, nor did we need to. I was full of wonder that we had made it safely, and I know Glen felt the same way. Moments later, Glen stood up, a bit shaky, and gently lowered himself through the escape hatch while I stayed seated, alone.

I patted the instrument panel and thanked *Ole Black* for bringing us here, knowing full well we should never have made it. *Ole Black*, after all our misgivings, was a stalwart plane that had carried nineteen grateful men back to a place not far from where we had left ten months before.

I must have sat there by myself for several minutes. Exhausted and depleted, I didn't have an ounce of strength left. I stripped off my parachute harness and placed my earphones on the instrument panel. I looked up to the sky and thanked God for being with us. I let my head fall forward, sinking into my cupped hands, and my eyes filled with tears.

Moments later, I'm not sure exactly how long, I looked back up into the deep, boundless sky, toward a place where I imagined heaven must be, a place where I believed Prudy rested peacefully. I had a sudden, unmistakable feeling of clarity and understanding, and I must have smiled, for everything made sense to me. "Prudy," I whispered, "You are an angel. You stayed with me the whole time. You were ALWAYS there with me like an angel on my wings." I stood up from my seat, walked toward the escape hatch, eased myself through, dropping down to the tarmac and onto my knees, and unashamedly kissed the ground.

Epilogue
Charles received the Distinguished Flying Cross and the Air Medal with Four Oak Leaf Clusters during WW II. He graduated from Yale University in 1947. In 1988 he retired and studied Ethics at Oxford University Graduate School in England. In 1989 he founded the Alling Institute for Ethics. The institute is affiliated with The Foundation for Leadership and Ethics in New York City of which Alling is Chairman Emeritus. Alling serves on the Board of Visitors of the Air University at Maxwell Air Force Base in Montgomery, Alabama. Charles and his wife Gail moved to RiverWoods from their home in Kennebunk, Maine.

Prior to retirement, Charles was a Senior Director at Spencer Stuart, an international executive recruiting firm.

This chapter, *"Flying Home on a Wing and a Prayer,"* is from Charles Alling's book, *A Mighty Fortress: Lead Bomber Over Europe,* published by CASEMATE of Havertown, Pennsylvania, in 2002.

The Great Anzio Rodeo

ROBERT H. BATES
Written by Gail O. Bates

B OB BATES has told his war experiences in his autobiography, *The Love of Mountains is Best.* The following is a brief account of one episode in a very large war.

Bob was one of the lucky ones in World War II. He already had abilities and experiences that made him useful in ways that saved lives rather than the other way around. He was called to Washington to advise on cold weather equipment for the Quartermaster Corps, due to his many expeditions to Alaska and the Yukon. After Pearl Harbor he was made an officer and spent his time designing and testing everything from clothing to rations under rugged conditions from Mount Washington to Mount McKinley. Layering of clothing rather than heavy outerwear, L.L.Bean shoepacs, wear resistant socks, a sweater with a collar with buttons in front, were innovations.

This led to his being sent to Italy with one other officer, Mike Slauta, as a two-man task force to test the clothing on soldiers under combat conditions. This was necessary as testing was required before any new improved clothing could be ordered by the millions.

Their destination was Anzio, where our troops were hemmed in on the beachhead. After settling into a local stable, Bob and Mike tested their equipment on the combat soldiers.

Meanwhile, as they awaited the eventual breakthrough, a Texan suggested they hold a rodeo. There were horses and cows wandering around and a field protected by low ridge was a suitable locale. A trade was arranged with the British troops of coffee for Cyprus brandy. There was to be "wild cow milking into helmets," "bare-back horse races," a concession stand, and a betting booth manned by a GI dressed in a woman's skirt and blouse, appropriately adorned. Mike couldn't resist the challenge, riding "Anzio Annie" racing in pairs. But alas, he flew off half way around the track. "Kraut Killer" and "Beachhead Beauty" ran neck and neck, with "Beachhead Beauty" the winner. Cyprus brandy was handed out all around.

Shortly after, Bob sent his report on approved new clothes and equipment back to Washington. The breakthrough out of Anzio took place and Bob rolled north as Rome was celebrating its survival as the Germans pulled out. Many of Bob's recommendations were put to use in the later fighting in the mountains of north central Italy in the winter of 1945 with the 10th Mountain Division.

In his photo Bob is wearing the sweater he developed for QMG.

Bob was born in Philadelphia, Pennsylvania, and received his secondary education at Phillips Exeter Academy. He earned an AB and an AM from Harvard before his war service, and a PhD at the University of Pennsylvania after the war. He taught English at Phillips Exeter. In 1962 he became director of the Peace Corps in Nepal for two years. His lifelong love of mountains led to many pioneering ascents around the world and to five books about mountains and climbing. Bob died in 2009.

Luck Runs Out

JOE BOYLE

TEN DAYS after Pearl Harbor I enlisted in the Army Air Force. I had been turned down for Naval Officers training, my first choice, because I was born in the Yukon Territory of Canada. One of the Navy requirements was you had to be a native born citizen. The fact I had derived my citizenship at age three when my father became a naturalized citizen, was inadmissible.

Basic training was a whole new bag of tricks; we were now in the military for real. We were formed into platoons, slept on iron cots, separated from our buddies, barked at by sergeants, hazed by upper-classmen, taught to march like a soldier, do an "about-face" when ordered, and salute our superiors whether we liked to or not.

Primary flight training required seventy hours of flying time, so-loing after seven hours. In six months the Air Force had trained thirty six aircrews in preparation for combat. Most of us were vain enough to think we should be fighter pilots. Almost all of us ended up in bombers. We got our wings and became second lieutenants in the Army Air Force on July 31, 1942.

At that time there were few planes and a limited number of trained aircrews. I was assigned as a copilot of a B-17 Flying Fortress, the workhorse of the air war in the European theatre. The pilot was a young captain named Martini, hence, the name of our plane, the *Dry Martini and the Cocktail Kids*. We were attached to the 305th Bomb Group led by Col. Curtis E. LeMay, who later became Commander in Chief of the United States Air Force.

We waited for our planes at Hancock Field in Syracuse. As the planes were flown in from the factory, they were equipped with autopilots and Norden bombsights. Gander was a stopping off place in our flight to England. It is where our Capt. Martini noticed the base personnel were wearing soft-leather, fleece-lined jackets. He was successful in convincing a supply sergeant to surrender four prized jackets for the navigator, bombardier, and two pilots. At that time we were the only fliers in the 305th group who were prepared for the cold wet English weather.

Arriving in England we learned the High Command and British had not determined how to use us. LeMay observed that bombing results were dismal, bombs dropped all over. The War would be lost with such lousy results. We weren't in England long before LeMay put his stamp on how things should be done.

Daylight bombing had been going on for several months before the 305th arrived. Review of photos and damage reports indicated the raids had been largely ineffective. Enemy resistance over targets was usually heavy. Pilots had been doing evasive action up to the last minute before releasing their bombs. LeMay knew that for the Norden bombsight to be effective, the plane had to be straight and level on the bomb run for at least seven or eight minutes. Also, defense and bombing accuracy would improve by tightening the formation. LeMay theorized by using the best trained bombardier in the group—give him all the time he needed to program his instrument, have the whole group drop their bombs when the lead ship did—should produce better results. Almost immediately the 305th proved him right.

Col. LeMay offered me a ride one day as I was walking to deliver a message to my crew chief. After a few silent minutes, the Colonel said, almost to himself, "I did something today, I hope I did the right thing."

I said, "Sir, may I ask what you did?"

He replied, "I bought an Air Base." He went on to explain actually, he was under orders to sign the papers transferring ownership to the United States. It was part of the deal for the fifty destroyers President Roosevelt had sold to the British before we entered the war. The deal was designed to wipe the debt off the books.

In 1942-43 most of our bombing runs were over France. Allied air superiority was a long way off. The odds were not favorable for completing the twenty-five missions required before we could return stateside.

Given the circumstances, I had numerous brushes with disaster. In January 1943 I was on my first real bomb run. It seemed like a "milk run". Pilot Martini was grounded by illness and had been replaced by our squadron commander. We dropped our bombs over Lille, France, without seeing any enemy fighters. We had turned towards home when I noticed a black speck on the horizon followed by a series of bright flashes. I blacked out. When I came to, the plane was in a dive and the pilot was dead.

I pulled the wheel to get the nose up. Not really sure how badly the plane was damaged, I headed back to base. Given the Air Corps rushed training, I was preoccupied the whole flight back with the prospect of making only my fourth landing alone at the controls. On my previous three flights I had a more skilled pilot by my side. I pulled it off but it wasn't pretty.

By February 1943 the 305th group had participated in about a dozen raids, usually consisting of sixty to eighty planes on a given raid. There were four bomb groups in England at that time. Each put roughly half their planes in the air on any given raid. The different groups would form up over an area and join together to form a continuous column of aircraft in tight formation. This brought maximum firepower against fighters and led to more accurate bombing.

As planes and crews were lost, new ones arrived from the States to take their place in our formations. As our losses mounted, pick-up crews were also used to fill the gaps.

My luck ran out in May 1943. On my fifteenth mission we were hitting submarine pens in Lorient, France. I was part of a pickup crew. In the flying formation of seventy we had the position of "tail-end-Charlie", the term for the most vulnerable spot, easiest to pick off. We dropped our bombs, turned toward home, when a crack was heard from the back of the plane. Fighters had knocked out our intercom. The group picked up speed, our plane falling behind—classic stuff. Fighters hit all our engines. Without an intercom the pilot rang three long blasts on a buzzer to signal "bail out" to the crew.

Not wishing to make a target for some eager German fighter pilot, I rolled into a ball and fell 6,000 ft. before pulling the ripcord. I immediately blacked out.

Landing in the French countryside I was quickly picked up by the Germans. Of the crew of ten, only four survived. The French underground got two of them first and later smuggled them to Spain over the Pyrenees. Fifty-five years later I was invited to return to the village of Brech for a dedication of a small monument to the plane and crew. I learned a French schoolboy had seen the crash and retrieved pieces of our wreckage and my parachute.

My interrogator was an English speaking German captain who had attended college in England. When asked how he liked his current assignment, he said to me, "How would you like it if every time you walked down the street of this village people stepped aside to let you pass, and you know they would shoot you in the back if they could!"

At an interrogation camp I met a young Norwegian pilot. He and several friends had sailed a small boat to England to enlist. While we stood visiting an airplane shrieked overhead. The Norwegian identified it as the latest weapon in the German arsenal, a jet fighter soon to be in combat, (1943).

Home for most of the rest of the war was Stalag Luft III, a POW camp known for the *Great Escape*. Stalag began with 200 POWs and ended with 10,000, all airmen. For the first six months Red Cross packages were coming through. Then they became scarcer as German rations deteriorated and theft increased.

By January 1945 the Russians were advancing from the east. With a half-hour notice prisoners were ordered to pack any belongings and whatever food they could gather and carry to begin the Long March. Eventually we reached our destination near Munich where 130,000 prisoners were corralled into a camp built for 14,000. Hitler was hoping to use us as pawns to negotiate a separate peace with the Western Allies.

While there I wrote in my diary dated February 1945, "It is probably safe for me to say that the sights and experiences connected with our evacuation from Stalag Luft III to here are far more to the point of what war is all about, than the worst of combat experiences, particularly from the standpoint of non-combatants who after all are in the majority in any man's war".

By April of 1945 Patton's 3rd Army liberated our camp.

> *TO B.R.P.- POW*
> The fate we share as prisoners
> Is drab and often grim,
> Existing on such scanty fare
> As Reich-bread, spuds, and klim.
>
> Beds and books and little else
> To fill Time's flopping sail,
> She makes or loses headway all
> Depending on the mail.
>
> Oh! Drab the days and slow to pass
> Within this barbed-wire fence,
> When all the joys of living are
> Still in the future tense.
>
> So here's to happy days ahead
> When you and I are free
> To look back on this interlude
> And call it history.

Born in Dawson City, Yukon Territory, Canada, Joe attended Lehigh University where he earned a BA in Business Administration. After the war Joe became Vice President of the Huffman and Boyle Furniture Co. and in 1957 he established the J.B. Boyle Co. Joe died in 2009.

The Red Ball Express

George Dixon

I WAS ATTENDING the Harvard Business School on a scholarship. I had tried to join the Naval Supply Corps, but flunked the physical exam on account of poor eyesight. In early 1943 sixty of my fellow students and I were drafted, having been assured we would all become Administrative Officers. That did not happen and we were sent to Fort Lee, Virginia, for basic training in the Quartermaster Corps. Two of us were selected to go to Officer Candidate School. I have no idea why I was chosen.

Once commissioned, I was sent to France as a Replacement Officer. I rode the Red Ball Express to become one of five white officers in an otherwise totally black trucking company hauling ammunition to the north side of the Bulge in Belgium. It was some kind of duty for a four-eyed, tow-headed, skinny, Harvard Business School type, and a long way from Administration! We worked mostly at night to try to avoid attacks by German fighter planes.

We gradually followed the Allied Forces' advances into Germany until we reached Leipzig. The war ended and our trucks were used to carry Displaced Persons from Germany back to their home countries—Poland and Czechoslovakia. Passing through the Russian lines was never easy.

I eventually wound up in Giessen, Germany, at a former German air base converted by the US to a major supply depot. I lived there for almost a year until I had accumulated sufficient time to be sent home and demobilized as a Captain, and returned to Harvard Business School to finish the requirements for an MBA degree.

I believed then that the Army made a mistake in segregating black troops into separate units, rather than simply treating them like everyone else and mixing them through the Army population generally. This practice has long since been adopted.

All in all, it was quite an experience, but was of little use in the career that followed. It was pretty boring work, but somebody had to do it!

Born in Rochester, New York, George added an LLD in Business and Finance in 1947. He held various financial positions and eventually retired as CEO of what is now US Bank. His travel adventures have included the North and South Poles and sailing his own boat across the Atlantic.

May 1945

HARRY HAMPTON

WHILE ONLY A few of us around now remember, May 7th marked the 65th anniversary of VE Day, the unconditional surrender of Hitler's German Reich, ending World War II. Invariably, every year during the first half of May, memory takes me back almost daily to where I was and what I was doing in May of 1945. Well, it wasn't the FINAL end to WW II, as four more months remained for Emperor Hirohito and Japan's military leaders to recognize defeat—but for me and the Weapons Platoon of Company L, 333rd Infantry Regiment, 84th Infantry Division, the war had ended. There was to be a month or two before serious thought was given to the possibility we'd be in the first assault waves hitting the beaches of the Land of the Rising Sun.

When the 333rd crossed the Rhine River on Easter Sunday 1945 our assignment was to take Berlin. That was the Ninth Army's goal before political considerations gave the honor to Russia. The US Ninth was to halt its advances at the Elbe River and await arrival of the Soviet forces on the far eastern bank. Company L was overlooking marshes on the Elbe's west bank by May 1st. With other units of the 333rd we had the distasteful task of discouraging and preventing German troops from crossing the Elbe east-to-west. We were obliged to be enforcers of Russia's roundup of hapless Wehrmacht soldiers, most of whom languished, over the next decade and longer, in Siberian prison camps. Relatively few were privileged to see home and family ever again.

That first week in May I was detached from my platoon with several non-commissioned officers, given a Quartermaster 6x6 truck and driver, and assigned to run the roads that spread out from the city of Salzwedel seeking American and British Prisoners of War. In some instances, the POW camps run by the Germans panicked and opened their gates. Others marched their prisoners considerable distances toward advancing US-British forces. Individuals and groups of Allied POWs were on the loose and needed rounding up. Over the next three or four days my detachment scoured hundreds of miles through dozens of rural towns within forty or fifty miles to the north and west of Salzwedel. With five or six similar detachments we brought in at least several hundred Allied POWs, all of them ravenously hungry and skeletons of their former selves. Within a day or two most all of the recovered POWs were flown to military hospitals in France or England.

Just as quickly, my POW recovery detachment was directed to become a Displaced Person (DP) recovery unit, operating out of what had been a Wehrmacht training camp a bit to the west of Salzwedel. The camp's facilities were concealed from aerial view in a pine forest.

Our job was simply to hunt down DPs, the men, women, and children corralled from civilian populations by German forces as they marched across conquered Europe. For the most part they were peasants enslaved as farm labor, harshly treated by their German masters, and aching to find some way to get back to Poland, the Baltic countries, the Ukraine, Hungary, Romania, Greece—wherever they had once called home. Once assembled in places such as the former German military encampment from which my detachment functioned, the DPs were hauled off in truck convoys, mostly British, to railheads where the International Red Cross or similar organization sorted them out by destination preferred.

The calendar was now bearing down on mid May. The rush was on to establish military zones of occupation. The Ninth Army pulled back from the Elbe, the British moved in, soon to be replaced by the Russians. For the last half of May, Company L was billeted in Bad Nenndorf. The town had its kurhaus, mud baths just like Baden Baden, Carlsbad, and numerous other places in Germany known as Bad-This-or-That. The major difference was no casino in Bad Nenndorf and a wholly rural atmosphere.

On the northwest edge of town was a street lined on both sides by thoroughly modern two-story residences—each had been built in the past five or six years—ultra new! Every member of L Company was privileged to be billeted in one of them. Most of my 4th Platoon was in what had been the home and studio of the town's professional photographer, complete with his gear and laboratory.

I had been tagged by battalion Headquarters (HQ) as Bad Nenndorf's Town Major. I'm clueless how such a post came to be, but it served as the interim authority of the occupying military units in towns, villages, and cities throughout the American zone of occupation until genuine military government could establish itself. In my limited experience, lasting not over ten days, a Town Major served as go-between for a burgomeister and other Germans who had fallen heir to the various posts and offices in a community's civil government upon the collapse of Nazi Germany. Those elements of the conquering American forces were able to keep the water works in operation, or assure supplies of coal for the electric generator plant serving the area, or maybe help the polizei limit depredations by DPs clamoring for more and better food as they waited impatiently for repatriation.

Luckily, I was not confronted by any of that, but there were forty or fifty Russians housed in Bad Nenndorf's school building, guarded by a unit of GIs taking their orders from either 333rd Regimental or Divisional HQ. Those orders were simply to keep the Russians in that schoolhouse or on its grounds, nowhere else except for a representative who might be allowed daily to meet the Town Major… me.

These were not the farm labor type DPs. There were about ten family units: father, mother, offspring, plus perhaps ten other adults ranging in age from late twenties to late forties. Nearly all the adults spoke English, some quite well. Their story of how they came to Germany differed from what the burgomeister said he knew for fact.

The burgomeister insisted it was well known that this group of Russians was voluntary defectors who had been long-time professionals in the motion picture industry of the Soviet Union, and saw their chance to escape the clutch of communism and Josef Stalin by offering their skills and talents in propaganda work for Nazi Germany. The Russians, of course, insisted they had been rounded up forcefully and sent to Germany. Was there evidence they'd done propaganda work for Germany? I never found out.

How and where this group of about fifty Russians had been rounded up and shepherded to confinement in Bad Nenndorf's public school, family groups still intact, also remained a mystery. But nearly every day during the last ten days of May 1945 I'd be visited by the eldest male and his lovely daughter in my Town Major office, escorted by one of their guards. Their plea, in perfect English: "Protect us, we beg you. Don't let us be sent back to Russia"… or words to that effect. Once or twice I'd be asked for help securing medical attention, and receive profuse thanks within a day or two for my intervention which had been nothing more than a phone call or hand carried message to the aid station of the 333rd battalion. Always the visit ended in a flood of Russian tears as I told them I was powerless to intervene in any way.

What became of them I will never know, but one early evening at the end of May, British Army lorries pulled up at the schoolyard—so it was told to me the next day—and all the Russians were forced to load onto them. My orders had been to avoid any and all contacts with this group of DPs except those that might transpire in my Town Major's office, so I had never gone to the school and did not see their departure from Bad Nenndorf. I was told it took over an hour for the British lorry unit to push and haul all the Russians and load them onto the vehicles with baggage. Most females were docile, but the younger men resisted, it was said. Daylight lingered long in late May, but finally in late evening the convoy moved out.

As it did so, gathering speed and with headlights not yet switched on, one of the older Russian men rolled off the back of a lorry falling onto the road and under the oncoming front wheel of the following truck and was killed. Was it intentional? A suicide to avoid repatriation to a guaranteed torturous death? Who can say? Do I really want to know—and should I?

There you have some of May that lives with me every year. It returns inevitably. Wars do end, but their aftermaths seem endless.

Born in Norfolk, Virginia, Harry attended grade schools in Florida, New Jersey, Illinois, and New York, followed by academics at Dartmouth. His college education, majoring in Government, was interrupted by military service and was completed after the war. In time he became executive director of two industrial trade associations: Institute of Makers of Explosives and Sporting Arms and Ammunition Manufacturers' Institute, who shared staff and office quarters atop Grand Central Station in New York City. He still had time for reading, travel, and carpentry.

Behind Enemy Lines

FRED JERVIS

IN JUNE OF 1943, a group from my advanced Reserve Officers Training Corps (ROTC) unit at University of New Hampshire (UNH) was inducted into the US Army. We finished our junior year in uniform, drawing military pay and unable to believe we were going to war.

After basic training, and Officer Candidate School (OCS) at Fort Knox, Kentucky, Armored School, several of us were assigned to the 55th Armored Infantry Battalion of the Eleventh Armored Division at what is now the Vandenberg Air Force Base in California where I became the Battalion Armored Reconnaissance Unit Commander. The remainder of my army time was spent in Intelligence and Reconnaissance. In California and later in England, I completed numerous advanced training schools in subjects like Mines and Demolitions, Foreign Weapons, and Intelligence Reports: The Movement of German Troops.

When the 11th Armored Division in Patton's 3rd Army arrived in Belgium in December 1944, the German's top SS and Panther divisions were massed on the German border, readying to break through the American front line. The 82nd Airborne was trapped at Bastogne. Much of our front line had been killed in action or captured. The Battle of the Bulge had begun. The 11th Armored was one of the divisions charged with blocking the advance of the Germans through Belgium and into Paris. My platoon ran night patrols, penetrated behind German lines, and kept commanding officers informed about location, strength, and movement of enemy troops.

Although the Allied troops pushed the Germans back to their border, these were still chaotic days. There was no defined front. Germans in the uniforms of captured American troops infiltrated regularly behind our lines.

We suffered heavy losses from injury and death, and whole divisions were decimated. Older family men and untried 18 year olds were arriving as replacements. Often they were injured or killed before we had an opportunity to learn their names. Eventually, a UNH friend and I were the only officers left in our battalion.

On the night of February 5th, 1945, my patrol crossed over the German border and entered territory behind the Siegfried Line. My jeep detonated a wooden Holtz mine, converted from a metal anti-tank mine, and my injuries resulted in permanent blindness.

I was first treated in a field hospital in Belgium where the medical staff performed remarkable feats of surgery, including the reconstruction of much of my face. I was shipped back to Cushing General Hospital in Framingham, Massachusetts, and then to Valley Forge General in Pennsylvania, for months of surgeries, and finally "social rehabilitation" at Avon Old Farms in Avon, Connecticut, before I was discharged on January 10, 1947.

I hold the most positive feelings and highest regard for the many individuals who cared for me. Nurses in the field hospital sat by my cot hour after hour, picking sand and debris from my face. Doctors, both overseas and in the States, performed surgery after surgery in vain attempts to preserve a bit of sight. All along the way, volunteers devoted uncounted hours to making my new world without sight a comfortable one. Most importantly I want to recognize the role my wife, Jan, has played to assure that my blindness would not be an impediment to a normal life for our three children and for ourselves as partners.

After childhood in Somerville and Cambridge, Massachusetts, and his military service, Fred earned a BA at the University of New Hampshire and a PhD at Columbia University. In 1971 he left academia to establish, with his wife Jan, the Center for Constructive Change. They managed this non-profit for 35 years. Fred's, and the Center's credo is "start at the end," i.e., focus on where we want to be instead of where we are.

A Ducky Barracks

JOHN MURRAY

IN APRIL 1943, I left my senior year of high school two months before graduation to enlist in the Army Air Corps to join a weather officers training program. After basic training, I was sent to Brown University for twelve months for fundamental education in math and the sciences.

The meteorological training I was scheduled for next was suddenly canceled. Instead I was sent to an electronics school for six months for training to become an operator for Ground Control Approach (GCA) radar, which was then in development.

After completing my GCA training, I joined the second team to be sent to Europe, where I spent a year at airfields in England and France. We were able to regularly direct airplanes within fifty feet over the end of a runway even in bad weather.

While living in our airfield barracks in England, we had a pet duck, which always hung around. I could never figure out why he chose us unless he thought he might need our services later. Fortunately, he did not and we did not.

I feel fortunate that World War II became a beneficial experience for me. It provided me with a free college education without the need to experience combat like so many others.

Born in New Hampshire, John was educated at Brown University and Dartmouth College. He worked as an automotive engineer at Chrysler for many years, but had time for his hobbies of organ playing, power boating, and skiing.

The First Special Service Force

ART REMIEN

THE FORCE WAS initiated by Winston Churchill and Gen. George C. Marshall in the summer of 1942 as a specially trained guerilla band with the objective of taking out Norway's hydroelectric stations. Named "Plough Project", the Force consisted of 2,500 men, half Canadians and half Americans. It contained a Service Battalion of which I was a member, non-combatants to work in maintenance, parachute packing, ordinance, clerical, etc. The Force was put through rigorous winter training in the mountains near Helena, Montana, but meanwhile the Army decided that attacking targets in Norway was militarily unworkable. Thus we were sent, in April 1943, to Norfolk, Virginia, for amphibious training, then to Burlington, Vermont, then in July by train to San Francisco where we boarded two Liberty ships for the Aleutians.

The Japanese had bombed Dutch Harbor in the Aleutians and deposited island garrisons on Kiska and Attu; these were the Force's first war objectives. After four days of heavy swells, bunk-restricted, we landed safely on Adak and then Amchitka. Mukluks were required in view of the tundra, soft clay, fog, etc. Heavy enemy resistance was expected against our attack on Kiska, but when the invasion began, it was found that the Japanese had secretly evacuated a few days before, thus negating the heavy Allied buildup here and for Attu.

The Force returned to California; from there to Vermont, and soon after, to Newport News, Virginia. There we boarded *The Empress of Japan* and proceeded to Casablanca and then to Naples, Italy. The 5th Army had been stalled in the Liri Valley by stiff German resistance. Joining the Allied forces, the Force was to spearhead the attack on the mountains where the German line was entrenched. It took six days of heavy fighting before the Germans retreated. From there we proceeded north, capturing other hills, to Monte Cassino and Anzio. There we joined other Allied forces in the liberation of Rome (we were first in the Eternal City), thence in the invasion of southern France. There we joined with Patton's Third Army across Germany until the surrender, on May 8, 1945.

Although the Force had disbanded in Italy to become the 474th Infantry Regiment, its exploits were ultimately made into a picture, *The Devil's Brigade*, starring William Holden. Further recognition has included dedications in Helena, Montana, by the US and Canadian governments, the naming of highways and more. Yearly meetings of the veterans in the US, Canada, and Europe have continued the recognition.

Born in the Bronx, New York, Art graduated from New York University in Accounting, Industrial Relations, and Personnel Management. He worked for Regal Paper Corporation for seventeen years, followed by twenty-eight years with Georgia Pacific. In retirement, he and his wife, Lorene, moved from Ramsey, New Jersey, to Exeter, New Hampshire.

A Seaman's Life

Stephen Richardson

FROM 1937 TO 1946 I served in the British Merchant Navy and was at sea throughout World War II. I went to sea as an apprentice and left nine years later qualified to be captain of foreign-going ships. Throughout my time at sea I kept a diary that formed the basis for my book *School of the Sea*, Whittles Publishing, 2009. The events here selected from the book occurred in January and February of 1944 when I was Second Mate on the *Kelmscott*, a cargo ship that carried newsprint from Newfoundland and eastern Canada to Britain.

Manchester to St John's, Newfoundland

During the passage we encountered a week of bad weather such as I had never seen before; even the Old Man said he could not remember the likes of it. The barometer bounced up and down at a speed of sometimes ½ an inch in four hours, and fresh gales swept down on us alternatively from the south and west. The wind set up a precipitous, confused swell, which threw us about with extreme violence. It was only possible to sleep when we were so dog-tired we could shut out the violent movement and the crash and rattle of the ship's goods and chattels careening madly about the accommodation and decks. No amount of wedging and lashing seemed to be about to restrain them. A raft was lost over the side; the pounding of the seas started leaks in number one hold, and two of the ships in the convoy broke up and sent out SOS messages. On one of those stormy nights, gunfire from one of the escorts on our side of the convoy indicated an attack by U-boats. The action lasted for several hours, but the following day we learned nothing of the result. At times like this, the weather seemed a greater menace than the danger of enemy action.

When the wind was from the south we got driving rain, and when the wind veered to the northwest it turned into hail and snow squalls. Any occupations except reading and trying to sleep were almost impossible, yet the cook, with great gallantry, kept to his work under appalling conditions to provide us with hot food. Meals were an exercise in balance. By now everyone had grown very tired of the incessant movement. The cheerfulness and good humour maintained by everybody was outstanding, with the most annoying incidents being laughed at. The great longing now was to have *Kelmscott* on an even keel and calm. The clinometers in the chartroom showed that we were rolling through 78 degrees.

On the last two days of the outward passage the weather moderated but the sea, refusing to lie quiet, would every now and again throw the ship into a sudden vicious roll as if finding vast amusement at our discomfort. Our first port of call was Bell Island, off the northern tip of Newfoundland, where we were to discharge our ballast. We then proceeded to St John's where we loaded a full cargo of newsprint.

St John's Bound for London

On February 9th I was called early and went out into the bitter cold. I was grateful to snuggle into the warm, hooded parka I had just bought second-hand from a local stevedore. After checking that the navigation equipment and steering gear were in order, I went to the stern to await orders to cast off. The tugs took our towropes and pulled us away from the dock into the black waters of the harbour. We headed out through the narrow gap between the high, snow-covered cliffs that flanked the port; then the tugs cast off, and the pilot left.

Once we were clear of the harbour I left my station aft and had breakfast. I was glad to be homeward bound, hoping we would be spared the gales and heavy seas that had broken up our convoy on the outward passage and made our lives miserable. I knew that German submarines had been reported off the Canadian coast, but they were an ever-present threat that I had learned to live with. After breakfast I relieved the Third Mate, who was on watch, so that he could have breakfast. By now we were proceeding along the channel, swept clear of mines, on our way to join a convoy. A salvage tug and a naval escort vessel accompanied us. As soon as the Third Mate returned to the bridge, I went into the chartroom to read over the convoy orders and lay off the courses that would enable us to join the main convoy.

Deeply engrossed in this work, I was suddenly interrupted by an explosion that shook the ship from truck to keel. I grabbed my coat and ran out on the bridge to see water, which had been blown high in the air, cascading down on the decks. Clouds of steam rose from a fractured steam pipe, and the *Kelmscott* was heeling over to starboard. My first thought was that we had struck a mine. Since the Captain and Third Mate were on the bridge, I went to the boat deck to be sure the boats were ready in case we had to abandon ship, and then mustered the crew. I made sure they all had life jackets, shared with them what I knew about what had happened, and told them not to leave the ship until ordered. I then assigned them different sections of the surrounding sea and told them to keep a sharp lookout for a periscope, since the submarine might be waiting for another opportunity to sink us. Reaching the stern, I found the gunners at their stations with the gun ready for use and gave them the same instructions. On the way back to the bridge, I saw the Steward and suggested he make a hot drink for all hands, because soon there would be no hot water left on the ship.

When I returned to the bridge I learned that the Chief Engineer had reported that the stokehold and engine room were flooding and it would not be long before the rising water would extinguish the fires in the boilers, the steam pressure would fail, and the engine would slow down and stop. The steering gear was intact, and Captain Pugh had already turned the *Kelmscott* back toward St John's. The First Mate had leaned over the starboard side to look at the damage. He saw a jagged gaping hole that extended down below the waterline on the side of number three hold, just forward of the stokehold and engine room. The explosion must have damaged the watertight bulkhead aft of number three hold allowing water to flow into the stokehold. He concluded that a torpedo had caused the damage, because a mine would have blown a hole in the bottom of the hull. We were fortunate to be carrying newsprint because it absorbed some of the shock of the torpedo, and would provide buoyancy until the paper became saturated with water. The Carpenter went round sounding the bilges in each hold to see if they were taking on water. He reported all holds were dry except number three.

We signaled our situation to the naval escort vessel. Shortly afterwards the rising water in the engine room caused our engine to slow and then stop as we lost steam. We signaled the tug and asked her to take us in tow. After what seemed an age of waiting—although I expect it was only a few minutes—the tug maneuvered to windward of us and fired a rocket, carrying a light line that landed on the foredeck. One of our sailors grabbed the line and took it up onto the forecastle. The Mate summoned everyone available to help haul the towrope aboard because we had no steam to power the windlass. The men pulled in three lines in succession each attached to the other: first the light line, then a heavier Coir floating rope, and finally the towing hawser, the end of which had a loop that we placed over the bitts (heavy metal posts on deck used for fastening ropes or wires). The tug went ahead slowly taking up the slack of the towrope, and then began towing us toward St John's. Shortly afterwards our electricity failed because the rising water flooded the generator. The sea was only moderate and the wind a fresh breeze, but unfortunately the temperature was down around zero Fahrenheit.

By then several naval vessels and aircraft had arrived and were circling in search of the submarine. At intervals of about half an hour we heard the sound of two muffled explosions and guessed that they might be distant depth charges. When the first shock was over there was little for us to do except wait and hope we would get back to port. Our four main holds were undamaged, the water was no longer rising in the engine room, and the tug was slowly but steadily moving us toward the land. It seemed we had a good chance of saving the *Kelmscott*.

About an hour and a half after the torpedo had struck us, a second explosion shook the *Kelmscott*, this time with still greater violence. Again, a great column of black smoke and water shot up several hundred feet in the air, and water rained down on the decks. At that time an aircraft was flying low directly above us, and it was thrown violently upward by the explosion.

The plane nearly crashed into the sea before the pilot gained control. It would have made history if the torpedo had downed the plane! The *Kelmscott* was listing heavily, and the bow was sinking lower. The second torpedo hit about fifty feet forward of the first and tore open number two, our largest hold. The forward starboard lifeboat was blown to pieces and, just aft of it, the second lifeboat had a side stove in.

The situation looked bad, and I heard the Old Man give orders to abandon ship. The crew lowered the two port boats, and men scrambled down the ropes and ladders and jumped into the boats. The Third Mate and the Cook were each put in charge of a boat. We told them to row well clear of the *Kelmscott* so they would not get caught in the downwash if the ship sank. For those for whom there was no room in the lifeboats, I released some of the emergency life rafts and, with help, brought them alongside telling the remaining men to get onto them. One of the firemen fell into the sea: a young Ordinary Seaman dived in, pushed a raft across to him and pulled him out of the water. (Seventy years later, while searching the Web, I found that the seaman had been awarded the British Empire Medal for gallantry.) A great deal was happening, but I was too busy to see much of it. The behaviour of the crew varied from panic to bravery, from bawling and cursing to being quiet and following around anyone who would lead and give orders. The gun crew had remained standing by the gun, so I went aft and told them to leave on one of the rafts.

Seven men stayed on the ship: the Captain, Mate, Fourth Engineer, a drunken Able Bodied Seaman, two gunners, and myself. Because we needed an escape if the *Kelmscott* sank I released the last life raft and pulled it round to the stern. We would not have had to stay on it long before being picked up by one of the circling naval vessels. On the bridge we gathered to assess the situation. The *Kelmscott* had settled lower, and the sea was lapping onto the deck forward on the starboard side. How long we could stay afloat was largely dependent on the newsprint. The large rolls that filled number two hold would initially check the inrush of the sea and provide buoyancy. How long this would take we did not know. If the watertight bulkhead between number one and two holds were damaged, water would flood into number one hold, increasing the chance that the *Kelmscott* would sink.

I went off with Finney, our senior gunner, to number one hold in order to find out. We made a sounding rod by cutting off the ends of a machine-gun ramrod. Through this hollow tube, we passed a piece of the rocket line that had been fired aboard. To get the sounding cap off, we had to use a cold chisel and hammer since the explosion had squashed the cap tight. To our relief, we found no water in the bilges. The Mate had signaled the tug and the escort vessel to let them know what had happened. The tug was still towing us, but at a greatly reduced speed because we were now much lower in the water. The escorts picked up the men in the lifeboats and rafts and took them ashore. As far as we knew, no lives had been lost.

The Old Man was on the bridge and the Mate stood by forward in case the towrope broke. As there was nothing for me to do, I went in search of food. The galley fire was nearly out, so I stoked it up, and then investigated the pots and pans. Most of the food was ruined by dirt and salt water that had poured in through the skylight, but the soup was intact, since it been covered with a lid. It provided the first course for dinner. There was roasted meat that had been taken out of the oven, so I put it back to warm. I then called Finney, one of the gunners, and using a fire axe, we went down into the food store, broke open the door and brought out some tinned peaches and cream. These provided the dessert. The only clean water was in a small tank in the galley, so we poured some of it in a kettle and put it on the fire to boil to make tea. Leaving the gunners to prepare and distribute the meal, I went out to see what was happening. The list of the ship seemed to have stabilized; she was down by the head and was lifting sluggishly to the waves. With the intense cold the water on the decks had frozen, making it hard to keep a footing.

Apart from the ship, my main concern was my clarinets. Not only were they my most valuable possessions but also they were a source of great pleasure and provided me with an entree to musical groups in ports we visited. In case the *Kelmscott* were to sink, I tied the clarinet case to a lifebuoy, went to the stern and floated the clarinets and lifebuoy on a long line close to the life raft that we planned to use. If we were to sink and had to use the raft I could retrieve the clarinets. Somewhat later I had to haul the clarinets back aboard because the line to the raft had broken and the raft was lost. Leaving the clarinets in the galley I went up on the boat deck to inspect the lifeboat that was our one remaining way of leaving *Kelmscott*. Though damaged, it would stay afloat if we had to leave. The falls (the block and tackles used to lower the lifeboat) were jammed, so I sent the gunners to fetch and load the rifles so, that in case of need, we could shoot through them. Returning to the galley I dried the clarinets and found they were not damaged. Some men were in the galley, the only warm place on the ship, so I gave them a short musical recital and then returned to the bridge.

While waiting with little to do, I was able to observe the behavior of the Old Man. He had had a very hard time during the war, having been bombed or torpedoed I think five times. About sixty years old, he was showing the stress of his experiences. He mixed blasphemy in his abuse of the Germans and the men who behaved badly on the *Kelmscott*, with affection for his ship. He was cheerful in an aggressive, rough sort of way, and it was only later that he began showing his reaction to the shock by drinking. While the rest of us were busy he would leave the bridge and wander about the ship, noticing the queerest details, and then come and talk about them with the Mate and me. He reported, with great excitement, that his bathtub had been blown across his quarters, and that a chip had been knocked out of one corner. A little later he came back, having inspected the cadets' room, and was indignant at the mess it was in.

The Able Bodied Seaman who remained on board was somewhat drunk and at times very annoying. While the men were taking to the boats, he followed me about doing what he was told in a slightly fuddled manner. He refused to leave the ship when I told him to get into the boats saying was going to stay and look after me. He was in the way; I got rid of him by giving him my clarinets and telling him to stay aft and make sure they didn't get lost. He obeyed and stayed away until he had sobered up somewhat. The Mate was rather short tempered with a strong aversion to drunks, and I didn't want a row between them.

During periods when there was little to do, I thought about what had happened. I was confident we would survive, whether or not the *Kelmscott* sank. We had the damaged lifeboat, naval vessels that could pick us up were close by and, as a strong swimmer I could survive for a short time in the water. Throughout the war I had known that we could be torpedoed at any time. Now it had happened, and we had escaped without death and suffering that so often came in the wake of a torpedo. I found the activity, and having to deal with novel situations, exhilarating—unlike most times at sea when, apart from routine activities, little happened.

Several additional naval craft had come out from St John's, and a launch came alongside. Captain Slope, Chief of Naval Staff at St John's, came aboard followed by a signalman. While he held a conference with the Old Man and the Mate, I went with Finney to sound number one bilge to determine whether the forward bulkhead was holding. To our relief we found no water in the bilges. By this time the water was lapping up onto the deck so there was only a foot or so of freeboard. In some places on deck, the force of expansion of the newsprint as it absorbed water had pushed out the sides of the ship and torn the deck and the sides of the ship apart. We reported our findings.

More tugs arrived. One of them brought out a pilot who came aboard and reviewed the situation with the Old Man and Captain Slope, while the rest of us went forward to make fast the additional tugs. There followed an hour or two of very heavy work, hauling ropes by hand as there was no steam to operate the windlass. Our difficulties were increased because many of the ropes were ice-covered and the ice on deck made us slip. We lost count of the number of towropes that broke. We hadn't enough men to pull the broken ends back on board, so just had to cut them away with fire axes. Soon all our good ropes on deck had been sacrificed in this way, so we went down into the forepeak and slowly hauled out a new 8-inch manila rope. Captain Slope had been busy on the bridge passing messages to the shore and nearby naval craft. Now he was up forward with us, hauling on ropes in a very sporting manner. The work enabled us to keep warm, as the sun by now was only a dull red ball close to the horizon. Every now and again great clouds would drift out from the land, and there were heavy snow squalls.

Our Pilot was a tall, elderly man with a great white walrus moustache and calm, kindly blue eyes. Nothing excited him. He spread peace of mind and confidence to everyone. As we drew nearer to the harbour, our confidence rose that we would get *Kelmscott* to safety. By the time we reached the narrow entrance to the harbour at about seven p.m. it was nearly dark. The port authorities weren't going to allow the ship to enter, fearing she might sink and block up the harbour, but Captain Slope overruled them. Close inshore, we were in smoother water. Additional tugs came alongside and we hauled still more ropes aboard and made them fast. Then slowly we moved into the harbour and approached the same pier we had left that morning. The Mate and I split our available manpower to go fore and aft to help us tie up the ship. He took three men forward, as he would have to handle the anchors, and I took one man aft. The task of tying up a ship without winches and with only two men would have been a tremendous undertaking, but to our relief, a boat came off from the pier with six stevedores to help us. By now we were very tired but we kept going until the work was finished. We were all heartily thankful when the ship was finally secured to the pier. Even if she then sank, she only had a foot or two to go before touching the bottom, as we were drawing thirty feet of water forward.

Once we were alongside, a big shore party came aboard. While the Mate interviewed officials with the Old Man, I finished tying up the ship and got a gangway between the ship and shore. Then I went round with men from customs, sealing the places most liable to be pilfered. By nine o'clock we had done everything in our power. The dry dock officials had sent powerful pumps aboard to combat the water that had risen in the engine room over the boilers and engine tops. Arrangements had been made for our accommodation ashore, and leaving the *Kelmscott* in the hands of a customs guard, the Mate and I went ashore.

Looking back we could see the chaotic state of the ship. The hatch covers on number two and number three holds had been blown off, the torn rolls of newsprint had been spewed up and were lying limply draped over derricks and winches. The heavy beams that held the hatch covers were lying scattered over the decks. Ventilator cowls, blown off by the explosion, lay battered and twisted where they had fallen. A tangled collection of ropes was hanging forlornly from the empty davits, and one of the davits was twisted as if a giant had been using it to vent his temper. Dirt and pools of frozen water gave the ship an unkempt, ragged appearance. Sticking up from the puddles of ice were debris and broken, buckled deck plates.

Many years after leaving the sea I found out that the German submarine that torpedoed us was the U-845. She was commissioned on May 1, 1943, and after a training patrol started on her first operational patrol on October 8, 1943. We were the first ship she torpedoed. In the book *U-Boat Adventures* by Melanie Wiggins, the subsequent history of U-845 was given. On February 14, an RAF plane attacked U-845 in mid Atlantic with eight depth charges causing the death of one crewmember. Then on March 10 she was sunk by depth charges from two destroyers, a corvette, and a frigate with the loss of ten lives and forty-five survivors.

In my diary I reported that there were two unaccounted-for explosions at intervals of about half an hour between the times the two torpedoes struck us. In a report obtained later from HMS *Gentian* which was escorting us it was stated, "At 1255 and 1308 two further heavy explosions were heard, but as no water disturbance was seen, it was considered that these were the results of torpedoes exploding at the end of their runs, or on the beach." Had those torpedoes hit us, we would probably have sunk.

This story is from a chapter in Stephen Richardson's book, *School of the Sea*, published by Whittles Publishing, Dunbeath, Caithness, Scotland, UK, in 2009. Richardson is the USA agent for the publisher. His book is available from him at e-mail: *stephen.arichardson@comcast.net* or by telephone at 603-778-8032.

Born in Yorkshire, England, Stephen was educated in pediatrics in Glasgow. He then obtained his BS at Harvard and PhD at Cornell. He became Professor of Pediatrics at the Albert Einstein Medical School in the Bronx. Richardson's interests are music, writing, and boats.

Army Air Corps Memories

JERRY RITTER

W E WERE a group of volunteers in the Army Specialized Training Program, whose college careers were interrupted and were being inducted into service at Ft. Dix, New Jersey. We were convinced that we had the "right stuff" to be turned into devastating fighting machines—surely at the officer level. However, it quickly became apparent that our Duty Sergeant—a crusty thirty-year veteran—did not share that exalted opinion of our potential.

We quickly learned from him the most basic truism of the army: NEVER VOLUNTEER! His call for a typist volunteer turned out to be "just the type for KP".

Those who volunteered as entomologists were delegated to capturing Japanese beetles.

His ultimate put-down, however, was "When you talk to me, shut up!"

Before being discharged after the war ended, our squadron in England, along with others, was assigned the task of making an aerial map of our area since some of the existing maps were not available or reliable. A new crew flew in and was assigned to our barracks. They looked to us, grizzled veterans, as if they had just gotten out of high school, which was probably true—green recruits, with very little flying time.

A group of VIPs had scheduled a scenic flyover. Major Brooks, our CEO, was assigned the task of arranging their trip. At this time most experienced crews were being discharged. The Major selected the new crew for a training flight prior to the VIP flyover.

On returning to the base after our day of map-making, we noticed that the bunks of the new crew had been stripped. On inquiry, we were told the Brooks flight had crashed, with no survivors.

This tragic occurrence is another illustration of the futility and waste of war.

Jerry was born in Pittsburgh, Pennsylvania, and grew up in North-field, New Jersey. After serving in the Army Air Corps with the Eighth Air Force, Jerry graduated in 1948 from Franklin and Marshall College with a BS in Chemistry. This led to a career as a sales engineer and consultant in the treatment and use of leather in industry and manufacturing. While serving in an Army college training program in Missouri, he met his wife, Louanna. They were married in 1946 and lived in upstate New York with their three sons and two daughters. After retirement they lived in Rye Beach, New Hampshire, before moving to Exeter.

A Lingering Look

MONTY SCHARFF

T HE TIME WAS September 1943 and I was on a Navy ship with hundreds of other very young men on the way to England. We had no escort so the Captain was zigzagging his way across the Atlantic, hoping no Nazi U-boats would find us and blow us out of the water. When we were about one hundred miles off the coast of England several British naval ships dashed out of the fog to escort us into a relatively safe harbor in Greenock, Scotland. We were sailing under a bombers' moon with dozens of other allied ships anchored hoping no German war planes would discover us and bomb us. The only moment of joy was a group of Scottish girls on the dock welcoming us to their world with hot tea and donuts. We also noticed a large crate of scotch being unloaded on the dock for the pleasure of some high-ranking brass.

We were soon put on a train headed for the suburbs of London. We were all terrified because when we arrived we were all dashed into bomb shelters seeking protection from German bomb raids. We were dumped into the middle of World War II and given a bunch of jobs, not very interesting, like kitchen police (KP) and guard duty.

A few weeks later I was given my first pass to take the train into London. Then came my miracle.

I was walking into Piccadilly Circus, a famous area in the middle of the city, in total blackout. Suddenly, I heard a sharp voice say, "Don't you salute when you see an officer?" He was a full colonel and I never saw him. I promptly saluted the officer and apologized. He took a hard look again and shouted, " Monty Scharff what the hell are you doing here?" I didn't recognize the officer. He added, "Don't you know me, I'm the father of your college roommate." I couldn't believe it and saluted him again. He asked, "How long have you been in London and what are you doing?" I told him I had just arrived and wasn't doing anything very special except for helping to put on musical shows for our airmen at bases around London. The colonel was impressed.

He then told me he had recently arrived in England and had been assigned as a senior officer to help plan and direct daytime bomber raids on wartime German industry. He said the US 8th Air Force would bomb during the day and the Royal British Air Force would conduct their raids at night. This was to become round the clock bomb missions on Nazi Germany. He asked me how I would like to join his staff and become a junior aide to his office. I said I would love it! The next thing I knew I was transferred to the American 8th USAF headquarters in the little town of High Wycombe, moving between London and Oxford.

I was billeted in the Wycombe Abby School for Girls. Unhappily, all the young ladies had already been transferred elsewhere. My new office had a sign on the wall that said, "Ring twice for the mistress." I rang that bell for three years and no mistress ever showed up!

The school was code named Pinetree and became headquarters for planning major bombing missions. The missions were all planned in underground locations behind the old school building. The Wycombe Abby itself looked like a gorgeous old castle.

I could hardly believe I was to become part of the 8th Air Force bomber missions. Our goal was to design air raids to destroy German production plants producing fighter planes, U-boat submarines, electrical plants, bombs, and all kinds of military equipment. I worked on a staff that carefully studied results of every mission, failed missions, and loss of planes and personnel. We were a twenty-four hour per day operation!

My commanding officer eventually became a brigadier general and I eventually became a 2nd Lt. On one memorable day we went to the 10 Downing Street office of Winston Churchill. Being the junior man I carried most of the secret reports. I was sure I was going to meet the great man but all I could do was sit in the reception area and watch the smoke from Mr. Churchill's cigar drift under the door of his office!

As the war wore on we used to visit our many 8th Air Force airfields to watch the bombers struggle home at the end of a long mission. It was often heartbreaking to see our planes come back minus one or two engines with wounded crew on board. The unhappiest thing was to see so many planes taking off in the early hours of the day and then wait and wait and wait for their late return, often to see less than half the bomber group return at all.

It wasn't till later in the war that we began to see fighter planes escort our bombers into combat and then help the bomber groups return. It's interesting to note in those early missions the famous Tuskegee fighters protected our bombers from German flak and Messerschmitt fighters. The Tuskegee fighters never lost a bomber in combat. There was a certain amount of prejudice among southern 8th Air Force pilots. They didn't want a black fighter around them. They soon got over that nonsense when they realized the Tuskegee pilots never lost a B-17. Many of the B-17 pilots didn't want to fly the missions WITHOUT the Tuskegee fighter pilots going right with them!

As the war was winding down in 1945 we received word from Intelligence that there was a secret little known slave labor plant with over one thousand people hidden in the Bavarian Alps high above the little town of Oberammergau. The plant was impossible to bomb because it was well hidden. The plant was building state-of-the-art Messerschmitt fighters with jet power in this underground Nazi factory. If these new jet fighters had ever gotten into the air they would have slaughtered our B-17 bombers.

The production of planes was stopped by General George Patton and his powerful tanks. General Patton blew open the factory doors, closed down production, and saved the lives of many of the laborers in the plant. Our group flew into Munich, which was then a holy mess, and when we drove up we saw the new jet fighters almost ready to fly out of the plant. We had nothing to compare with the new jet fighters. Of course many of the slave laborers were delighted to get out from under the clutches of the Nazis and we of course did everything we could to help them.

I recall a particularly warm friendship while living in High Wycombe. The local people used to invite the Yanks to tea, donuts, and music at the local high school. I loved going there and became friends with Mae Fowles, a delightful local lady. One evening she invited me to visit her home to meet her husband. Jack was headmaster in one of the local schools. He was a classic Englishman with tweeds and pipe. I'm not sure how delighted he was to have a Yank visit his sanctuary of his private home!

We soon became great friends. The Fowles had no children and I soon became part of this lovely family. While they never asked for anything it was always my great joy to bring the eggs, steak, vegetables, and all kinds of things they could not get because of rationing. It was a wonderful friendship, three thousand miles from home, and lasted for many years after the war.

It's all a long time ago now, but we must try to keep alive the extraordinary memories of our WW II lives. Most of all I remember and respect the British people who had great courage and spirit. So many times I would see moms, daddies, children, and grandparents spending long nights in the silent London subways, trying to keep alive, despite the threat of air raids from Nazi bombers and V1 and V2 robot bombs. When the robot engines stopped they could crash anywhere.

Following four years in England with the US Army 8th Air Force Command Headquarters, Monty returned home to complete his college education at Bard College, a part of Columbia University, where he met his future wife, Edwina. Monty became a pioneer in the field known as Industrial Relations and formed a national consulting company headquartered in New York. Monty's goal was to offer consulting services to public companies seeking to build a following in the Wall Street world. After forty years of consulting, and serving on numerous boards of directors, he and his wife retired to Kennebunkport, Maine.

POW

Bill Smallwood

WHILE STILL an undergraduate at Wesleyan University I enlisted in the Army Air Corps and was called to duty in January 1943. I'd always wanted to fly a B-17 "Flying Fortress", but after a series of tests I decided to request training as a bombardier rather than as a pilot. The long arduous training was interrupted by an outbreak among the troops of spinal meningitis, which landed us all in quarantine for two weeks and did nothing to lift morale.

We were sent to Los Angeles for classroom work in meteorology, navigation, theory of flight, Morse code, and aircraft recognition. Then we went to New Mexico to learn use of the Norden bombsight and to practice bombing runs on synthetic targets. After a twelve week program I was commissioned a Second Lieutenant and assigned to still further training in New Mexico, then in Washington state where our crew of four assembled with pilot Dale Tomlin in command. We continued to practice bombing runs, weather permitting, and learned deflection shooting with 50 caliber machine guns. Finally we were sent to a base in Florida to await orders to proceed overseas. It had been just one year since I had first reported for duty in Nashville.

Overseas

The Tomlin crew departed the US on New Year's morning. In our brand new B-17G, we ached to know where we were being sent, but our pilot was under orders not to reveal the destination at first. A jubilant mood pervaded the plane, tempered with the knowledge that, as a replacement crew, we would soon be entering a combat zone. Finally, in Natal, Brazil, our final stop in the Western Hemisphere, Tomlin opened the sealed orders. Our assignment was the 15th Air Force, headquartered in Foggia, Italy. Disappointed at not being sent to England to join the 8th Air Force, we four officers tried to console ourselves at an officer's club adjoining an airfield in Dakar, Africa. At the next table four flyers wearing 8th Air Force insignia sat, quietly drunk, having completed their prescribed quota of missions.

"They won't talk about it," reported Mac, our co-pilot who had attempted unsuccessfully to learn from them about aerial combat in the European Theater of Operations.

Foggia, Italy

Following arrival in Foggia we turned our plane over to Operations. Here one could feel a seriousness of purpose all around. The Tomlin Crew was assigned to the 346th Squadron of the 99th Bomb Group, with its base at Tortorella Field, six miles east of Foggia. We settled in, tents perched atop gooey mud. Our Squadron Commander, Captain Schroeder, proved to be a no-nonsense guy. On the first few missions our crew was separated, each of us to fly with veterans. When we finally did fly together we were conscious of other crews watching, waiting to see if we could hold our own against sophisticated German flyers. After dinner in the mess tent you would learn about a crew which hadn't returned—shot down somewhere. You tried to get sleep, to be ready for the morning, for another mission.

Five of the fifteen missions I flew on are described in my book, *Tomlin's Crew*. The first was to Poggibonsi, in Central Italy. It was my baptism, flown with a veteran crew. The target was obscured by cloud cover, so we sought an alternate site. German flak gunners managed to place some shots close enough to put holes in the Plexiglas nose of our plane, convincing me of the reality of combat. The second mission, when the Tomlin crew was together again, was to Sofia, Bulgaria, to hit railroad marshalling yards. As a result of total cloud cover, the Wing of seventy-five planes circled and circled, failing to locate the target. The formation became separated and our plane soon found itself alone. I managed to bomb a small airfield, a "target of opportunity" on the way back to Italy. We became so low on fuel that we had to land at Bari. When our wheels touched down, two of the engines quit.

The tenth and eleventh missions came on successive days, each one really an emergency. The tenth, to Anzio, was an attempt to support our ground troops, forced into a desperate position on the beach; our job was to bomb German infantry, to prevent them from pushing our men into the sea. The following day, at Monte Cassino, we were called upon to destroy a monastery, supposedly filled by German soldiers. Many of us questioned the wisdom of this attack, but we followed orders.

Big Week

My final mission took place on February 25, 1944, on a raid to a Messerschmitt aircraft assembly plant in Regensburg, Germany. We had no fighter escort. Our squadron was subjected to repeated attacks by swarms of German fighter planes, resulting in the fatal wounding of our pilot, Lt. Tomlin, and the serious wounding of our engineer and me. Three of our engines were hit, two catching on fire. Eight of our crew bailed out initially, leaving Mac, the co-pilot, and me. The co-pilot's parachute had been struck by German 20 mm shellfire, bursting the pack open. Once the bomb bay doors were opened, to salvo the bombs in order to lighten our stricken Flying Fortress, the flow of air from the bomber's belly sucked the fabric of Mac's parachute back through the fuselage. Mac was in a predicament. I gathered up his chute, pulling it back into the cockpit, and together we folded it carefully in his bent arms. Then he bailed out and made it safely to the ground. I was the last to leave, as I had attempted to maneuver our wobbly plane over Switzerland, in order to bail out over neutral territory. But in the end I was forced to bail out over enemy country.

This had been "Big Week," a series of raids by US heavy bombers against German oil refineries, ball bearing plants, and aircraft assembly works. The mission to Regensburg was the final day of "Big Week," and the American bombers, some accompanied by US fighter planes, had met the German Luftwaffe interceptors head on. Both sides experienced severe losses. In the end it was the Nazis who suffered most, as they were unable to replace the pilots shot down. This loss of hundreds of their seasoned fighter pilots was never made up. I feel that during the invasion of the European continent on June 6, 1944, Allied troops were spared the opposition of the Luftwaffe primarily because of "Big Week."

Capture

Armed German soldiers awaited our landing and saw to the capture of co-pilot Mac and me. Our engineer was eventually ordered repatriated because of the severity of his arm wound. I was placed in an Austrian hospital, where I was operated on for shrapnel removal and remained for a month of recuperation. The co-pilot was sent by train directly to prison camp. Following release from the hospital, and after a bout of solitary confinement, I joined my co-pilot and navigator in Stalag Luft I, a prison camp for Allied flying officers, on the shore of the Baltic Sea in northern Germany. It was in this prison camp, while taking a delousing shower, that I was amazed to see my close friend from cadet days showering. When he told me the third buddy from our cadet days together was here also, I almost fainted. Our enlisted men were sent to various camps—none of our crew managed to escape.

Life in Stalag Luft I during my fourteen-month stay was a combination of tedium, inadequate food, and those rare moments of intensity when something unusual took place—the shooting of a fellow prisoner was one such occasion. Once a month our room would be entitled to the use of a battered, hand-cranked Victrola, courtesy of the YMCA, complete with worn records of popular band music. Lying on our bunk beds on excelsior-filled mattresses, after lights out we twelve Americans would listen to strains of

Tommy Dorsey's trombone playing *Night and Day*, our thoughts a million miles away.

Escape was constantly in the thoughts of a Kriegie, as we called ourselves, after the word *Kriegsgefangener*, prisoner of war. I participated in one abortive escape attempt because of my ability to speak German. I became part of a tunneling operation, a "digger" working eight feet underground, lying flat on the stomach, passing back dirt loaded in wash basins to the next man, to be disposed of, we hoped, undetected by German guards. Our effort failed, but we heard about one escape attempt elsewhere that almost succeeded: A Royal Air Force officer had had himself concealed under a load of garbage on a horse-drawn trailer leaving camp to go to the dump. In a moment when the armed guards were inattentive, the officer slipped away into the forest, and walked some distance before he was confronted by a German patrol which demanded his papers. He produced forged papers stating that he was a French worker. The German officer in charge then spoke to him in French. He was unable to respond, so back to camp he went.

We learned later, however, that many—an estimated total of 35,000—Allied POWs escaped the camps. A good third of them reportedly were aided by a scheme devised by the British Intelligence Service, which was declassified and came to light only in 2007. Maps, obviously, are indispensable aids to an escapee, but paper maps have drawbacks: they're noisy, they wear out rapidly, they turn to mush when wet. But someone in MI6 thought of printing maps on silk: durable, scrunchable into tiny wads, noiseless when unfolded. At that time there was one manufacturer in Great Britain that had perfected the technology of printing on silk, the John Waddington Company. The firm was only too happy to do its bit for the war effort. By pure coincidence, Waddington was also the UK licensee for the American board game Monopoly. It so happened that "games and pastimes" was a category qualified for inclusion in CARE packages distributed by the International Red Cross to prisoners of war. A group of sworn-to-secrecy employees, in an inaccessible and securely guarded old workshop on Waddington's grounds, began mass-producing silk escape maps so fine that when folded, they could be stuffed into a Monopoly playing piece. While they were at it, these clever workmen managed to add playing tokens containing a small magnetic compass and a two-part metal file that could be screwed together, and useful amounts of genuine high-denomination German, French, and Italian currency hidden within the piles of Monopoly money! British and American air crews were advised before taking off on their first mission how to identify a rigged Monopoly set, by means of a tiny red dot that looked like an ordinary printing glitch. A CARE package was much to be desired!

Liberation

The most vivid event in our camp was liberation, when an advance unit of the Russian Army arrived and opened the gates which had denied us freedom for so long. To this day, when I meet a fellow Kriegie from Stalag Luft I, we will go over a number of things, but always the liberation, with those Russian troops—Mongolians, many of them—offering us vodka, attempting conversation. I tried to converse with one of our liberators while sharing guard duty with a short Russian assault trooper. We couldn't use words, but when I fished out a package of Camel cigarettes from my blouse, he saw the silhouette of the camel on the side and immediately began jabbing his finger excitedly at this animal, something, no doubt, reminding him of his homeland.

Once the Russian Cossacks had arrived and our euphoria had died down, our main interest shifted to thoughts about leaving the camp and returning to Allied lines. This hope turned out to be premature, as a delay set in while Russian officers made contact with Moscow for further instructions. Consequently Col. Zemke, our commanding officer, decided to take action himself. He sought out a pair of RAF flyers and ordered them to attempt to exit the camp during darkness and try to make contact with the nearest body of Allied ground troops, presumably British ones, with instructions to pass along word of our plight to Field Marshall Montgomery's headquarters. Zemke's move turned out to be fruitful, as it resulted in bringing about our eventual departure by air.

The air plan was to make use of an 8th US Air Force group to transport all nine thousand of us POWs to France, an undertaking which would last three full days. The plan was to use an airport runway near Barth, a town on the Baltic coast. However, neither Zemke nor his British counterparts knew whether this runway was of sufficient length for bomber use, nor could they be sure the runway hadn't been mined by departing Luftwaffe personnel. I knew that my barracks neighbor, Major Fred Rabo, played a part in our departure, and that he had the confidence of Col. Zemke as being cool under fire.

In the late 1990s I obtained his telephone number in California, phoned him, and heard in his own words what had actually taken place that day. Rabo said Zemke had directed him to visit the airfield to check out the runway's length, and also to see if there was any evidence of mines. Fred told me he found a German bicycle left behind and proceeded to pedal the three miles to the Barth airport. Once at the facility, Fred decided the runway appeared long enough to accommodate bombers. Then he looked closer and spotted the telltale signs of dirt piles running along both sides of it, six piles to a side. In a moment a man in uniform appeared, riding a bicycle. He approached, saluted, and gave his name, Lt. DeLury. He was an American paratrooper, trained among other things to know how to de-activate mines by disconnecting the detonators. "What a stroke of luck!" Rabo told me. He said the two of them worked together with ropes they found in a nearby barn. They carefully withdrew the mines away from the runway sides and then deactivated them, rendering them harmless.

Satisfied that the assignment had been carried out, he returned to the camp with DeLury. On the way back, however, the paratrooper volunteered that the wily Germans could have placed a second mine below the top one, though he had seen no evidence of it.

"I told the Colonel what I had done," Fred said over the phone, "but then he asked me, Major, are you certain you found them all?" On telling me this, Rabo paused.

I jumped in. "Fred," I asked, "this is all news to me, but what more could you have done?"

He laughed a little at that, but then resumed his story to describe a final return trip to the runway. "I went back alone and looked things over. I made my decision, took a deep breath, climbed back on the old bike and pedaled down the runway. Nothing happened. So I turned around and pedaled back again."

"Wow!" was all I could say. Then I added, "That was brave. You could have been killed…. I'm glad it worked out."

"Me too," Rabo replied. There was a silence till the major said, "Guess I'll get back to my pecan groves." That was all.

"So long, Fred," I said. "If you ever come east I'd be glad to see you."

The balance of our stay was merely preparation for departure. No one in Allied authority really knew what the Russian attitude would be should American bombers suddenly appear, intent on removing Allied airmen. In the event, our liberators chose to stand aside. Soon the "Forts" flew in. I was pressed into service as a loader, checking to see that only thirty-five men climbed aboard each B-17, fitted now with bucket seats in the waist section. Departing in one of the flights, as our plane headed for France I took a last look out of a waist window back toward Stalag Luft I, with its barbed wire. Fifteen months ago our crew had penetrated German skies in a Flying Fortress, and now here I was, leaving in one.

This story, *POW*, is based on a book by the storywriter titled, *Tomlin's Crew: A Bombardier's Story* published by Sunflower University Press, Manhattan, Kansas.

Born in Glen Rock, New Jersey, Bill was raised in Ridgewood, New Jersey, and later graduated from Wesleyan University. He was a Partner at Carl Pforzheimer & Company in New York City, later a Vice President at Burgess and Leith in Boston, and past president of Oil Analysts of New York City. In 1980 the family retired to Brownsville, Vermont.

Wartime

ROBERT A. SOUTHWORTH

I SPENT FIVE YEARS in the US Navy and to put it briefly—I had a great time. I traveled over much of the world, served on many different types of ships, was temporarily attached to the Army, and to the Marine Corps. My assignments were always unexpected, but almost always turned out to be extremely interesting. Being twenty-two years old and single, it was not a hardship to be away from home. I took a destroyer out of Norfolk "all by myself" (with the assistance of some 300 other men), drove a tank in Africa (and threw a tread), piloted many sorts of ships, had command of a tug in the Chesapeake, was flown off an aircraft carrier, and landed again! I was Naval liaison and drove a jeep for Army General Lucian Truscott in Africa, was strafed by German planes in Sicily, and had a two-engine bomber assigned to me in Australia to deliver a letter to Manila. In addition to the landings in North Africa and Sicily, I made three amphibious landings in the Pacific.

It began in New York City where I had gone to work for Socony-Vacuum (later Mobil Oil) after graduation from Dartmouth College in 1938. In 1940, after talking to several people about the certainty that war was coming, I made inquiry about joining the Navy at a ship tied up in the Hudson River, and after producing my college diploma and a cursory physical exam, I was sworn in.

The first thing we did was a thirty-day cruise on the USS *New York* as part of a V-7 program. Later we were known as "90-Day Wonders." The *New York* was a World War I battleship and I thought it was a wonderful ship. We cruised to Panama. It was September of 1940. On the way back we had gunnery practice off Guantanamo

Bay with our 14 inch guns. We attended classes and were required to visit every part of the ship. The engine room was enormous and had a reciprocating steam engine. After this cruise we were graded and almost all 700 of us passed. They were in need of naval officers. We were then assigned our next duty and I drew Annapolis.

Three months elapsed and in February of 1941 I reported to the Naval Academy at Annapolis for "90-day Wonder School." There we were instructed in Seamanship, Navigation, Gunnery, and how to be an officer and a gentleman. I loved the time at Annapolis and on May 15, 1941, was commissioned an ensign, United States Naval Reserve (USNR). I then began a series of five schools in rapid succession—Armed Guard School at Annapolis, Local Defense Force School in Boston, Small Boat School in New Orleans, and two others, after which I was ordered to Parris Island for a session with the Marines.

In October I reported to Quantico where for the first time the twelve men, who had been selected as Naval Gunfire Officers, met each other and our Marine commanding officer. The training began—providing shore fire from the supporting naval ships for the landings. There were two real problems. One, naval gunfire is very high velocity and flat trajectory, hence not useful against an enemy behind even low hills. Two, there was no way to communicate between those on the shore and those on the firing ships. This was one of the challenges to resolve.

While at Quantico we drove to Washington for some reason, with a Colonel from the First Marine Raider Battalion and we got lost returning. I mentioned to the Colonel we were going north, not south. He said, "How do you know?" I replied that I had been watching the stars. And it turned out to be true. Wouldn't you know, next day I was detailed to address the battalion officers on finding your way by the stars at night.

My log shows "Dec. 7 Japan jumps in."

In March of 1942 I was assigned to the light cruiser USS *Brooklyn*. There was a ship I loved. She was a real fighting ship—fifteen 6-inch guns in five turrets. I was delegated as Assistant Navigator and went in a 29-ship convoy to the Canal Zone. My log shows, first day out "sick as hell." And for the first time the realization came to me that there were enemy submarines out there. At Panama we had no liberty, picked up the RMS *Aquitania* and sailed with her and four destroyers to Scotland. I had a great time exploring Edinborough, after which we headed back to Norfolk. My log shows that at 0615 the lookouts reported a periscope. "The Captain ordered hard left rudder, I gave the order and blew two blasts, but we flew the wrong flags, gave the wrong signals, and in a word lost our collective heads in the first attack."

In June of 1942 I was transferred to the Amphibious Force, US Atlantic Fleet, in Norfolk, Virginia. I made Lieutenant Junior Grade at that time. There I became involved with Bloodsworth Island, which had been donated to the Navy for a firing range. Our part would be directing naval gunfire in support of landings and shore operations, and none of the destroyers had ever engaged in naval gunfire on a shore—so we had this island as a target. I got involved in building the lookout towers, two of them, 40' high, made of wood (as there was no steel available). I went, by air no less, to Washington to assist in designing them. Obviously I don't know any more about designing a wooden tower, 40' high, than you do. But I persevered and was listened to most respectfully by the Bureau of Ordinance engineers. We spent many, many days going up and down Chesapeake Bay. Sometimes I would be assigned a tug for my use, and several times the Admiral's private yacht.

At Amphibious Force headquarters, the Hotel Nansemond in Norfolk, we got down to planning an invasion. Where, we didn't know, but no matter. The log shows, "not enough radios of the right kind." We were trained by the Marines to spot the fall of shot, but we had to talk to the Navy on the ships that were doing the firing. And we trained and trained, we made rehearsal landings, and the Underwater Demolition Teams (UDT) had all their special gear, and the officers played Acey-Deucy and went to the Officers' Club and drank, and everything got pretty hectic.

I thought maybe I would go with Admiral Hewitt in the USS

Augusta but sort of wanted to be assigned to the USS *Green Hornet* with General Patton. As it turned out I was assigned to Army Brigadier General Lucian K. Truscott in the USS *Henry T. Allen*—a troop transport. That suited me fine. All our gear was marked "Delta T" and for all intents and purposes I had joined the Army.

Now begins the start of the real war as far as I was concerned. This was Operation Torch (North Africa), and the extent of the foul-ups only became apparent later. Task Force 34 (the entire convoy) was under the command of Admiral Hewitt, the Army under General Patton, and my General Truscott was in command of the sub-task force, Goal Post. The convoy was 102 ships. Ten miles ahead was a screen of ten destroyers, the main convoy was nine columns and five lines with the battleships USS *New York* and USS *Texas* on the forward outboard corners. Twelve miles astern was the air group the USS *Ranger*, four escort carriers, a cruiser, and nine destroyers. It formed a space 20 x 30 miles. Our mission was to steam 4,000 miles and make a night landing. I think it was considered the largest armada ever put to sea.

Two of our concerns were the German battleships, particularly the *Tirpitz* with eight 15 inch guns and capable of speed of 34 knots, and German submarines. We had the great advantage by then of having broken the German code (Ultra) by means of capturing their coding machine (Enigma). We also had their position charts so that we could intercept messages sent by Admiral Doenitz to his boats (submarines are boats, not ships).

In the convoy we had many merchant ships that did not use Navy-signaling procedure; sometimes one sent them a signal and they just hoisted the flag "Answering." So we arranged that hoisting "EASY" and sounding one long blast meant "All ships turn 90° to the right and continue steaming." We did this once or twice when Washington signaled submarines in our path. But you can imagine it took us hours to get ourselves straightened out afterwards. There were sixty-three ships in the main section of the convoy, they all had different turning radii, and to get this massive conglomeration of vessels turned around was something else again! Meanwhile the naval ships in the rear of the convoy all had to shift to new positions. The World War I battleships, USS *New York* and USS *Texas* had a hard time in a rough sea. They had to turn their turrets sideways to avoid flooding. The ocean-going tugs had a difficult time in heavy weather, but we did not lose a ship to enemy action.

Let me try to tell you about an amphibious operation. It resembles nothing so much as one hundred Chinese fire drills held in the middle of the night on a seething ocean. To begin, the transports anchor ten miles off shore. How far depends on what we think they have on shore in the way of guns. They begin to unload their boats. Each davit holds three landing craft, (ten davits = thirty landing craft). The men are called to clamber down the landing nets and into the boats, which continue to circle. If they weren't seasick before, they are now. Finally, in the pitch-black night the boats are dispatched to the Line of Departure, about two miles off shore. H-Hour is usually 4 a.m. and a ragged line of boats heads for shore. We were new at this and had not perfected the technique of rolling rocket fire on the shore. So the boats go in. Some become stranded on a sand bar fifty yards off shore and the men have to swim or wade in from there. It is just beginning to get light and thousands of men are milling about on the beach.

The plan is to have the men get ashore and inland, clear of the beach. It seldom works smoothly or quickly. We had 9,000 personnel and sixty-five light tanks and it was extremely difficult to walk around on the beach in soft sand.

We arrived in the transport area around midnight. I was on the bridge of the USS *Henry T. Allen*, scanning the shore. I was astounded to see five ships, lights ablaze, steaming out of Port Lyautey, French Morocco, in column and heading south. One ship blinked at us "Beware, the shore is alerted." This was four hours before our landing. So much for surprise. We never did find out how the shore knew. It was disheartening to have steamed 4,000 miles and there was the enemy waiting for us with open arms.

At any rate, the initial troops got ashore and eventually the General and I went ashore. You should have seen my triumphant entry onto Africa's sunny shores. The General and a few others of us set out about 10 a.m. in a small boat. We were well equipped. I had my tin helmet, Colt .45 pistol, and I had also picked up a couple of hand grenades. I mean they were passing them out, so why not? Plus I had 100 rounds of ammunition and the water jug. It was pretty exciting, I can tell you, and a few honest-to-God bullets were flying. As the boat touched the shore, the ramp went down, and the General walked ashore. My foot caught in the ramp and I fell full length in the water. I managed to get up with all my heavy equipment and was wet for three days.

How come we were fighting the French? Well, it worked out this way. France fell in 1940 and Germany gained control of the French in North Africa and the French fleet. During the summer of 1940 the American President decided North Africa was the place to halt the German encirclement of the Eastern Atlantic. Churchill and Roosevelt decided a major offensive against Europe must be undertaken in 1942 at the latest. Further, Rommel, the Desert Fox, was going great guns in Northeast Africa. The reason we went in to Port Lyautey was because it had the only all-weather concrete landing strip in Northwest Africa.

We had hoped the French would welcome us. Not so. I think the French were frightened, they were under the leadership of Marshal Petain who was a collaborator with the Germans, and they were taught to fight.

We were determined to try our best to work with the French, so as soon as we landed we sent a jeep with Colonel Craw and Major Hamilton through the lines under a white flag of truce and an American and a French flag. The jeep came over a rise and the Colonel was shot dead. The message that they were trying to deliver to the French commander was delivered and on November 10 General Mathenet agreed to capitulate and the formal surrender took place at a meeting arranged by Major Hamilton.

Colonel Craw's death had a profound effect on all of us on the General's staff. Remember, we were new at this war business and we felt that a white flag offered protection, as it had in most instances in previous wars.

The General said that he had to deliver a message through the lines to Rabat, with some details of the arrangements for the cease-fire. I volunteered and leaving all weapons behind we roared off in a half-track with a white flag, an American flag, and a French flag. We got to Rabat all right, delivered our message, and tried to return. Somebody had not gotten the word of our mission and I saw tracers arcing over toward us from our right—from our own anti-tank guns. The driver went like hell and we got through safely. We had landed November 8, 1942; the armistice was three days later on November 11. It was a long three days.

After that, I stayed on with the General and we took up offices in the town. The General assigned me to get the stranded landing boats off the beaches. What a difficult job! First we tried to tow the boats off with a tug. It did not work. A bulldozer pulled the boats across the sand to the jetty on which there was a crane, and a reluctant crane operator lifted the boat over the jetty into the Sebou River. We towed them upstream and repaired them.

I was with General Truscott when he visited sickbay in a make-shift hospital. The General had a cardboard box of Purple Hearts and he gave one to each wounded soldier. We had 250 wounded, eleven dead Navy. We dug a cemetery inside the Kasbah and there we buried Colonel Craw and eighty-four other officers and men.

I was awarded the Legion of Merit for this operation, but felt I had not really done anything to deserve it. In later operations I felt I did deserve some recognition, but got none. I have a theory about decorations: (1) you have to be there, (2) you have to do something—almost anything, and (3) you have to have someone see you do it.

Some conclusions that I reached after that first battle experience remained in place throughout the rest of "my" war. The armed services don't really get along. The Army doesn't trust the Navy to deliver them to a destination on time and intact. The Navy regards the Marines with mild suspicion; the Marines regard the Navy with open derision. The services cannot even agree on how to divide a circle. The Navy uses degrees; the Army divides the circle into 6400 bits called "mils." They will not use the same maps and charts—

a big problem for shore fire control. The Navy's charts go to the shoreline, and that's it. The Army maps extend from there inland and use a different grid system. In Africa we got around that by issuing a road map to the troops—figuring that any American boy could read a road map.

The Army and the Navy did not use the same radios, nor did they have access to each other's frequencies. There was no Talk Between Ships (TBS) when we started. All Navy radios had to be adjusted to include Army frequencies. Our radio communications were medium frequency, and 2182 was the emergency frequency. No high frequency, no ultra-high frequency. The radios we lugged ashore were SCR 584s. They were two big boxes, two and a half feet long, plus a generator. It took three men to operate them.

Communication, speed, versatility—that's what makes a war go. Our tanks were effective because they were fast, even though they were so high you could not easily conceal them.

I had a unique opportunity to participate in a small battle, which served me well as I next was involved in the invasion of Sicily, for which I was back in the Navy where I served as Assistant Flag Navigator. My next assignments were in Pearl Harbor, then New Guinea, and the invasions of Halmahera, Leyte, and Lingayan Gulf. I retired from Active Duty in the United States Naval Reserve in 1945 as a Lieutenant Commander.

Born in Boston, Massachusetts, in 1917, Robert spent his early years on the coast of New Hampshire at Little Boar's Head. After the war he returned to Mobil Oil, and married Katherine Hobson in 1957. He completed thirty-five years with Mobil in 1973, mostly involved with Marine Retail Division. Retirement involved nine years as a Selectman in North Hampton, completion of forty-nine years as Commissioner of Little Boar's Head.

A Bad Night

Bob Spang

I WAS IN THE US Navy in WW II from 1942 to 1946 and had destroyer duty for over three years, mostly in the Mediterranean Sea. The most hairy experience I had was off the coast of southern Italy in 1944 when German planes were overhead dropping bombs on our group. It was dark and we were zigzagging at 20 knots to make a poor target. One-at-a-time the bombs came at us. The first one had a light on it, which I could see getting nearer and making a screaming noise. As the first one approached I was sure it would destroy our ship. I was on my knees until the bomb exploded astern. We lost one destroyer that night.

One of the worst things about war is that you could be shooting and killing a good friend. Max Schaeder, a German soldier and friend of my wife and me was captured and imprisoned on a Liberty ship in the Hudson River. As the Gunnery Officer on a destroyer I was giving orders to shoot and kill, which could have resulted in the death of a good friend.

Bob was born in Marshfield, Massachusetts, and graduated from Williams College in 1936. After his service in the Navy he obtained his Law Degree from Harvard and practiced Tax Law for several years. His later career led to investment management, where he became Senior Vice-President of the Fiduciary Trust Company. Prior to retiring, he and his wife raised six children. They later moved to Florida where Bob was active in community affairs. He later moved to RiverWoods following his sister, Barbara, who had previously become a resident.

East Of The Elbe

DAVID WARNER

No DOUBT about it. Ed was in a fury.

"Dave, you wouldn't believe it. I had it right in my hands, the biggest bag of stuff you've ever seen. Pistols, cameras, watches, daggers. Then this f----- lieutenant comes along. He asks me what outfit I'm with and doesn't even wait for an answer. He just took it!"

It was late April in 1945, and the 291st Field Artillery Observation Battalion, like dozens of other US Army units, was bivouacked just west of the Elbe River. General Eisenhower had made the deal with the Russians. They could have the area east of the Elbe River, which made a clear and unequivocal dividing line between them and us. Of course it meant that the honor of capturing Berlin had been forfeited. Some glory! The Russian Army suffered over three hundred thousand casualties in the vicious fighting that occurred during the last convulsive throes of the Nazi regime.

But for the last several days, tens of thousands of beaten and dejected soldiers of the Third Reich had been drifting by us. These men had crossed the river to our side by some means, even though the US Army decreed that no more should be allowed to cross. Prisoner of War (POW) enclosures, sometimes little more than a strand or two of wire enclosing an open field, were filled to capacity with these pitiful remnants of a once great German Army. Gone were the stiffly efficient soldiers I had seen upon occasion through field glasses. These men were beaten, in both body and spirit.

Dull eyes, slovenly stance, dirty and bloody clothing. Sometimes one could see a smile and a friendly wave of the hand, "*Kamerad*". It was the realization that they had made it. They had been captured by the Americans! The fate of those still east of the Elbe was not pleasant to contemplate. Siberian work camps or even death awaited those who fell into Russian hands.

In order to implement the "no-cross" order, stringent measures had been put into effect. The few bridges in the area had been put under heavy guard, with instructions of "shoot to kill" if any German national tried to cross. For several days, boats and rafts of all sorts had been employed all up and down the river, but now most craft had either been destroyed or pulled up on the west bank of the river, out of reach of those desperate to cross. Whether truthful or not, I never learned, but a tale was told of a young girl who swam to safety across those frigid waters.

Now had come the breaking point. Army authorities felt they could absorb no more. Already the tactical situation had come to a place where handfuls of American soldiers were guarding thousands of prisoners. There was no danger of their attempting to escape ... where would they go? It was more a matter of space. Facilities to feed or care for that many were stretched to the limit. It is certain that the US Army realized the humanitarian aspect of the situation. Allied forces were, in fact, the salvation of those they accepted. Conversely, of course, they destroyed those they denied.

"Dave, let's give it another try. Things are pretty quiet along the river. If we don't get up there soon, the whole damned war will be over and we won't have any more chances for souvenirs." Ed had recovered a bit from his dejection and still showed signs of his irrepressible spirit.

"But, Ed," I replied, "we'll just be kicked out of there again. The 291st doesn't have any assignment to be up by the river."

"Naw! There wasn't much of anybody around. And besides, it was just a stroke of bad luck." Ed sat on the stone steps of the small farmhouse where we were billeted and lit a cigarette. "Maybe a few stragglers will get across and we'll get lucky."

He cocked a speculative eye at me, a small smile flitting across his face. "Ah, come on, Dave, if we don't go now, it will be too late and we won't ever have anything to remember the war by."

I hadn't told Ed that I already HAD a war trophy, a good-sized Nazi flag. A few weeks before I had won a foot race to get it from a second floor window in a small town we had passed through. It rested securely in a tight bundle in the bottom of my barracks bag.

"What do you say?" Ed gave me a sardonic grin.

"What the hell," I thought. It was only a short half-mile to the river from the small farmhouse that was our billet. We would be there and back before anyone would even miss us.

In the few days that we had been in the area, I had not seen the Elbe, so it was a surprise to me to see how broad and swift it was. Running bank-full from what must have been early spring rains in the high country to the south, it was a shock to see how rapidly the current of muddy water swept to the north. Only a few trees bordered its edge. On the distant shore, a good two hundred feet away, were barren fields that seemed to stretch endlessly to the horizon. How far one could see! Low clouds and smoke hugged the horizon on that early April afternoon, and we could see flashes of light from what must be distant artillery. How far away? Certainly it must have been dozens of miles since we could not hear anything but a muted rumble.

Not a single soldier was in sight. After several tumultuous days, the great masses of German soldiers were gone, now imprisoned in the make shift stockades to our west. There didn't even seem to be anyone on the far shore.

It was immediately apparent that war souvenirs would be hard to come by. Ed, walking at a brisk pace, was already scouting along the edge of the water.

"What are you looking for, Ed?" I asked.

He kicked at a rough tangle of lumber that obviously had been a raft of some sort. Had some Wehrmacht soldiers used this to cross? A short distance down the riverbank we came upon several boats that had been disabled, large holes punched in their bottoms. Obviously, the US Army didn't want MORE prisoners. Far to our south there appeared to be the dim outlines of a bridge. Was that why we saw no Germans across from us? Were they all heading for that bridge as the way to their salvation?

Hands on hips, Ed was the picture of frustration and determination, gazing across the river where he felt SURE there must still be a chance for souvenirs.

"If we can just find a boat," he said. "There must be Krauts over there who have what we want."

"Ed, are you crazy!" I replied incredulously. "Even if we find one, that river is damned swift. We'd be miles to the north before we got across."

But Ed was not to be deterred, and didn't even seem to have heard what I said. He was poking along the brushy riverbank, while I kept in hailing distance from the small dirt path that paralleled the river.

"Hot damn! Look at this." Ed had found a good-sized inflatable boat, one of these cumbersome things meant to be manned by a dozen men. By poking around the brush, he uncovered one usable paddle and a short piece of plank that could serve as a makeshift paddle.

Ed was in a hurry. "Come on. Let's get this thing in the water." He was so impatient to get started that he didn't even look back to see if I was coming to help.

There are times in a person's life where snap decisions are made. Why did I not look at the recklessness of the venture? Six months of being in combat with nary a scratch. The war was practically over. Why top it off now with such insanity?

Nonetheless, I found myself scrambling down the low embankment and pulling at the ropes threaded along the gunnels of the boat. It was all that two could do, but finally the thing was afloat. The current quickly grabbed us and we were spiraling slowly in the water as we dug in with our paddles. This craft was never meant to be propelled by only two, and it quickly became apparent that we were going to be swept downstream a considerable distance before making landfall.

With hard work and aching backs, we seemed to be making progress towards the east shore, when around the curve from the north appeared a large inboard motorboat. US flags snapping smartly from both bow and stern clearly showed it was one of ours.

It bore directly down on us, and a bullhorn was poked out of the cabin window. A heavy male voice thundered over the water, "What the f--- are you guys trying to do? Git your ass back on the west side NOW."

Without waiting for a reply, the pilot gunned the motor and was soon out of sight to the south.

"What the hell was THAT?" Ed stood momentarily in the boat and gazed upstream at the wake of the fast-moving cruiser. "To hell with them. Not again. No f------ officer is going to do us out of our chances," and he immediately began digging in with the paddle at a furious rate, trying to make up for the distance we had lost.

At this point the stupidity of our venture should have told me that the guy was right. "Git your ass back on the west shore," was sound advice. But somehow Ed's resolve carried the day, and by determined paddling we finally hit the east shore, a scant quarter-mile north of our embarking point. Alder-like bushes lined the riverbank, and we quickly tied up to a small tree. There wasn't even a steep embankment to deter our idiotic adventure.

"Come on, Dave. Let's get cracking," Ed was already out of the boat and headed south along the bank. No one was in sight. Where was everybody? The gradually rising ground that we had seen while crossing, stretched away to the east had been barren of soldiers, and even buildings. The only explanation had to be that the bridge to the south was the magnet that drew all the traffic.

It was going to be difficult finding souvenirs. But a short distance from our mooring, we ran into several dejected Wehrmacht. After their obvious amazement at seeing us, they clustered around Ed. A barrage of German, only a little of which I could understand, ensued. Ed's proficiency in Yiddish was coming in handy. "*Haben ze pistole?*" was the only thing I could understand.

They shook their heads and gestured towards the far bank. What idiocy that we did not foresee what was about to occur?

When the handful of soldiers did not produce any souvenirs, Ed set off again due south as determined as ever, leaving a puzzled and embittered group behind him. I followed. Surely there must be others around who could fulfill Ed's burning desire to replace that lost sack of war souvenirs.

Going over a gradual rise of land, we found that we could see a considerable distance to the east. Not one soldier or person of any sort was in sight. It was enough to give pause to Ed's mission. Simultaneously, a blinding revelation! It occurred to us that our boat, our means of retreat, was in peril.

As fast as we could, we scrambled back to the point where the boat was moored. Our worst fears were realized. It was gone! Surely this was where it had been. There was the bush broken over where I had marked the place for us. A few muddy footprints sunk into the shallow mud. Looking out across the water to the north, I thought I could see the outlines of a boat on the water, already nearly across.

What idiots we had been! What lunacy had blinded us to the obvious?

I have to hand it to Ed. Already he was engaged in the only action that would help. We HAD to find another boat. But after an hour of careful searching, nothing was found, not as much as a floatable log.

It was getting late in the afternoon, and the patrol boat had passed us once, going north. We had hidden in the low brush. As a last resort, of course, we could hail it, but such a course came with consequences. Courts martial, maybe. Certainly more than a reprimand.

Time went by slowly. The patrol boat again passed at high speed, this time going south. With all hope of finding a serviceable boat, we had run out of options.

We had just about decided to hail the patrol boat and cast ourselves on the dubious mercy of the military, when, out from the far bank, there appeared a good sized inflatable boat manned by at least a half dozen strong paddlers. We were saved! Gauging the boat's progress, we were at the shore immediately as they touched ground.

These guys were bent upon the same sort of mission as we. Mindless souvenir hunters! With Ed's encouragement, these soldiers set off enthusiastically to the north. I couldn't believe that not one man was willing to give up the venture to guard the boat! Certainly I wasn't going to leave the boat unguarded.

As their voices faded into the distance, I felt our vulnerability. ONE man left to guard the boat? Perhaps it would be OK, but I would be counting the minutes until they returned.

Time passed at an excruciatingly slow pace. Nothing to be heard except the soft gurgle of the water as it pulled at the bushes dragging in the water. Even the low rumble of distant artillery seemed to have subsided. The quiet seemed to portend SOMETHING was imminent.

I sat down on the end of the boat. These inflatable boats didn't have a front or rear ... that's what made them so unwieldy. I lit a cigarette, picked up my carbine and laid it across my knees.

How much time had passed? Five or ten minutes? Surely the group would be gone for quite some time yet. Just as I was about to relax a bit, the dense shrubbery a few yards upstream started to shake. A head appeared, followed by the body of a surprised and disappointed German soldier.

His dismay at finding me there was palpable. Quite logically, he had backtracked the group, and had every hope of a quick ride across the river to freedom and safety.

"*Kamerad*," followed by a babble of German that I could not understand.

"*Nein spreken Deutch*," I said. Despite my fractured accent, he seemed to understand, and he quickly resorted to hand gestures that consisted of pointing across the river and mimed paddling a boat. The message was clear. In reply, I shook my head and waved vaguely to the east, holding up ten fingers.

For the first time in the war I was facing a German soldier at uncomfortably close quarters.

True, I had witnessed stiff bodies in the snow of the wintery Ardennes forest, and seen thousands in the last few days plodding along with their hands clasped on the tops of their heads. But this was the first time up close and personal.

He appeared to be of middle age and clothed in a uniform that was grimy and torn. A bloody and blackened bandage partially concealed one eye. Was he armed? No weapon of any kind was visible. The one eye watched me carefully as I tried to appear casual in my stance at the end of the boat.

What was he thinking? Certainly I was the one who was armed, but for the life of me I could not remember whether I had a loaded clip in my carbine. Not the best of tactics or the time to check, either. He had settled into a silence that was more disturbing than conversation.

More noises emanated from upstream and I was congratulating myself on a successful standoff when two more Germans emerged. This time it was an older man with a youth in tow who looked as if he could not be more than fourteen. Both, however, wore tattered distinctive uniforms of the Wehrmacht and they too appeared to be unarmed. These two immediately began a conversation with the first man, while I, trying to feign indifference, lounged on the edge of the boat. If I were to speculate upon what was said, I would guess that he told them OTHER American soldiers were close by. If they behaved properly, they stood a good chance of getting across the river.

The minutes dragged by slowly. Where WERE those guys! Before five minutes had passed, another man hobbled into view. This soldier looked like bad news. He had the look of the individual hardened by the long war. I could not tell whether he was an officer, but his demeanor seemed to say that he was. His talk with the others was brief and rasping, and I could not feel that he was in favor of just sitting there, awaiting the return of other American soldiers.

Just how this would have played out, I will never know, for the sudden appearance of the American patrol boat seemed to quell their desire to commandeer the boat. Almost simultaneously, the seven souvenir seekers came crashing back. They had had no luck at all.

Immediately there arose from the Germans a babble of pleas and gestures to be taken back across the river. Ed interpreted. There was ample room in the boat, and I was in favor of it. Wasn't it the humane thing to do? If left to the dubious mercies of the Russians, no one had any doubt of what would happen, but a majority of the GI's was against it. How would we explain having German prisoners? What if the patrol boat came again and caught us red handed? Their frame of thinking was that "we didn't owe these sons-of-bitches anything." All risk, no reward.

The matter was decided quickly, much too quickly. We cast off without them. I can still remember the desolate and beseeching expressions of these three men and a boy as the widening water gap between us spelled their fate: capture by the Russians.

And so, by late afternoon the eight of us returned to our unit without ever having been missed, but minus the war souvenirs so coveted.

Years can cloud memory, but some things are etched in one's mind forever. As I sit at my desk some years after the event, I know why I have never had the desire to set down on paper the foolish and illogical events of that day. I have related this crazy escapade to a few people, but have always, until now, left out one crucial piece of the story.

I HAD my souvenir of that day. The first German soldier who had come to the riverbank that fateful afternoon had given it to me. He had raised his hands, palms forward, and then carefully reached inside his shirt, withdrawing a small leather holster. With measured gestures, he showed me that it was not loaded. It was a small 32-caliber Shuer automatic.

A gift? Hardly. Between us there was the unspoken message that this was to be his ticket to safety. And I had failed him, and all of them. In the heat of impatience to be back on the other side, we had not done the humane thing. It would have cost us little. Why didn't we do it? The consequences of being caught with or without prisoners would have been little different. That knowledge will stay with me always.

So now, after the passage of a ridiculous number of years I have been trying to find Ed, with no success. Where are you, Ed? Your unquenchable spirit, your impulsive way of pursuing what you wanted, your derision of anything military. Did this carry on into your adult life and get you into trouble? I hope not.

As for me, I still ponder why he led and I followed. Was it because the Army taught you to never let your buddy down, or could it have been the proverbial game of chicken played out with such tragic finality for those left behind?

A moment of compassion. A two hundred foot boat ride. To four people whom I will never know it would have made all the difference. It is seldom in life that a person has the opportunity to make a material difference in what happens to someone else. We failed the test.

Born in western Pennsylvania, David earned a degree in forestry after the war. He worked as a forester on the Yakima Indian Reservation in Washington State. Later he joined his father in the trucking business in Pennsylvania. He retired in Hershey, Pennsylvania, and later moved to RiverWoods where he utilizes his woodworking and forestry skills.

The Captain And
The One-Arm Bandit

John Wicklein

What follows is an edited version of a story I wrote shortly after WW II about a happening in which I took part. The basic facts are all true; only the names have been changed, to protect the guilty. - JFW

AT THE SURRENDER of Japan, my destroyer found itself moored to a buoy in the middle of mud-green Guantanamo Bay. There was a sense of Whoopee! among the crew that, contrary to expectations, we were not going to be sent to the Pacific to take part in the invasion of Japan.

On nights we were in port, the officers not on watch (I was communications officer), would hit the Gitmo Officers Club, buying 15-cent whiskeys and playing the nickel and dime slot machines.

One night our ship's Captain proposed a scheme to win us a lot of money with the machines—a scheme that might have won him a court martial instead. The Old Man was a thirty-three-year-old Annapolis commander to whom the war had given gray hair, the beginnings of a paunch, and an inordinate consciousness of rank. When we were at sea and a lookout spotted another US Navy ship on the horizon, he had us check the Signal Number Book to find out if the other captain had a lower number, and thus a higher rank, than he. If the other captain out-ranked him by as little as one number, he ordered the signalman to flash the message, REQUEST PERMISSION TO PROCEED ON MISSION ASSIGNED. This was stretching Navy protocol, but the Captain wanted to be sure.

Our Captain liked to ride our whale boat over to the club's landing every night, to schmooze in the bar with some of his Annapolis Trade School buddies, and also imbibe with us, his officers. We were delighted to learn the low cost of alcohol and looked around for other places to invest savings accrued at the bar. We found them in the dozens of slot machines, in the large room just beyond the bar.

Usually when we were playing the slots, the club's Commandant—a short, unimposing-looking commander with close-set eyes, a small black moustache, and a bald spot showing through his shiny black hair—hovered close by. The take from the one-arm bandits must have paid much of the club's upkeep, because the Commandant seemed to take a special interest in their well-being. He cautioned us not to smack their fronts when they didn't pay off, not to rock them on their bases after we had played for hours with no appreciable return. For his looks and personality, we named him The Beetle.

One night while Otto Heinrich, our bull-necked gunnery officer, was cursing and shaking a machine, The Beetle scuttled up and peered round his shoulder. Otto glanced bleary-eyed at him and yanked the handle. It broke off in his hand.

The Beetle scowled. "Now that will just cost you fifteen dollars," he said.

"The hell you say," said Otto. "The way you set the payouts, I've bought this handle ten times over." For emphasis he prodded The Beetle in the stomach with it and started to walk away.

The Beetle clapped a hand on his shoulder. "Give me that handle!" Otto's meaty face turned red. He swung the metal arm backhand to thump The Beetle across the chest. Just then our Captain stepped between them, taking the blow on his upper arm.

"This is one of my officers, Commandant," he said. "What's the trouble?"

"Your officer deliberately broke the handle off this slot machine and now he won't give it back."

"Give him back his handle, Otto."

"If I gotta pay for it, I keep it."

The Captain twisted the handle from Otto's hand and plunked it into the Commandant's. "C'mon, Otto—I'll buy you a drink."

"He can't stay here," said The Beetle. "He's got to leave the club."

The Captain gave him a contemptuous look and pulled Otto into to the bar. The Beetle started after them, then thought better of it. He turned back to the broken machine and slapped the handle down beside it.

After that, the Captain steered clear of the slots, because every time he looked, The Beetle seemed to be watching over them. Mostly, he sat drinking beer with Arne, the ship's Paymaster.

"Pay," a Wisconsin fullback in '36, had the most sensible attitude regarding the slots—he never played them. A bottle of Cerveza Hatuey before him, a mischievous twinkle in his blue eyes, he watched good-naturedly as we dumped streams of coins down the various drains.

One evening some of us were sitting at our table, talking about our losses to the bandits and Otto's run-in with The Beetle.

The Captain looked concerned. "Pay and I think you guys are going at this all wrong," he said. "You don't use any concerted effort to lick the bandits. We ought to do something about it." The Captain drained his glass. "Now," he said, "we've been thinking we should do this in orderly manner, using some Navy know-how. We'll set up a continuous watch schedule at one machine, with each of us standing a half-hour watch. With seven of us playing, it's got to hit the jackpot sometime. And then each of us will get an equal share, regardless of rank."

"That's decent," said Doug, the ship's First Lieutenant.

"So each of us will kick in two bucks," said Pay, a smile on his face. "That will give us $14 in nickels to work with." Each of us shoved $2 across to Pay.

"The next thing is to select the right machine," the Captain said. "Which one pays off the best?"

Doug's cheery face lighted up. "The one I play is by far the best."

"He's right," said Pay. "I've watched—It takes him longer than any of you guys to lose his money."

"Very well," said the Captain. "We'll play Doug's."

The Captain drew up the watch schedule, assigning Doug the first watch, the 1930 to 2000. With ceremony, we formed a semicircle around the machine, a fruit-wheeled slot near the wide doorway to the bar. The gathering immediately attracted The Beetle—he lodged himself behind the Captain, watching apprehensively.

"Ready, Cap'n," said Doug.

"Very well, Mr. Cass, set the watch."

Doug snapped to attention, saluted and, doing a smart about-face, inserted his first nickel and pulled the handle. The wheels came to rest with two plums side-by-side. Three nickels trickled into the payoff slot. It was a good omen; we cheered.

"Excellent, Mr. Cass," said the Captain. "Carry on." He stepped backwards and collided with The Beetle. "Why don't you look where you're going?" he asked, when he saw who it was.

"Why don't I look where I'm going?" The Beetle said. "You bumped into me."

They scowled at each other, and then The Beetle scowled at us as we stepped aside to let him pass.

"Damned Reserve," said the Captain, ignoring the fact that so were almost all of his own officers Reserves.

Near the end of the sixth watch—Otto at the slot and the last few nickels left—it happened. "Sonoma B!" the gunnery officer roared, and from wherever they were in the club came running the other officers from the ship. We found Otto on his knees scooping together a pile of spilled nickels. "It hit, dammit, it hit," he said, grinning inanely up at the Captain.

"Very well," said the Captain, "the watch is secured."

Otto and Pay carried the loot over to a table in the bar. Pay stacked the nickels in piles of tens and announced the result: "Ten dollars and eighty-five cents."

He looked at our expectant faces. "Gentlemen," he said, "subtracting $10.85 from almost $14 we put into it, we have taken a loss on the operation of just about three bucks."

We looked at him blackly. To make matters worse, The Beetle, who had watched the accounting, walked away with a grin on his face.

"That son-of-a-" the Captain began, starting to get up. The paymaster's ham-sized hand pulled him back down into his seat. For a moment, the Captain fumed. "Men," he said, snapping out of it, "we haven't lost to that damn sea scout yet. That slot machine belongs to us, after all the money we put into it tonight and what Doug has put into it all this month."

"Bully for you, Cap'n," Doug said. "Let's carry it out to the ship and set it up in the wardroom."

"Who'll get the take?" asked Otto, looking suspiciously at Pay and the Captain.

"We'll use the money to pay our mess bills," said Doug, illogically. Then he saw his error—we'd be paying for the mess with our own money. He smiled a bright-eyed smile. "Maybe we should set it up on the quarterdeck, Cap'n—then the enlisted men could play, too."

"I'm not sure that would be ethical," said the Paymaster.

"Ethical, hell," Otto grumbled. "The men will have just as much chance of hitting a jackpot as we have. Give 'em somewhere else to spend their cash rather than on lousy Cuban beer in the Slopshoot on the base."

The logic of this won Pay over. "All right," he said, "but how will we get the machine out to the ship?"

"I've got an idea how to do that," said the Captain, looking around to make sure The Beetle wasn't within earshot. "Just before the club closes at 2300, Otto and Pay, you two start a wrestling match at the opposite end of the room from our machine. Make it rough and noisy. Everybody will run over there, and The Beetle will rush over to stop it, sure as hell.

"Then, Doug, you and I will grab the machine and make a run for it out the door and down to the landing."

"That's a dandy plan, Cap'n," said Doug. "I always knew you weren't the ol' s.o.b. the men say you are."

"Good thing we are both drunk, Doug, or I'd put you in hack."

At 2245, as I stood near the club's front door, I saw a light flash from our whaleboat at the landing. Turning toward the open doorway to the bar, I held my arms out horizontally, forming the semaphore "R". Through the doorway I saw the Captain raise his arm and bring it sharply down. Immediately I heard a table overturn in the slots room beyond, and I knew Pay and Otto had started their fight. It got very noisy in there, and I started to go in just as Doug and the Captain came lumbering out with the heavy machine.

Half way to the front door, Doug sank to his knees, crashing his end down on a coffee table. "I can't go on, Cap'n," he sobbed.

"Bear a hand, man," said the Captain, "bear a hand!" He reached down and lifted up his side of the machine.

Ominously, the noise of the fight had ended. The Beetle burst through the swinging doors of the bar, followed by four officers pulling the outraged Otto and Pay along by the arms.

"Stop!" cried The Beetle, spotting Doug, the Captain, and the slot machine. He scooted past them and held his arms out to bar the front door. "Put that thing back where you found it."

Doug was impressed, but the Captain was not.

"You, Sir, are speaking to a line commander of the Regular Navy."

" I, Sir, am also a line commander of the Regular Navy."

The Captain was taken aback, but he regrouped quickly. "What's the date of your commission?"

"That's it, Cap'n, pull rank on the s.o.b.," urged Doug, who had recovered from his breakdown and was enjoying the drama. "Ask him what's his Signal Number—ask him, Cap'n."

"My commission dates from 1933," said The Beetle. "Annapolis '33."

"That's my class, too," said the Captain, trying to picture the man minus his moustache and 12 years younger.

"Ask him to tell you his Signal Number," goaded Doug.

"My Signal Number, lieutenant, is 3369," said The Beetle. "And what is your Signal Number, Commander?"

The Captain looked distraught. "My number, Commandant," he admitted, "is 3453."

"Very well," said The Beetle, "Put that damn slot machine back where you found it and leave the club immediately."

"Aye, aye, Sir," replied the Old Man. The Beetle might be able to do something to damage his career. He motioned to several of us and we lugged the machine back to its stand. The Beetle, arms folded, was still standing at the front door as we shuffled by, single file, on the way down to our whaleboat. Nobody said a word until we reached the landing.

Then Doug, always for the underdog even if it happened to be his commanding officer, said, "Don't take it so hard, Cap'n—The Beetle mighta had a higher Signal Number than yours. Then we woulda had the slot machine, fer sure."

The Captain was not consoled. In silence we stepped down into the boat. Doug's face was as plaintive as the Captain's was grim. He made one last try, "Cap'n, I know where we can forget all this— I know where we can go to forget."

The Captain grunted. He stood distracted in the stern beside the cox'n, who was looking to him for instructions.

"We can go to Caimanera, Cap'n. They've got women in Caimanera—they'll make you forget."

At the mention of the infamous Cuban town, the Old Man perked up, "Which way to Caimanera?" he asked, to no one in particular.

Otto spoke up. "Up an inlet on the north side of the base," he said. "But you've got to get past a gate boat at the boundary, and the guards have machine guns."

"On this gate boat," the Captain asked warily, "are there any officers?"

"Just the duty officer," said Otto.

"Would he have the rank of commander?"

"Hell, no," said Otto, "just a lieutenant or a J.G., I'd think."

"Cox'n, shove off," commanded our Captain, pointing an outstretched arm to the north. "On to Caimanera!"

Born in Reading, Pennsylvania, John was educated in journalism at Rutgers University with a BS in 1947 and at Columbia with a MS in 1948. He served in the Navy in the Atlantic 1943-1946 and is now a freelance writer and consultant to newspapers. He has three children.

Well-Trained And Fortunate

Robin D. Willits

I WAS NOT A young man who had grown up excited by airplanes and eager to fly. However, I could not see myself as a ground soldier sleeping on the ground and living outdoors. Nor was I a sailor. My only sailing experience left me clinging to the bottom of an upturned sailboat, off the distant coast of Maine. I had an older family friend, a Navy pilot, who described flying as "better than skiing!" So, I enlisted in the Army Air Corps.

Training

The military took me, of untested aptitude, and in less than a year trained me to fly a B-17 bomber, at the time, one of the world's largest airplanes. It then made me the 1st pilot (captain) of a nine-man crew. Two events give evidence of the training the co-pilot (Jim Willingham) and I had. First, Jim and I ferried a B-17, and our crew, to England, landing at a number of unknown airstrips. We flew from Georgia to Bangor, Maine, landing on a runway that was not completely level. It had a very significant dip across the middle of the runway. From there we flew to Goose Bay, Labrador, landing at night in a quiet snowstorm. We had done several night landings before but never in a snowstorm. Next we flew to Greenland, where the airport was at the end of a narrow fjord. As we started up the fjord, I thought of the uphill landing ahead. The runway was 30 feet above sea level at its start and 130 feet at the other end. It was a "land-it-or-else" runway. With high mountains on both sides and at the end, once committed to land you could not go around for a second attempt. Obviously, we made it on the first try. Thereafter, we flew to Iceland and the next day to Wales. Our training prepared us to handle airports with different conditions.

The second event, that also gave evidence of good training, was a day I took off with a full bomb load to climb through a solid layer of clouds. As I started a climbing turn to the left I noticed that the main instrument for flying when you can't see anything, was not working. I was flying blind! I knew immediately what was wrong and what to do. I had not unlocked the instrument when Jim and I had gone through the pre-flight checklist. I switched to out-of-date instruments (needle, ball & air speed) that we had used in our first instrument flight training. Reverting to old skills, I stopped the turn, climbed straight ahead until we got above the clouds, and joined the other planes. The training we'd received was crucial and instinctive.

Life in Combat

Our home was an airbase (one runway) in East Anglia, England. For each mission we flew across the English Channel and the Netherlands, or Belgium, or France to our targets in Germany.

Our airbase was located about a mile from the small, rural town of Elmswell, about seventy-five miles northeast of London. Our quarters consisted of a one-story wooden building, with cots lined up on both sides of one large room. The cots were separated by small bureaus that defined each man's space. Coal stoves at either end of the room kept us warm in the mild English winter. We ate in a central mess hall that also served for briefing sessions before and after each mission. Our planes were parked on individual circles of macadam alongside the runway. The nearest thing we had to snow was a few days when the ground was covered with hoarfrost. We could walk to Elmswell, but there wasn't much contact with local people.

The days we were scheduled to fly on a mission, we were awakened around 3 to 4 a.m. After breakfast we attended briefing on the day's target and were taken to our planes by trucks. There we loaded our gear and prepared for takeoff. Subsequently, each plane took off in sequence, climbed to an assembly area above and near the airport, and arranged themselves into a formation. This formation consisted of twelve planes arranged into four levels of three planes each. At each level the three planes were in a vee grouping next to each other at the same altitude. When all were in position we headed east, climbing to our bombing altitude, typically at 23-27,000 feet. Upon reaching the target area the formation turned onto a bombing run with the bomb bay doors open and every plane in a fixed position. After dropping the bombs all at the same moment, the formation turned and headed home (England). A typical mission lasted 8-12 hours.

How often did we fly? This was 1944, and on average we flew one mission per week. Usually we didn't fly two days in a row. Instead we would have a day of training or rest while another crew flew in our position in the formation. Sometimes we flew three or four missions in one week. Some days, bad weather prevented any flying. From late September to VE Day in May, I flew thirty-four missions (one less than a complete tour of thirty-five missions.)

Fear

Fear is not a topic that I've seen much written about in articles or books on war. While I didn't have any dramatic or terrible experiences, perhaps the fear that I did have might be of interest.

On my first mission I flew as co-pilot with an experienced crew. For a while it looked like it might be my last mission! Just after dropping our bombs we lost two engines to flak (fire from German anti-aircraft guns). We could not maintain our speed and dropped out of the formation. We continued losing altitude and flying alone across Germany.

I knew we were in a very dangerous situation. If we continued to lose altitude we might eventually have to bail out while still over Germany. Even worse, if we were attacked by two or three German fighter planes, we probably would be shot down with our plane damaged and out of control. I felt that the danger was real, but I was neither panicked nor trembling with fear. Instead, I was very calm, fearfully calm. I probably would have felt strong fear if fighter planes had appeared, but none did! As we lost altitude and got down to 10,000 feet, the two engines regained power. The flak had knocked out the turbo-boosters that allow engines to work at high altitudes. The flak had not damaged the basic engines. We flew home.

I felt more active fear on the mission when the whole formation was told to land in France because of bad weather in England. We were above a layer of clouds. We were to peel off from the formation one by one, fly down through the cloud layer to land at a US airport. But when our plane came out of the clouds no airport was visible, just snow covered trees and fields! As the navigator sought to find the airport my discomfort, anxiety, fearfulness began to rise. What if we didn't find an airport? What then? Fortunately, the navigator got us to a British airport where we landed for the night.

I felt terrible fear for several moments one morning, as we were getting ready for another mission. I had just started one engine when I looked out and saw a crewmember stepping toward the rotating propeller! I yelled, but that was futile. He could not hear me over the sound of the engine. I was helpless. What an awful feeling! Fortunately, he realized his danger in time and turned away. My fear at that moment was huge.

In addition to such fears as those described above, I had a steady, underlying awareness that we were engaged in a dangerous activity. On the way to the target and on the way back we could be attacked by German fighter planes, and could come under fire from flak. We could be severely injured or killed. The purpose of our mission was to wreak damage and kill. That was also the German goal. It was fear, not very active and mostly not in my conscious mind, but always present underneath all.

Fortunate
The timing of our going into combat was fortunate. The days of heavy losses of bombers and a tour of twenty-five missions were over. Our tour was thirty-five missions. German fighter planes sel-

dom attacked us. Germany had lost so many pilots that it was sending up pilots who had no instrument flight training. They could attack only on a clear day with no cloud layer through which to fly.

I was fortunate in having Jim as co-pilot. He was as well trained as I, and as good a pilot. He exhibited no envy for not being the 1st pilot. Also he had greater rapport with the crew. One early time the crew was at a roadhouse together to celebrate one member's marriage, and I was out on the dance floor dancing alone to the music despite have had no alcohol. Jim told me afterwards that the crew's reaction was, "My God, he's a human being after all!" Jim added a lot to the functioning of the crew. He and I worked well together.

We were also fortunate in the character of the crew. They cheered each time one of them got "stick time" (at the controls learning a bit on how to fly the plane), without concern that they each get exactly the same amount of time. In addition, the radio operator was a voice of experience. He had already flown twenty-five missions and was back for a second tour.

I was personally fortunate that my unrealistic youthful choices were ignored. During training, when asked whether I wanted single-engine or multi-engine, I said single. I was given multi. Later I said I wanted P-38 fighter-bomber, not B-17 heavy bomber. I got B-17. And that is where I belonged. While I participated in sports at college, I am neither a well-coordinated person nor a person with quick reaction time. In basic pilot training I got through acrobatic training (loops & spins) always on the edge of getting airsick. I would have washed out of fighter pilot training. Fortunately, I wasn't given the chance.

Finally, the crew and I were fortunate to not be flying on the mission on which one plane, when dragged into clouds, suddenly pulled up into the plane above it in the formation. Both planes crashed. The plane flying the upper position was in the slot that we filled on alternate days.

Why wasn't I a CO?

My parents were members of the Religious Society of Friends (Quaker). I went to Quaker Sunday School, and to a Quaker boarding school. I am a Quaker. The Quaker church is one of the so-called Peace Churches. It would have been no surprise if I'd applied to be recognized as a Conscientious Objector (CO).

I certainly knew that application for CO status was an option. I understood the Quaker view that war is organized killing, is immoral, and violates the commandment, "Thou shalt not kill". I knew of Gandhi and the use of non-violent resistance to oppose the British. But, I could not see how the world could stop Hitler or the Japanese except by military force. Also I knew that draft boards, when judging an application for CO status, defined a CO as someone who would not serve in any war, no matter whether it was a so-called "just" war. I did not see that I measured up as a CO. I felt that I should serve, and so I enlisted.

Mine was not a decision based on thorough and careful study and reading on the issue, nor on the options open to me such as serving as a non-combatant in the military. Today I know much more about the full nature of war, including the inevitable killing of civilians, often unavoidably.

Soldiers are killed during war and many are crippled, physically and emotionally, Post Traumatic Stress Disorder (PTSD), suicide by those on active duty as well as veterans, etc. War is financially costly, with money spent for destructive purposes—explosives, military equipment, etc.—that could have been spent to further human life—roads, health care, water systems, etc. War often leaves anger and hate that can lead to future wars. War can beget war! War often entails societal disruption, such as limitations on civil rights for security concerns and relocation of people as homeless refugees.

Furthermore, the massive dreadful consequences of atomic weapons threaten human life. How can we foster public understanding, emotionally and intellectually, of the full realities and costs of war so that we come to use better ways to solve international disagreement and conflict?

Mine was an impersonal war compared to that of a ground soldier, or even to earlier B-17 crews bombing Germany. I never saw bodies blown apart, nor heard screams of injured people, nor saw buildings blowing up. All of that was out of sight and hearing nearly five miles below. Since we were seldom attacked by German fighter planes and could not hear approaching flak, we had little direct contact with German pilots, or soldiers and civilians. My war was much more impersonal than many other veterans'.

When the war was over and I was home, for some time I didn't want to fly on a commercial airliner, in part, from a superstitious feeling that I'd been drawing on my "safety-bank account" and didn't know how much was left.

A Post-war Happening

During the Vietnam war, my wife became a paralegal with knowledge of the draft law and a little of military law. In that role she volunteered to give young men information on their options under the draft and also to men in uniform.

One day when she got home she told me about a young Air Force pilot back from flying transport planes in Vietnam. He was applying for a Conscientious Objector Discharge. She had not learned his name, but had learned that his father, who was from Texas, had been a pilot in WW II but lost his life shortly after the war in a crash while flying a commercial airliner. She also learned that he was an infant when his father died, and that his mother had remarried.

We thought, could the improbable be happening! Could the young pilot be the son of the co-pilot of my crew? His background certainly fit!

In a further meeting, we verified that he was my co-pilot's son, including having the same name as his father, Jim Willingham! I have kept contact with both Jim and his sister ever since. But for the Air Force, he might never have come to New Hampshire.

It reminds me that good things can happen to individuals during war. A number make close friends. A few meet and marry. Many travel to lands they knew nothing about and their awareness is broadened. A few find a career. Some learn of a capability they never knew they had. But overall, for a great many more people, war is not a positive experience, be they soldiers or civilians.

Born in Philadelphia, Robin earned bachelor's degrees from the Massachusetts Institute of Technology and Middlebury College. In 1965 he earned a PhD in Industrial Management at MIT. He worked for thirteen years in industry, followed by twenty-five years as Professor of Administration and Organizations at the University of New Hampshire.

Air Transport Command

MADDIE WOODWARD

LESS THAN one week following the Japanese attack at Pearl Harbor and the US declaration of war against the Axis Powers, I graduated from college with no entanglements, plans, or responsibilities, but into a world committed to the task of ridding the world of the evil forces aligned against us. Thousands of my peers, male and female, were joining the war effort. I had recently made inquiries about the newly organized Women's Army Auxiliary Corps (WAAC). With the enthusiastic support of my family, I applied and was accepted as a candidate for officer training.

After commissioning in September 1942 and six months as Commanding Officer (CO) of a WAAC basic training company in Florida, I was reassigned to the Army Air Force, Air Transport Command (ATC). The ATC was a noncombat division of the Army Air Corps. Its mission was the movement of personnel, aircraft, and supplies to theatres of operations wherever needed. This included servicing, processing, and transporting, often under hazardous conditions. WAAC did not serve on aircraft crews but functioned on all other activities on an ATC base.

I was CO of the WAAC Squadron. Our members served in every department on base: Motor Corps, Control Tower, Adjutant's Office, Quartermaster, etc. I served on ATC bases in Homestead, Florida, and Dow Field, Maine, before going overseas.

In the meantime, the status of the women's role changed; no longer auxiliary to the army but fully accepted members of the Air Force, from WAAC to WAC. I received two promotions, First Lieutenant and Captain.

We received orders to proceed to an embarkation center for overseas assignment. Our destination was undisclosed until the last day of our voyage. I awoke to discover that our ship was flanked by destroyers at port and starboard, a US naval escort guided us into a safe harbor, Liverpool, England. We disembarked to an assignment on the Isle of Anglesey, Wales.

When the European War was nearly over, bases began to rapidly close. In Wales we processed hundreds of planes every day, e.g., small fighter planes with two-man crews who crossed the Atlantic Ocean night and day. During the period I was there, a plane was not lost. In fact, in all the three plus years that I lived on the air base, I recall only one fatal plane crash. That was from two young boys playing games in small trainers, quite a different story from those involved in combat.

Finally, after very brief assignments in Germany and Paris, I was released from active duty in 1946 at the Separation Center in Ft. Dix, New Jersey.

Born in Brookline, Massachusetts, Maddie was educated at the Abbot Academy in Andover, Massachusetts, and at Radcliffe, where she received her BA in sociology. She was a US Army WAC 1942-1946, and in 1947 married the Rev. Donald Woodward. She has been active in social, community, and church work, and in barbershop, madrigal, and quartet singing. She served on the Board of Education in Bennington, Vermont, and in Kansas. She has four children.

Stateside
Military Service

SPARS

Peggy Aplin

WHEN I WAS in college in 1943, many of my male friends were in the service, either overseas or in this country, or about to be drafted. The president of our freshman class, a pilot in the Air Corps, was killed and we all mourned for a good friend. At the end of my sophomore year, I decided to join the service.

I had been working in the Cape Cod Candle Factory and other jobs to pay my tuition and living expenses. It's hard to imagine today, but the atmosphere in those days was VERY patriotic. Everyone wanted to do his or her part, e.g., to relieve a man on the home front to fight on the war front.

This was the incentive for many women to join the service. In June 1943 I went to Boston and joined the United States Coast Guard (CG). I chose the CG because I had always admired them, and preferred navy blue to khaki. I had to get my mother's approval because I was under twenty-one. She reluctantly gave it with the promise from me that I would go back to college after the war.

I went to Palm Beach, Florida, for training at the Biltmore Hotel that had been taken over by the CG during the war. Florida was hot in June! The Biltmore sounds pretty swish, but with six girls in a room, it was not quite the same as vacationers experienced before and after the war.

We had the regular basic Coast Guard training: marching, parades, seamanship, and CG history. I spent most hours on the beach or in the outdoor pool in my "uniform", a white sharkskin bathing suit and sun helmet. I also taught huge classes on Coast Guard history, seamanship, and First Aid in the auditorium, in my regular uniform. I once met a seaman (girl) in the elevator in the hotel who said, "Oh, I didn't recognize you with clothes on!" She had never seen me in anything except a bathing suit. We seamen also did practice and research on various methods of rescuing people in the surf, how to launch surfboats, ordinary rescue in the water, etc.

On our off time, we explored Palm Beach and the surrounding territory, walking or on bicycles. We took trips to Miami by bus. My mother came down to visit and we had a grand time. She had been worried about her little girl, but was relieved to find I was pretty strictly supervised, while still enjoying life.

After several months there were no promotions, even though we were instructing others, including new officers. Several of us put in for transfers. Being a bit homesick, I requested "New England or as near to there as possible." I was sent to San Francisco.

San Francisco was a good liberty town and especially nice to women in the service. I remember the Pepsi Cola Center as being especially hospitable to women. One of my duties was patrolling the beach on horseback. However, I was still homesick for New England, so I requested a transfer to radio school in Atlantic City. I thought it would be a radio technician school, as I liked to take things apart and put them back together. It turned out to be a radio operators' school, which I did enjoy and came out at the top of my class. I asked for a station in New England, and this time they sent me to Boston, and then to Rockland, Maine.

I loved Rockland, Maine, where the people were so friendly and helpful. At church, we met many interesting and caring people. They took us SPARS for rides to show us the countryside (even though gas was rationed). Because of the war there were no buses to Portland, so we hitchhiked there for brief weekends now and then.

Eventually, I was stationed at the east end of the Cape Cod Canal. I enjoyed that station because I had been at college on the Cape and had friends there. Among our duties there, we put pilots on board ships going through the Canal. We used radio and Teletype to communicate with other stations. If I were going to Boston on free time, I would connect with the SPARS there to see what the weather was or to get suggestions about what to do in Boston.

Epilogue

In July 1945, after two years and twenty-seven days, I was discharged, did as I promised my mother, and went back to college. Hyannis State Teachers College, which I had attended, was closed so I chose to go to the University of New Hampshire in Durham—and haven't left New Hampshire since!

I'm very glad I went in the service and feel I helped with the war effort at the time. I was most grateful for the GI Bill, which helped with tuition and made my work time less. The two years in the Coast Guard gave me time to grow up and to have more purpose in my life. I studied much harder and got a great deal more out of college.

Although born in New York City, Peggy has spent most of her adult life in New England. She earned a degree in education at the University of New Hampshire and did graduate work at Springfield and Dartmouth Colleges. A teacher of English and science in secondary schools as well as a recreation director, she has also worked in a family resort business in East Madison, New Hampshire. For twenty years she volunteered at the Mt. Washington Observatory as Registrar.

The Navy V-12 Program

DON BASSETT
As told to Nancy Taylor

IN 1943, the Navy created the V-12 College Training Program. The Navy wanted their officers to be college graduates, and the program enabled both current college students as well as enlisted sailors to apply. While I was at Franklin and Marshall College in Pennsylvania I applied to the program, took the necessary tests, and was accepted. I was particularly interested in this program as my father was a Navy Ensign during WW I.

The program emphasized sciences and math courses, but as I was in a pre-dental course as a chemistry major, this was not a problem. We also had hours of physical training including calisthenics and running timed miles.

Once I started Dental School at Temple University in Philadelphia, I was on active duty and drew seaman's pay as well as receiving a uniform allowance and a food allowance. Shortly after I arrived at Temple it was discovered that twelve people, including me, were a few hours short of the 120 semester hours required for graduation from college. That meant that we had to take one more course, which was set up just for us. On Saturdays we traveled to Franklin and Marshall for a course in Korean and Japanese history. It was an easy course with an even easier final exam, so everyone passed.

By the time I finished dental school in 1947, the war was over. However, I owed the Navy five years of active duty. Although I never went out on a ship while I was at Franklin and Marshall or Temple, I had many experiences on ships as well as shore duty during my thirty-two years in the Navy.

Don was born in Palmerton, Pennsylvania, and graduated from Franklin and Marshall College and the Temple University School of Dentistry. Retiring from the Navy after thirty-two years of service as a dentist he became a professor at the Tufts School of Dental Medicine. He and his wife raised five children and eventually moved to Durham, New Hampshire. Don was a University of New Hampshire Marine Docent, sang with the Sea Chanty Singers and is a regular singer with the RiverWoods Chorus.

Service In The States

LEWIS KELVIN DOYLE

EARLY IN 1942 I attempted to join the Navy but failed to qualify due to poor eyesight. However, the Belmar, New Jersey, draft board was quick to send me a draft notice, and in May I found myself in the Army at the Ft. Dix indoctrination center. After a few weeks there, I was on a train, which ultimately deposited me at Biggs Field in El Paso, Texas. It was at this installation I received military police (MP) training and began checking passes at one of the entry gates. After several months I was told that I could apply for Officer Candidate School. I was accepted and was assigned to an Air Force, non-flying, school in Miami Beach, Florida. After graduation in December, I was sent to Olmsted Field, Middletown Air Depot in Pennsylvania where I was assigned to the 881st Guard Squadron (Aviation). I understood that after three months training the unit would be sent to England.

In late January I asked for and received a three-day pass to visit my parents and girl friend in Sea Girt, New Jersey. It was an unfortunate trip as I had a bad automobile accident on black ice, skidding into a trailer truck coming in the opposite direction. I suffered a fracture of the pelvis and fractures of several of the transverse processes of the lumbar spine. I was taken to the Indiantown Gap Military Reservation Hospital. Three months later I was discharged from the hospital and after a month's recuperation leave, I returned to Headquarters, Middletown Air Depot.

At the Depot I was restricted to limited service and assigned to Personnel which involved administrative assignments—ground safety in particular. I served in that capacity until late 1944 when

I was transferred to the 855th Aircraft Storage Depot in Philadelphia, Pennsylvania. Occupied with many administrative duties I remained at that location until I was discharged from the service at Westover Field in Massachusetts during April of 1946 with the rank of captain and approximately four years of service completed.

Post Script

In late spring of 1951 I received a letter from the Air Force Reserve requesting that I report to Camp Kilmer, New Jersey, for a physical examination. When I had been discharged five years previously I had not signed up to be an active reservist, but I was curious and went as requested. I passed the exam and was informed that I would be contacted in several weeks. Subsequently, I received orders to report to Kirtland Air Force Base, Albuquerque, New Mexico, within three weeks. Again I followed orders and contacted the base personnel officer who informed me that I would be the base Ground Safety Officer. I served for 19 months and was discharged. I enjoyed the work and my wife and daughter could join me. Our second daughter was born in Sandia Base Hospital. And my employer at home said my job would be there when I returned.

Kel was born in New York City and attended Dartmouth College. His fifty-year career (eighteen in the US. and thirty-two in Toronto, Canada) was spent with the Philadelphia-based Crown, Cork & Seal Co. where he rose to be Vice President of Sales. The Company is a producer of beverage containers and beverage filling equipment. Kel also served as President of the Canadian Manufacturers of Chemical Specialties Association.

Luck Of The Draw

CARL IRWIN

IN EARLY 1944, as a newly selected Aviation Cadet, I was sent to Tyndal Field near Panama City, Florida, for Air Gunnery Familiarization.

My very first flight at Tyndal Field could have been the beginning of a very short Army Air Corps flying career. My first flight in an Army plane went well until it was time to land. At that time the instructor sent me and two other cadets to the nose of our B-17. As we approached the field the pilot apparently felt we were too low, and decided to try another approach. Unfortunately, we did not have sufficient airspeed and we pancaked into a field of stumps at the end of the landing strip. The Plexiglas nose of the plane popped out and we jumped to the ground uninjured. Tragically, the plane caught on fire and at least eight cadets perished.

The next morning an Air Corps doctor asked me if I wanted to continue flying. I said, "Yes," and continued bombardier-navigator training with no further incidents.

Talk about the luck of the draw!

Born in Sikeston, and raised in Springfield, Missouri, Carl graduated from Cornell University in 1949, following service in the Army Air Corps. While working in Seattle, Washington, for the Ingersoll-Rand Company, he met and married his wife, Betty, from Victoria, British Columbia, Canada. His sales and marketing assignments took them to New York, St. Louis, and points in between. With two sons in the Chicago area, a daughter in Maine, and another in the Boston area, RiverWoods and the seacoast of New Hampshire proved to be an excellent place to retire.

Celestial Navigation

Bob Shealor

I WAS A freshman at Lehigh University at the time of the attack on Pearl Harbor. I finished the semester, learned to fly, and enlisted in the Army Air Corps on November 14, 1942. I wanted to be in a flight crew.

Upon reporting for duty I was required to have the physical exam. We were stripped down to only our shoes and marched down the street for everyone to see! (I still have bad dreams.) I was sent to Brown University to study meteorology where I became an instant big shot—promoted to Cadet Captain by a fellow cadet who was a fraternity brother. However, advanced calculus was not my forte and I washed out of the program.

From there I went to Langley Field for navigation training. Was I finally making it to a flight crew? No, I was off to Charleston Air Force Base in South Carolina where I was going to operate a Link Celestial Navigation Trainer, an amazing gadget. The navigator's compartment was high up in a silo-shaped building with maps and aerial views from ten thousand feet up. They covered from take off to target, which on our Trainer was Cologne, Germany. I had the opportunity to ride with navigators on several training flights, one of which was to Batista Field in Havana, Cuba. I was discharged on February 16, 1946, and returned to Lehigh.

Born in Brooklyn, New York, Bob grew up in Greenwich, Connecticut. After the service Bob graduated from Lehigh University in 1948. Following a few years with a CPA firm he spent twenty years in sales in the office equipment industry, after which he moved to Wall Street and retired in 1988 as Vice President for Investments at Prudential Securities. Bob, and his wife, Dorothy, moved from their Florida retirement home to RiverWoods.

A Newport Experience

ROBERT C. WADE

FROM BOOT CAMP I was assigned to the Construction Battalion (CB), Davisville, Rhode Island. I taught a course in chemical warfare. There I met Jim, Yeoman First Class, who had served in several Seabee assignments in the European Theater and was battle hardened.

Both of us were Episcopalians and occasionally attended the oldest, beautiful little Episcopal Church in America in nearby Wickford, Rhode Island. This early colonial structure was pure white, inside and out. The pews were the antique box pews with small doors on the aisle side. This Sunday, Jim and I chose to sit up front. The pew contained a beautiful Bible, Book of Common Prayer, and Hymnal.

Just before the service was to begin, a very distinguished elderly lady came marching down the aisle and came to a halt opposite our pew. She looked us over, reached into her expensive handbag, took out a lorgnette, peered again at us, and then took out a small note pad and pen. She proceeded to write a note. When finished she handed the note to Jim. He read it.

"I pay $5,000 to sit in this pew. M.L.W."

Jim looked it over, then took out a chewed up pencil and wrote on the back of her note.

"You pay too damn much. James, Yeoman 1C."

He handed it back to her. As she read it, there was obvious shock on her face. Slowly, the visible anger gave way to a smile, and then a soft chuckle. She quietly asked us if she could sit with us. We quickly made room for her, and the three of us prayed together.

After the service she offered to drive us back to our base. We gladly accepted and thoroughly enjoyed the company of one of Newport's most distinguished ladies.

Robert was educated at Lakewood High School in Ohio and received his Chemistry BA at Oberlin. In 1944 he married Diantha Adams and they had seven children. He was a member of the American Chemical Society and served in the US Navy. Robert died in 2010.

Medical Service

A Night To Remember

GAIL O. BATES

I WAS IN bed in an American Red Cross Hostel in London, dead tired after a day-long trip from the north of England on a crowded troop train. The soft roar of planes overhead lulled me to sleep. It was the night of June 5th 1944.

I had spent a year at an American Air Force repair depot, where I helped run a Red Cross Aero-Club for the GIs who were doing the heavy repairs on the shot-up bombers from the bases in the south. Our clubhouse was open from 6 a.m. to midnight every day and it was always full as the GIs came off their shifts. For reasons unknown (the Red Cross operated like the Army—no explanations) I was reassigned to join a P-38 Fighter Group in the south of England. The morning of June 6th at breakfast we listened to the wireless reporting that D-Day had begun. This was, of course, news to all of us.

Two days later I arrived at Stoney Cross in New Forest, Dorset, a barren airstrip surrounded by giant rhododendrons in full bloom, and gray Quonset huts. As our Aero-Club was already set up, Nancy, my co-worker, and I started dishing out coffee and doughnuts to the GIs who were working around the clock to keep their planes flying, and mourning the loss of the pilots who didn't make it back across the English Channel.

It was another month before our outfit was completely moved across the Channel. St. Lô had fallen to the Allies, General Patton was mopping up Brittany and moving east, and the 367th Fighter Group was spread on three different airstrips, flying missions on a daily basis.

Nancy and I were the least important, and the last to fly over the Channel. We arrived at Sainte Mère-Église in Normandy, which we learned was the first village in France to be liberated by the Allies. The French were very happy to see the Americans and even happier when they greeted the first French tanks, rumbling through their village with the Croix de Lorraine painted on their sides.

We camped in pup tents by a wheat field between apple orchards and ditched hedgerows. Evenings, we toasted k-ration cheese and crackers over little fire holes in the ground until sundown when all blacked out.

We waited anxiously for our supplies to arrive to start serving doughnuts and coffee in our Aero-Club tents, furnished with chairs, tables, a victrola, and a piano. And then our outfit decided to have a party for the children of Sainte Mère-Église. Tootsie rolls and chocolate Mars bars were contributed by the GIs from their rations, and our field was filled with happy children dressed in their best clothes, including one little girl in a camouflage silk dress. Then the Mayor, Paul Renaud, gave a dramatic account of the arrival of the parachutists and gliders on the night of June 5th, first in French to the children, then in English.

Colonel, Ladies and Gentlemen,

It is from the bottom of my heart that I am thanking you for the Wonderful Welcome that we have received from you.

In my little town, we knew that the Americans when they would jump from the top of the sky on the land of France, not only would deliver us from the German slavery, but would be real friends to us, just as these American soldiers who landed in Saint Nazaire in Nineteen Hundred Seventeen with the shouting "Lafayette, Here we are."

Two months ago, during the night from fifth to sixth of June, it was the first time that in a growling of C-47s, in the moonlight of a lovely summer night, we have seen, appearing in the sky the first airborne troops.

In a part of our city, a fire, most likely set by German tracing balls, was destroying a cottage. Deprived from electricity since a month, we had been hurrying with only a hand pump to try to save the house from fire. From the steeple of our old church, the bells rang the alarm, calling for the men's help.

Above us, the big bombers passed and in the West, towards the illuminated sea lighted by the star shells, we could hear the big bombs explode.

The German Flak troops looked at us.

Suddenly, from a heavy C-47, all lights on, flying at tree top level, the first American parachutists jumped down. We did our utmost to help them hiding from the Germans and thus many were safe. But the others were received by the Flak with the shots of their automatic rifles. The tracing balls crossed the air like huge glowing flies. A C-47 crashed on the ground and soon her fire was raging a few hundreds yards from the first one.

Then, the Germans realizing the danger for them, threatened to shoot at us at once if we did not go home straight away.

All night, we looked at the wonderful scene from our windows. As far as we could see, we saw parachutists appear and jump down on the earth in a hurry. They came down in the trees, in the orchards, on the roofs of the houses, in the yards. The large gliders seemed to slide on the air.

At dawn, we saw the parachutists occupying the market place. Some of them were hidden behind the walls; others sitting at the feet of the big trees were smoking cigarettes quietly. The windows opened and at once it was a frantic rush of the inhabitants towards them. THE PARACHUTISTS. We found them fine, in spite of their black grime. In the town it was quite calm, not a ball was shot, not a shell...The Germans had gone.

IT HAD FALLEN TO THE LOT OF SAINTE-MERE-EGLISE THE GREAT HONOUR TO BE THE FIRST VILLAGE OF FRANCE DELIVERED....

From nine o'clock in the morning, here and there, a few bullets began to hiss, and later on a volley of German shells burst on Sainte-Mere-Eglise.

At two o'clock in the afternoon, the situation in Sainte-Mere-Eglise was getting dangerous. The captain of parachutists, Chouvaloff, called upon me to say that it should be prudent to evacuate the place, or at least to stay into the house. German counter attacks were going to start. I was told that the Infantry and the Second Battalion of the same regiment, both commanded by Lt. Colonel Benjamin Wanderwoorts and Lt. Colonel Edward Krause.

Then, for thirty-six hours, those two battalions already diminished by the night casualties, posted at the point of the struggle, separated from the sea by six miles of enemy space, resisted the German counter attacks coming from north, south, and west. They did resist by themselves with their machine guns, two heavy machine guns and two small mortars dropped out of the gliders, against complete German battalions and supplied with plenty of guns and tanks.

Three times from the north, twice from the south, the Germans managed to get inside the town, but the soldiers of America were here. They got hold of the city and did not let it go.

These men, I have observed them very well during the battle. They did not boast, they spoke but a little, one would think that they were having drill. They went, with their cigarettes between their lips, or chewing their gum, holding to the walls, but so straight and with a firm step, beneath the fire of large shrapnells laid down incessantly from Azeville and Saint Marin batteries.

In the evening of the sixth of June, from the ditch where I had taken refuge with my family, I realized that the fight drew near. Two Germans were creeping close to us in the bushes slipping into the town and the Parachutists passed by afterwards. One of the Airborne whom I spoke to answered: "We launch an attack. The reinforcements will arrive from the sea, O.K."

The following evening, they were still expecting their reinforcements: "There is a delay," said one of them, "The sea was rough," and as the woman wept and supplicated: "For God, don't leave us." He answered with a large smile: "We never abandon, we die on the spot."

At the moment, when the reinforcements arrived from the sea, with twelve hours delay, in that moment when, full of joy, we heard the rolling of the tanks on Ravenoiville road, the Airborne had nearly no more ammunitions. "Now," they said to us, "we must shoot but very accurately and certainly. And morover, we have our bayonettes and knives."

DURING THAT NIGHT, THE FIRST BATTLE HAD BEEN WON BY THE AIRBORNE TROOPS. They had caught three hundred sixty four prisoners, and the tanks pursued the beaten enemy.

THE FIRST AMERICAN BRIDGE-HEAD WAS BORN.

COLONEL, LADIES AND GENTLEMEN, I was just telling the children: You have been living the most tragical fairy tale that has ever been written, and I explained to them, an evil spirit has spread over our villages and threatened to destroy us forever. He had plundered our nation, he had put our young men in prison, he had taken all our butter and cattle from us. Because of him, our good white bread had turned into black bread.

The good fairies had sworn to fight against him. They manufactured arms in a large island and also in a huge country very far from us, at the other end of the world.

We were waiting for these good fairies, we have been waiting since such a long time that some people here began to doubt they would come.

And suddenly, in this night of nightmare and dreams, before our amazed eyes, just like once upon a time Saint Michel throwing down the Devil, they did jump down on our earth in the thunder of the planes, among fire works like children's eyes had never seen.

There has been the fight between the good and the bad. Blood has been spread, men have died here in this field where we are today. The earth has been dug, bruised by the bombs, grenades and shells and finally the bad have been defeated.

Two months have passed away. Blood has ceased to flow on this spot of Norman land. In that same place, some tents have been set up on which the Red Cross of charity and peace is drawn.

And the good Fairies have welcomed the French children, they have spoilt them, they have given them plenty of candies, chocolates and sweets unknown to the babies and that, they believe, but heavenly hands can dispense.

FRIENDS, for us the grown up and also for the future generations, you are our good fairies.

France, during the same generation has been devastated by two horrible wars. It has been weakened by the loss of its best blood and the destruction of many artistic treasures. For thus, France needs you for a long time.

COLONEL, LADIES AND GENTLEMEN OF AMERICA, in the decisive moment the parachutists have not abandoned us. Do not abandon us in the future. THREE times, the French have fought with the Americans side by side, and NEVER we have been enemies.

WE MUST STAY GREAT FRIENDS, NOT ONLY FOR A WHILE, BUT FOREVER.

He was describing the same night when I was sleeping soundly in London. It took almost another year and many lost pilots, but the liberation of France had begun.

Born in Cleveland, Ohio, Gail earned a BA Degree in Italian and Art History at Vassar College and a MS Degree in Social Work at Columbia University. She served in the American Red Cross in England, France, and Germany from 1943 to 1945 attached to the US 9th Air Force.

Promises, Promises

KERWIN HYLAND

SEVERAL MONTHS after celebrating my seventeenth birthday, when I graduated from high school, I began thinking about college and a career in the field of entomology. I had already chosen to attend Penn State, and it was one of the few colleges in Pennsylvania that offered a major in entomology.

Early on the morning of December 7, 1941, we were awakened to learn that the Japanese had bombed Pearl Harbor. Obviously, this news hit the town of State College like a bombshell. We were all aware of the war in Europe and the fear and anticipation of war in the Pacific. The entire campus was thrown into turmoil. There were numerous students who were already expecting to be drafted and others who feared that if they did not enlist immediately, they would likewise feel the pinch. The University shifted to an accelerated program of three semesters per year so that students could graduate in less than three years.

One program which was available was the Army Reserve Program in which the Army promised to sign up students so they could continue at the accelerated pace as long as they remained in good standing. If and when they were called to active duty, they would have their choice of the branch of the Army they preferred. I enrolled in the Army Reserve and continued my studies from 1941-43. With the three-semester program in force, I was able to complete five semesters by the spring of 1943. Since I was an entomology student I envisioned service involving some phase of insect or vector control, or parasites in the Pacific Theater.

My fellow reservists and I received notice from the Army that we were to report for active duty in mid-May 1943. On May 27th I said goodbye to my parents in York, Pennsylvania, and hello to the Army at Fort Meade, Maryland.

Remembering what I had been told upon enrolling in the Army, I announced very confidently that I was an entomology student and interested in parasites. Little did I expect that when the time came I would be separated off with the Anti-Aircraft group. I couldn't believe my ears when I heard this, but was still sure that the moment would come when I could explain that I had been misclassified. Nothing seemed to change my listing until it was noted that I had played the trumpet in the high school band and orchestra. Since there was a dire need for a bugler, I was brought in to be the bugler for the company. This was a new experience because except for playing a few calls in Scout camp and on the high school practice field, I knew very little about the Army bugle calls. In any case, I became the Company Bugler, played reveille, first call, assembly, and taps. Somehow I found myself set aside from the other troops because by the time I played the various calls to assemble there was little time for me to take my bugle back to the barracks and to get my hiking gear in order for marching.

At the end of basic training I found myself at a desk in the classification center, explaining again my conviction that I had been poorly classified. Everyone felt sorry for my situation but they seemed unable to ship me off to medics or sanitary corps. When they noticed that I had taken college physics, their eyes lit up and they suggested electrical school. I attended electrical school for eight weeks, followed by study of power plants to energize the anti-aircraft equipment.

At a certain point I had a physical examination and mentioned my disappointment at not reaching my desired branch of the Army. I was told that I should never have been assigned to Anti-Aircraft in the first place. A few weeks later my wish came true when I got orders to go to Camp Van Dorn in Centerdale, Mississippi, to join the 126th Evacuation Hospital, a new unit which was being established for service in the European Theatre.

Upon arrival I received more basic training with other new entrants. Most had not been trained in any specialty. As an option I chose surgical technician training in Atlanta, Georgia, and a short stay at Fort Bragg, North Carolina, for experience, and then back to Camp Van Dorn.

Somewhere between our basic training and our bivouac experience, the "handle" of our unit became "Wild Bill and his Medicine Show." There was a certain covey of musicians among the enlisted personnel who volunteered to try their luck at organizing a seven-piece dance band with piano, drums, two trumpets, two alto saxophones, two clarinets, and a trombone. We were able to practice during our off hours and put together something of a dance band. Remember, this was the 1940's when the greatest of the dance bands were at their height. We did our best to beg, borrow, or steal instruments and used the barracks or service quarters to practice. I kept my job as the bugler for the hospital, and the other trumpet player took my place when I was absent for any reason.

It seemed that every day we packed and unpacked some of our gear and equipment. Whether it was a collection of tents, surgical instruments, sterilizer, operating room lights, or cooking equipment, we were always packing or unpacking. What monotony, but this was the Army you know!

At last "this is it" was broadcast throughout the hospital and we prepared to leave Mississippi. Where to? West Coast or East Coast? Soon the news spread that we were headed for New Jersey, a happy event because most of our hospital crew was from the Northeast. So what was our next surprise? After marching our first mile, the SS *Queen Elizabeth* came into view. What a magnificent ship she was, waiting to take us to Glasgow in Scotland. It was quite a surprise to see the ship, but a real letdown to have cold fish, yes, cold fish for breakfast! Yet we survived the five-day trip to the Firth of Clyde and the tender into Glasgow. We were greeted with coffee and donuts upon arrival and very soon encountered the almost constant fog. We were housed in a compound in a series of Nissen huts with our beds equipped with straw mattresses. It was so cold in our huts that we slept with our clothes on plus whatever additional coats we could collect.

Glasgow is the largest city in Scotland, but there were many places we could not visit because of the threat of possible destruction. For example, the municipal museums were closed and the treasures were packed up and moved for safekeeping. Word was received that our vehicles had been commandeered for use in the Battle of the Bulge and that we would be stuck in Glasgow until replacements could be delivered.

During this period many of us were put on various forms of temporary duty. In my case, I was selected to help with the transportation of casualties onto the SS *Queen Mary*, which had docked in the Firth of Clyde. The casualties were taken on a tender to the *Queen Mary* and then carried onto the ship and up the stairs, since many of the patients were in casts or on stretchers and could not be taken by elevator. This was an extremely arduous task because the soldiers with casts were not only heavy, but also very difficult to move.

Another of our activities continued to be the dance band. We were invited by the United Service Organization (USO) in Glasgow to play for their Saturday night dances. We continued to do this during a series of weekends, and in addition we played at the Air Force base in Prestwick, Scotland.

Finally, we headed to Southampton by train to board the *Llang Libby Castle* destined for Le Havre in France. We were greeted by nothing but devastation. We then boarded Forty and Eights, railroad cars fitted to bunk forty soldiers or eight horses, made famous in World War I. Traveling through France we witnessed the shambles, pill boxes, destroyed airplanes, and foxholes. This was our first look at the results of REAL WAR. Eventually a long winding mountain road led us to our destination at Corbion, Belgium. At the edge of the Ardennes Forest we made final preparations for combat on the outskirts of the town. It was here in Corbion that I visited a very small bookshop in the middle of town and met the family of the proprietors. I was invited into their home and received various gifts, including a few schoolbooks in French and a tobacco box for my pipe tobacco. This latter was a gift for my twenty-first birthday. I still cherish it although I no longer smoke! It was here that I fell in love with Belgium and started learning French, which I am still working on today.

After spending about a month here, long enough to experience the spring thaw in March and April, we left for Germany. The war was ending and we encountered little resistance from the Germans who were mostly fleeing. We passed through a series of cities and towns beginning with Korbach and then on to Gotha, Erfurt, Weimar, Jena, and finally Gera. Along the way the unit was sometimes separated into small segments on Temporary Duty (TDY) to go into smaller captured towns.

In the process of fleeing, the Germans had left many of their wounded troops behind in small makeshift hospitals, in schools, churches, and town buildings. Three or four of us with an officer would enter these "hospitals" and ask questions about the needs of the patients. The technicians and doctors would sometimes examine the patients to determine if they were well enough to be released. Those determined to be sufficiently improved to leave the hospital were sent to prisoner-of-war camp. We would help these soldiers board the US trucks and we never saw any of them again.

It was a difficult job to make a truly accurate assessment of the soldiers—especially the officers. Any officer, especially one of rank, would continue to remain sick or injured for an extended period of time to deter being transported to the prisoner-of-war camp. We had a language problem, of course, but in addition it was not efficacious to remove complex bandaging and casts. Our other responsibility was to determine whether each "hospital" unit was adequately supplied with food, surgical instruments, and hospital supplies.

As we journeyed along the back roads we saw some marvelous architecture and beautiful scenery. It was still spring in Germany, with wonderful vistas in spite of the destruction everywhere. For the most part there was very little antagonism expressed by the populace as we drove along or inspected patients. Our hospital unit finally settled in the outskirts of Gera where we set up our complex establishment and began admitting patients. Fortunately, the war ended on May 8, 1945, and although the hospital's activities diminished we continued to have a plethora of activities including items such as automobile accidents, souvenir gun accidents, and even sick prisoners of war.

Finally the time came to pack up, ONCE AGAIN, supplies, equipment, vehicles, and tents of all types. Word filtered down that the 126th was destined for redeployment. Yes, redeployment. We left most of our equipment in a Quartermaster Depot and rushed back through Belgium. After a night in Liege and a stay in the staging area, we boarded the USS *Monticello*. After a reasonably quick, but rough, trip we arrived in New York and proceeded on to Camp Bowie in Texas to be redeployed to the Pacific. We dragged our feet hoping to wait out the trip to the Orient. Fortunately, the war in the Pacific ended before that happened.

I was sent back to Pennsylvania for discharge and returned to York to be greeted by my overjoyed parents. I had been many places, seen many things, and it was heavenly to be home to enjoy my mother's real Pennsylvania Dutch cooking once again.

After discharge from the Army in the fall of 1945, Kerv returned to Penn State where he completed his BS in Zoology and Entomology in 1947. He also married that same year and thanks to Uncle Sam and the GI Bill, he enrolled for the Master's Degree program in Parasitology at Tulane University. While teaching at the Christ Church School in Virginia, he completed his PhD in Zoology at Duke University and received an appointment in the Zoology Department at the University of Rhode Island where he taught until his retirement in 1999. During his academic career Kerv spent three sabbatical years in Belgium working at the Institute of Tropical Medicine in Antwerp, once on a Fulbright Grant and once on a grant from the National Institutes of Health.

Three Years On Liberty
or How Not To Wage A War

Joe McCarthy

February 5, 1943

THEY SAID this was the coldest night of the year at Fort Devens Induction Center—34 degrees below—so cold that the steam train that was to have taken me and about a thousand other shivering recruits to a Basic Training Camp, "somewhere in the South," could not move. "Next day," they told us. But that departure never did happen for eleven of us who were routed out of bed very, very early the next day and put on a bus for Taunton, Massachusetts, where we began months of training in a base hospital for "service at sea."

An Observation: The Army had given me a choice—although I did not know it at the time. One option was to go through Basic Training that would prepare me to sleep on the ground, live in a trench, and eat K-rations. The other option was to complete a medical training program that would enable me to live in my own cabin, sleep in a clean bunk every night, eat "three squares" a day, and have someone do my laundry once a week. I'd like to say that I chose the second option; but the truth is that the Army made that choice for me—just as it continued to make "my choices" for the next three years.

September 23, 1943

I went to Norfolk, Virginia, to board the *Alfred S. Moore,* a Liberty Ship retrofitted to accommodate five hundred troops. I was one of two medics assigned to her. We also had a second lieutenant to supervise cargo handling and a platoon of twenty "Armed Guards," sailors who manned our anti-aircraft guns and small cannons in the event of an attack. Our training as medics had been intensive and certainly audacious! The objective was to equip each trainee with the knowledge and skills to act as medical officer on the small troop transports that were being launched at the rate of one a day. We could cope with routine illnesses and trauma in a small clinic and operating room. Seasickness? Broken limbs? Acute indigestion? Nasopharyngitis? We could take care of all those problems and, in a pinch, perform an appendectomy. As an appendage, we were shown how to run a motion picture projector to sustain morale throughout the voyage. On a stormy night, a Betty Grable movie was arguably the best medicine at my disposal!

October 1, 1943
We steamed down the James River with five hundred infantrymen of the 45th Division bound for England. And now a surprise: instead of heading due east, we turned south to a spot just north of Cuba where we were scheduled to join a "slow convoy" of Liberties and other merchantmen which could not exceed 13 knots. Finally the navy directed us to our assigned place in this checkerboard of about 120 freighters with a destroyer and three small Destroyer Escorts to maintain discipline and protect against the subs that patrolled our route. On the third day, signals were flashed from ship to ship and the whole convoy began to move east at 11—then 12 —and finally 13 knots; all but the *Alfred S. Moore* which fell behind, further and further, spewing telltale black smoke in a vain effort to keep up. Before dark the Navy order was flashed down: "*Moore*, return to port!"

October 11, 1943
We found that we did not have to return to Florida or Norfolk. Our Chief Engineer solved the smoking problem and assured the Navy that we could maintain 12 knots cleanly if they could assign us to a slower convoy. Five days later we set out again in a convoy of decrepit colliers, oilers, and Victorian Era tramps, steaming more

or less due east on a zigzag course at 10 knots! Now we had a new worry: food for the troops. With a thirty-day supply of food in the hold, would we make it to England? But the Army knew what to do: Order the *Moore* into another closer port. So we split from the convoy together with thirty other ships to discharge our troops in Oran, Port Mers-el-Kebir. In a few days we boarded another five hundred troops bound for Sicily, the first of several trips shuttling across the Mediterranean from Oran to Sicily and eventually to Italy, all at no more than 10 knots: "The Slowest Ship in the Med!"

December 15, 1943

Our Captain and Chief Engineer had told the port command in Oran that the *Moore* desperately needed an overhaul and perhaps a new boiler. So rather than chance leaving American troops adrift in the middle of the Mediterranean, the Army directed us to take a "cargo" of five hundred German POWs to Boston and to refit the ship there. This was a new experience for my partner medic and me but we scrounged port storage for essential medical supplies and even a couple of Marlene Dietrich films. What a surprise when the commander of the German troops appeared in the clinic the following day to say that he had three graduate physicians in his command and to ask whether he might simply assign them to us, handling sick call and emergency duties! We agreed readily, introduced the doctors to our facilities, and arranged that they prescribe medications that we would fill. There were several seriously ill men among the prisoners and it was a rough and tedious crossing across the North Atlantic. But, thanks to those doctors, we delivered every man to America and for a few brief days, we could imagine that there was NO WAR.

March 6, 1944

We had boarded troops in the Brooklyn Port of Embarkation for delivery to Naples in a small convoy bound for Liverpool. Since the threat of subs in the North Atlantic had diminished sharply during the winter there was no armed guard and we were ordered, together with about a dozen other ships and a single escort, to swing west out of convoy about two days out of Gibraltar. Weather and yet another engine failure intervened, however, and we found ourselves alone on a vast sea, steaming at eight knots under clear skies for the safety of the "Rock."

But we were not alone for long. "Submarine to Port," the lookout screamed. Then we saw the torpedo, streaking through the water on course to hit us amidships. The Captain rang General Quarters, ordered full speed and hard to starboard but the *Moore*, ever unresponsive, continued to plod along its course. "Clang!" The torpedo hit our plates just aft of the engine room. And we waited for a ten-second eternity. Again the lookout shrieked: "She's a dead fish." And we watched the torpedo sink out of sight. Only then we noticed that the submarine was rising out of the water, as the crew prepared to finish us off with what looked like a five-inch cannon. Even more quickly we saw a bomber flying in from the west, a British two-engine Mosquito, the celebrated "plywood plane." The pilots read the situation quickly and maneuvered to drop some depth charges on the now submerging sub. Just in time: "BRO-O-O-O-M." By this time the *Moore* had responded to command and was headed away from the neighborhood at full speed, leaving a blanket of black smoke behind. We never did learn whether the sub sank. Years later I met a Gibraltar Mosquito pilot and learned that he was in fact the man who saved our lives. But when I pressed for details— "Look, Laddie, I don't recall that day—we saved so bloody many Yanks. But I am glad you are here today!"

September 28, 1944
We continued to shuttle between Africa and several Italian ports all summer. But in August we learned that we were scheduled to go to southern France with the invading forces, carrying assault troops and heavy gear, tanks, field artillery, the real stuff! But there were delays and it was not until late September (Marseilles was fairly well secured by then.) that we steamed alone out of Mers-el-Kabir with over seven hundred sword-swinging soldiers from French Sene-

gal—all handsome, enormous, ebony guys, with their camp follow-
ers, French officers and their wives, replete with kitchens, stringed
instruments, flutes and drums, and a vivid green jeep for the Com-
mandante. Never had our ship been so crowded, so noisy, so in-
credibly joyous as when the Senegalese mounted a dance on deck
to welcome the full moon on our second night out of port. But that
was the last we saw of the moon or the sun for a week. We were hit
by a Mistral, the vicious storm that whips up the Mediterranean in
the fall. Much of our deck gear was washed overboard, including
the precious jeep, and we had to keep all hands below deck.

On the 28th, two French officers brought a Senegalese patient
into the clinic. I noted giant skin eruptions, buboes, fever, and a
purple skin hue. Bubonic Plague! Our instructors had not prepared me for this! We did what we could to quarantine the passengers and to keep our ship's crew out of harm's way. But, once I
got confirmation of my diagnosis from a doctor on a nearby hospital ship, there was little more to be done other than to preserve
the bodies in our freezer for autopsies and keep the clinic free of
sepsis. The port authorities did not exactly welcome us. Rather
they ordered us to anchor to the west of the port where a proces-
sion of amphibious trucks (DUKWs) transferred the troops to a
vacant camp. All of the merchant officers and crew, and I, had to
find accommodations in Marseilles for a week while the ship was
fumigated. But the Army did award me with a star for my part in
the invasion of Southern France.

February 11, 1945

We were at anchor in Mers-el-Kabir when we learned that, for
many reasons, the *Alfred Moore* would no longer transport troops.
We were ordered to steam immediately to Norfolk where the ship
would be refitted for cargo only. "What will we do with you, Mac?"
the Captain asked. I had no orders and his effort to get me reassigned to another transport had yielded nothing, nothing! He invited me to stay aboard for the twelve-day crossing to Norfolk. I
accepted and we got out the cribbage board. Thirty-two days later

we steamed up the James River leaving a black cloud that probably still hangs there. I bade my hosts farewell and took a jitney to the Army's Transportation Office. Once there it dawned on me that my uniform, part khaki, part blue, all that I could find after the fumigation, might seem a bit strange in this tight-laced GI Office. I reported to the staff sergeant: "Hi, I'm Joe McCarthy, fresh off the *Alfred S. Moore*." Sergeant: "But you're missing. We've had you 'Missing in Action' for a month. Corporal, call your family, right now!"

Summation:
I was required to spend a couple of months in the Norfolk Base Hospital just to be sure that I had no lasting effects from the Bubonic Plague. Then, after a few days leave in Andover, Massachusetts, I took a train to Mobile, Alabama, where, on VJ Day, I boarded the SS *Hagerstown Victory*, a bigger version of the *Moore*, fast, clean, but with no dancing allowed on deck—dull, unspeakably dull. I made a few crossings, one with a "bananas only" cargo from the island of Guadeloupe. Finally, on January 31, 1946, we returned to the Brooklyn Port Offices where some lovely person noted that, with the extra citation I had earned in the "invasion" of southern France, I had enough "points" to quit the Army. Which I did—promptly!

Note: The dates cited in this account are taken from my notes, not from Army or Merchant Marine records. I am persuaded that my records are in many instances more accurate.

Born in Andover, Massachesetts, Joe attended Tufts University before his Army service and continued there after the war to receive an AB degree in 1948. Following graduate study in scenography at Western Reserve University, both Joe and his wife, Marcie, were involved in community theatres for ten years. A graduate degree from the University of North Carolina propelled Joe into teaching at several universities in New York and Pennsylvania and in 1966, while teaching at Bucknell University, he was asked to devise a "Pennsylvania Plan for Teacher Education in the Arts." Retirement brought them to Cape Cod and in a subsequent move they settled in Exeter, New Hampshire.

An Army Surgical Nurse

Lucy Grover Parrella

M Y LAST six months of nurse's training were spent as a cadet nurse in a large Army General Hospital, mostly in surgery, for $50 a month. It was during WW II with nurses in great demand. My father was very sad when I told him I had joined. He already had four sons in the service.

As an Army nurse I went through basic training where I learned to march; wear fatigues, boots, cap, and helmets; dig holes; share a pup tent; use slit trenches; eat rations; drink from canteens; and receive lots of medical shots. We hiked one to five miles and bivouacked overnight. I learned to shoot (Maggie's drawers). After a final review in front of ranking officers, we were awarded officer's uniforms, a gold bar, and $150 a month.

I was given further training in new surgical procedures before assignment as a surgical nurse to a team, ten nurses and four doctors, in the First Service Command. The team was moved every ten days to a hospital wherever the need was greatest. The locations were often close to enemy lines. When you worked as a team it was always "We", seldom referring to "I" alone.

One memorable procedure was to build a face. A young soldier had lost one side of his face. Working in a new field, plastic surgery, required one surgeon and one nurse to assure strict sterile technique. First, a metal cap was placed over the front lobe of the brain and forehead. Second, a floating rib was removed to make a jaw and, eventually, to have false denture plates put in place. Third, a cheekbone and eye-socket were created; a remarkable resemblance of color and features was accomplished. Eventually, the rest of the repair required skin grafts. The field of plastic surgery was greatly furthered during WW II.

In addition to assisting in surgery I taught WAC's and Ward Boys to aid in hospital care. Some of the boys were from rural mountain areas and could neither read nor write but had great sympathy and tenderness toward the soldiers and were dependable workers. They also learned sterilization techniques and how to assist in administering drugs.

Serving as an Army nurse was one of the most challenging, rewarding, and enduring times in my life. The American wounded were brave, resilient young men looking forward to going back to school, home, family, and jobs.

My role as an Army nurse was meager compared to others. Many outstanding and accomplished doctors joined the service and were invaluable, bringing in new medical treatments and requiring more sophisticated equipment and medicines. They were also teaching new doctors who eventually went into their own practices.

Born in Rowley, Massachusetts, Lucy married Dr. Jack Parrella after WW II and lived in Milford, Connecticut, for fifty years. In Milford, she volunteered with Red Cross Blood Banks, Cancer Research Detection, and the Hospital Auxiliary. Her most rewarding work was in the later years when her husband had restricted his practice to office surgeries and she was his assistant. Following her husband's death, Lucy moved to Newburyport, Massachusetts, where she was active in the Episcopal Church and the Historical Society.

American Field Service

ALLAN B. PRINCE

D URING THE early spring of 1943, while completing my freshman year at Rutgers University, I received notice from the local draft board to report to the Newark, New Jersey, US Army Induction Center for a physical examination. A medical officer told
me my punctured eardrums made me ineligible for the US Armed
Forces and I would be classified 4-F. When I asked why, I was told
that those people with this condition were likely to have middle-ear
infections, which would incapacitate them. Since I was determined
not to remain uninvolved, my father inquired about an ambulance
service, the American Field Service (AFS), which had been active
during World War I, and discovered that it was once again serving
with Allied Armed Forces. Volunteers were accepted within certain
age limits and with certain types of physical disability.

On June 29, 1943, I reported to American Field Service headquarters in New York City and five days later boarded an armed freight-
er, *Robin Tuxford*, at the Brooklyn Navy Yard. The following personnel were on board: ship's crew, US Navy (to operate the guns), US
Army Medical, Office of War Information (OWI), British Fleet Air
Arm, and American Field Service.

The ship sailed, without convoy or escort, south along the US
east coast, through the Panama Canal, south along the west coast
of South America, around Cape Horn, across the South Atlantic
into the Indian Ocean, and north to Mombasa, Kenya. There, AFS
personnel transferred to the ship *Lancaster* and proceeded north
through the Red Sea, reaching Cairo, Egypt, on September 2, 1943.

On September 7th my unit proceeded by train and truck to Baalbek, Lebanon, in the Bekaa Valley where we were housed in some former French Foreign Legion barracks. It was here we were assigned our Dodge ambulances and given instruction on vehicle operation and maintenance. For the next two months the platoon operated out of various posts in Lebanon and Syria.

Word came on November 20th that our unit was to be transferred to Italy. We proceeded to a staging area outside of Cairo, where our ambulances were prepared for battlefield conditions, and then to Alexandria to be loaded on a ship named *Uradyesse*. On December 17th our ship joined a thirty-ship convoy bound for Italy. On the way one ship was lost when German planes based in Crete attacked the convoy. We off-loaded our ambulances at Taranto and from there drove to the Naples area. The next two months were spent carrying out routine assignments in the Bay of Naples area including such towns as Pompeii, Castellammare, and Sorrento.

At the end of February we moved north to the front at Cassino. Here Field Marshall Kesselring had established a German defensive position known as the Gustave Line that extended all the way across Italy. In January the US 5th Army troops had failed in an attempt to break through this line into the Lire valley.

We were given some burlap bags, told to fill them with earth and place them on the floorboards and under the seats of the ambulance. The purpose was to give us some protection should we run over a mine. One problem with the idea was it forced us to operate the clutch and brake pedals with our heels instead of our toes. Double clutching with thick layers of mud on our boots became an art.

Four of us were posted to a New Zealand Advanced Dressing Station (ADS). While talking with one of the AFS drivers from 567 Company, who was being sent to another post, I noticed that leaves were falling off the olive tree under which we were standing and at the same time there was a whirring sound. He calmly informed me that it was shrapnel from the shells landing on the other side of the hill.

My friend Joe and I decided rather quickly to construct a dugout that both of us could sleep in. As added protection we filled wooden shell boxes (four feet long and twelve inches square) with earth, placed them around the perimeter of the hole and banked earth up against them. Our pup tent was then pitched over the top. We would lie in our bedrolls at night and count the German shells passing overhead, trying to guess which ones would be duds when they hit. We quickly learned that we would not hear a shell destined to hit us. The Germans could easily see the red crosses on our tents and vehicles identifying us as a medical unit. They would shell all around us and we liked to think that they were respecting the Red Cross. Nevertheless, we could not always rely on their accuracy.

Just before dark each day we would get some charcoal from supplies, place it in a #10 tin can which had holes punched in the sides and fire up the charcoal using gasoline. It did a pretty good job of reducing some of the chill in the dugout. Sometime during this period a field mouse took up residence. He/she was quite tame. Once I woke up in the morning with the mouse perched on my feet at the foot of the bedroll watching me.

Our assignment was to evacuate wounded to a Main Dressing Station (MDS) twelve miles to the rear. The evacuation track was shelled every day so we tried to do much of our work at night to avoid enemy observation. Nevertheless, the Germans had all of the roads and crossroads zeroed in with their artillery and were shelling at night as well as during the day. Sometimes they would send up a flare to spot our road traffic.

One night a shell landed so close that my ears were ringing for fifteen minutes. I traveled over the evacuation route without lights. Moonlight helped on some nights, but on others my orderly, Wonga, a Maori from New Zealand, had to walk in front of the ambulance to help us stay on the track and avoid some of the shell and potholes. Patients with stomach wounds or broken bones were particularly sensitive to any jarring, but it was almost impossible to avoid causing them additional pain. The groans of the wounded and the sounds of machine gun and shellfire created a lot of tension. One AFS driver said, "The whole journey was uncanny—a sort of naked feeling—your progress being watched by countless pairs of enemy eyes."

On our return trips to the ADS we passed through our own artillery on either side on Route 6. Shortly after that, moving toward Cassino, we would pass a large sign with the message, "Achtung! Why go further, only Jerry lives down yonder." At night I would use this as an indicator that I was getting close to the turnoff to our ambulance track. The sign was put up after a female news correspondent got too close to the front and was killed.

A few days after our arrival at the New Zealand ADS, Joe, my dugout mate, was wounded when a shell landed next to his ambulance, filling it full of holes and killing a patient in the back. I had the job of evacuating Joe over the same area where he had been wounded.

The ambulance track from the ADS to the MDS linked up with Route 6 in front of our artillery near Monte Trocchio. One night I arrived at this point in the midst of an artillery duel with the Germans. The noise was deafening and the gun flashes blinding. While I was passing through our gun emplacements, I was flagged down by a soldier who asked me to pick up wounded. I already had a full load of patients, no additional stretchers, and no bandages. Nevertheless, we piled the more seriously wounded on the floor of the ambulance. The blood was running out the back door. I can only hope that they all survived. At least they were still alive when I delivered them to the MDS.

On March 15th the New Zealand troops attempted to break through the German lines and capture the town of Cassino as well as the Abbey on top of Monte Cassino. A massive bombing of the Abbey, which the Allies believed was being used as a German observation post, preceded the attack. Allied officers were standing in a field watching the beginning of the bombardment. As I drove by them, they began diving to the ground. Then a shock wave lifted the rear of my ambulance off the roadway. Several of the bombers had mistaken the target and dropped their bombs behind our lines, killing a number of allied personnel.

I watched the bombs landing on the Abbey for several hours, followed by dive-bombing on the slopes below and wondered how the New Zealand troops were doing. Towards the end of the day a tank came up the road and reported that the bomb craters were so large that they couldn't get through to support the troops.

Following the failure of the New Zealand attack and the inability of the Allies to break out of the beach head at Anzio, there came an extended period of relative calm. During this time there occurred a build up of troops, equipment, and supplies in anticipation of the next attempt to break through the German defenses. The attack finally began on May 12th, preceded by a six-hour artillery barrage. The casualties on both sides were very high. The commanding officer of my platoon was killed.

This time the Allies prevailed, and there began the long and very difficult task of pushing the Germans northward and ultimately out of Italy. The Germans made good use of the mountainous terrain to set up a series of defensive lines to be overcome and so the battles continued through the rest of 1944 and on into the spring of 1945.

My fifteen-month tour of duty was almost up when we reached Siena, just south of Florence. Having spent more than four months within range of German artillery fire as well as suffering chronic fatigue and intestinal problems, I was ready to return home!

Born in New Jersey, Allan attended Rutgers University, where he received his PhD in 1950. He later taught agronomy at Clemson College 1950-1954 and at the University of New Hampshire 1954-1980, where he was also Vice President 1971-1988. He later played various roles at Whittier College, the University of New Hampshire Foundation, Duke University, and University of Washington 1965-1966.

Home Front

Life During World War II

ESTHER BERKOWITZ

I HAVE RECOLLECTIONS of several aspects of World War II.
I experienced some inconveniences as the wife of Lt. Harry Berkowitz. Housing was in short supply around many bases. One attic apartment we rented for a month had a kitchen that didn't look right. I discovered there was no sink. Dishes had to be washed in the bathtub! Another apartment had a special refrigerator. When I pushed the door with my foot, a hole appeared. It was cardboard with enamel over it. We were able to repair it.

The nuclear bombs dropped on Japan have a special meaning for me. My husband was on Okinawa ready for the conventional invasion. He and millions of others, on both sides, were spared by this US action.

He was on the USS *Missouri* at the time of the Japanese surrender. He said one of the Japanese signers was so upset with the situation that he vomited.

During the war, Harry lost forty pounds because he did not want to eat pork. He felt uneasy being the only Jew in many assignments, and had to cope with some hostility.

At the end of the war I was pregnant, due in early September. If the baby was born by September 2, Harry would have gotten ten extra points toward hastening his discharge. The baby arrived two days later, and we coped until Harry was discharged in March.

Housing was still short in the New York City area at the end of the war. Consequently, we (three by then) lived with Harry's brother, his wife and daughter, and sister. When we heard of an apartment becoming available a few months later, we took it before even looking at it!

After living in the New York City area for several years, Esther moved to Florida. She and her husband loved to travel, chalking up ninety Elderhostel trips. Esther is a soprano, and has sung in many choruses, currently with the RiverWoods Chorus.

Celebrations

JOAN BROWN
As told to Jack Taylor

IN AUGUST 1945, my family was able to vacation at our summer place in North Lovell, Maine, and prepare for my wedding there. We had no electricity and difficult radio reception. Consequently, we were a little late in hearing about the end of the war. Even though gas was in short supply, my father splurged to put some in the boat and motored around the lake with a megaphone to shout the good news!

Tires were well worn by then, but several guests made it to the wedding. Everyone left so that we could spend our honeymoon there. Eventually some neighbors learned that we wanted to drive up Mt. Washington as part of our celebration, but couldn't because of the threadbare tires on our car.

One evening, there came the knock on the door. It was one of the neighbors, who offered the use of his pickup truck for our expedition up the mountain. He was pretty sure that his tires were adequate—and they were.

Born in Mt. Vernon, Ohio, Joan was educated at Wheaton College, the US Cadet Nurse Corps at Mt. Auburn Hospital, Cambridge, Massachusetts, and at Northeastern University. Her hobbies are bridge, following the financial news, ice dancing, and watching figure skating, swimming, and gymnastics. Her volunteer work included PTA and the Lake Kezar Watershed Association.

A Driver's Education

BETTY COLLIER

I DID NOT learn to drive at the usual time. My widowed mother needed the only car and the rationing of gas further delayed my driving education. When Stan and I were married in 1945, his mother loaned us her car and we headed slowly toward Newport News, Virginia, where Stan would report for duty on the USS *Solomon*. He rented an apartment for us and there began my acquaintance with heat, humidity, cockroaches, and Dr. Pepper.

Stan dropped the keys to the big Buick in my hand and wished me luck. I was a twenty-one year old non-driver. I walked to the nearest gas station only to discover that all drivers' schools had closed for the duration of the war. However, the garage owner kindly offered to teach me in his smaller car. He had enough gasoline left so was able to provide for my lessons for about a week. He offered to drive me in his car to my appointment for the license test. I cheerfully accepted the wee slip of paper, the temporary certificate of a driver's license, with a sigh of relief.

As luck would have it, the ship's orders came too quickly and the wives were to go south and meet the ship in Mayport, Florida. The first impossible task was to board the Newport News Ferry. I was petrified to park so near the other cars, and if first in line, thinking I would drive right into the water!

The captain's wife was to be chauffeured by a sailor, and she offered to have him drive the Buick for the ferry ride challenge. We met somewhere beyond the Norfolk city congestion and I was to follow them. They drove a bit too fast for my new-driver skills, but I managed to keep up until I saw the sailor make a left turn, through a yellow signal light. That was my undoing! Too many things at once: braking, shifting down, signaling, and turning left. The local policeman was kind when he realized I was such a new driver who didn't even have a real driver's license and had to drive to Florida. Poor young Navy wife with no map and no directions to Mayport, Florida. He noted the tears in my eyes and said, "Never mind, dearie, there is only one road to Florida. We'll find your captain's wife and the sailor."

Of course they had stopped and waited a few miles down the road, but were a bit surprised to see the friendly cop and me pulling up behind them.

Eventually I arrived in Florida, in one piece, and quite an experienced driver.

Born and raised in Glastonbury, Connecticut, Betty graduated from Smith College. While in college she met Stan Collier whom she later married. His career took Betty and their family to live in several places: Rochester, New York; Ann Arbor, Michigan; Scotland; and Orlando, Florida. Betty's great loves are her family, playing golf, and Scotland.

War Concerns In Nebraska

JOAN DARLINGTON

M Y SISTER and I were in school in Lincoln, Nebraska, when World War II finally arrived. Our father had been in World War I, and he was keenly interested in international affairs. He read the New York Times daily and he consulted the Congressional Record frequently.

I remember one day when he came thundering up the front steps, calling my mother with his bad news voice. I asked what happened. "A new dictator," he said. "Is he worse than Mussolini?" I asked. "Yes, because Germany is a more powerful country than Italy," my father replied.

Neither my sister nor I learned to drive while we were in high school. Our old car had to last indefinitely so that my father could drive to work at the university. Mostly my sister and I walked to school, a distance of two or three miles. I enjoyed the walk and we could save money for war bonds by doing so. But at night after "sock hops" we had to depend on a bus, and bus service ended early in the evening. The high school prom was cancelled for several years.

On his trips to work my father often took a friend and colleague, and they would discuss the war and its implications. Sometimes I rode with them. I learned a lot from their discussions. The friend persuaded my father to give a course on the background of the war to a group of Air Force cadets stationed at a nearby air base. My father loved teaching those young men. Their eager questions pleased him. For the course, the military provided huge brown maps, four feet square, and my father asked me to color them so that important features would show from a distance. Thus I learned the importance of rivers and of towns reached by a double track railroad.

Victory gardening during the war led to my life-long love of growing vegetables. We also did busy work like picking lint off bandages to help the war effort. We baked bread and we lost the taste of sugar. We lost friends who moved away for war jobs in other places. We knew grieving sisters of killed or missing soldiers.

Later in the war when my sister and I went to college, we found college filled with GI Bill soldiers and widows. There were seven unmarried girls to every unmarried boy. Harvard was so short of students that my older sister got a huge scholarship to bring western students east. She was able to bike around empty Cambridge streets.

My mother, as the daughter of two American artists, had grown up on the northern coast of France. As D-Day approached, both my parents worried about the terrible losses that a Normandy landing would entail. In Nebraska they watched the tides and the full moon information as they knew that was the best time for a landing. Sure enough, the landing occurred on the first day of a full moon.

At the end of the war we worried about the atom bomb. I heard the doubts of one scientist who thought the atmosphere could be turned into flames. I heard about the Holocaust of the Jews and other scary details of that period. I listened in fear to the great winds crossing Nebraska.

After the war my grandmother wrote and sent CARE packages to her former maid, Marie. Later still she went back to France to search for the grave of my grandfather who had died in 1914. She never found it. Perhaps it had been destroyed in one of the wars.

Born in Pullman, Washington, Joan attended the University of Nebraska and received a BFA Degree from The School of the Art Institute of Chicago. She has been a teacher of arts and crafts and an illustrator of children's books as well as spending six years in New York City as an artist. She has also taught in Dover, Massachusetts, and Lake Placid, New York.

A Boy's Take On The War

Bob Gustavson
As told to Margo Harvey

I GREW UP in Pontiac, Michigan, which was the heart of the auto country at the time. I was just a little guy then, about eight years old. My father was a highly skilled machinist in the plant, which of course had been converted to produce tanks and half-tracks and carrier busses and so forth. He knew the kind of equipment that was needed. He also had some asthmatic problems, so he was not eligible to go to war, but his experience and skills were highly required in the plant. He was also assistant air raid warden in our neighborhood. My family consisted of my parents and one brother, four years younger.

We had a small, relatively new neighborhood; maybe eighty families in small two-bedroom houses, with a lot of woods around where we kids could just play freely. There were about six of us boys, and we had our little makeshift guns, sometimes made out of cardboard, usually some sort of wood, and we would pretend that we were in the Service fighting. We were always the good guys, of course. The road up to northern Michigan where they had the proving grounds and testing areas ran not far from us, and when we heard the rumbling from the tanks and the half-tracks coming toward us, all the little boys ran out to the highway to watch and salute the guys who were moving all this equipment up to the testing grounds and points of embarkation.

We used to have a lot of formations of aircraft flying directly over us, following I guess the same road going north out of the big aircraft manufacturing center down in Detroit. Willow Run I think was the plant that built the planes. We would always run out to see these big flights of planes go by.

As kids we didn't know exactly what was going on but we knew there were really two wars, one in Europe and one on the other side of the world in the Pacific area. All those little islands that had names you couldn't even pronounce.

Of course we heard the radio announcements every night at dinner; there were two or three news reporters I remember specifically, and things that were talked about, like the D-Day invasion of Normandy and the Battle of the Bulge. The war I was familiar with was in Europe, where we had ancestors. My grandmother in fact lived in Sweden, and several of my uncles and aunts, so we were aware of what was happening when the Germans marched through Sweden and into Norway. That made a lasting impression on a lot of Swedes in the US, I tell you. There was a great effort among the Swedish lodges and the ladies' aid societies and so forth to provide bandages and blankets and sheets and towels. My mother, who was a very fine seamstress, would get together with other ladies and make up these big packages of different things and send them over. We were pretty proud of that effort.

I remember a lot of specific things we as kids had to do to help the war effort. We had to take all tin cans, for example, wash them out, cut both ends out and stick them inside, then step on them and flatten them. We'd put these in a bag and take them to school, and we had a contest between grades to see who got the most pounds of tin cans. There was a drive to save newspaper, and any scrap metal we could find—an old stake, or fencing or anything like that—we'd gather it up and take it to the scrap yard. It was a pretty major effort. We had a special kind of fund-raising, for the purpose of buying—paying for—one of those so-called ducks that were made there in Pontiac, the amphibious vehicles that go in water and also on land. I clearly remember the one sitting in front of our school: that was the one we were going to be buying. It was there as an incentive, and it was pretty striking.

In our neighborhood we had several young men who were in the Army or the Navy or the Air Corps. Our neighbor across the street had two boys in the Service, one in the Navy and one in the

Army. The one in the Army I knew quite well. He brought things home for me, like his insignias when he got promoted to whatever the next level was, he'd bring me his old stripes and I'd have them sewn onto my shirt and wear those proudly. His brother brought me a navy hat, one of the old original ones that stood up and you'd pull it down over your ears. Both of those boys got back all right at the end of the war. But one of our neighbors died. I think he was a tail gunner in a B-29 or something; he got shot up pretty badly and did not make it home. He had a son who was a little younger than I was, so we felt very badly about that, that was a tough one. A couple of the other families had boys missing in action; one was found, the other was never found. Their mothers had their gold stars in the window. It was a pretty close neighborhood, so everybody knew what was going on with their children.

It's a pretty distant memory now, but a very distinct memory for me when the war ended in 1945. We all had our bicycles decked out with streamers and red, white, and blue crepe paper. We rode around the neighborhood in a big parade. There were all kinds of shouting and joy. It probably meant more than we realized, but we were in it and did it. Of course, that was the most fun part of the whole deal when it was over.

Bob grew up in Pontiac, Michigan, earned a BS at Michigan State University, went on to Duke for a Master's Degree in Natural Resources Management, where he found Willie, his wife-to-be, and finally to Harvard Business School for his MBA. He then worked for several firms, mostly in the Boston area, in venture capital, acquisitions, and mergers. Wanting finally to work in a non-profit setting, he moved to LaJolla, California, and then back to Concord, Massachusetts, where for fifteen years he was business manager for two large independent schools. The Gustavsons have a son and a daughter.

Memories Of Auburn, Maine

FRANK GUTMANN

I WAS SIX YEARS OLD when the war began, so what I now remember of the home front is somewhat thin.

My father was in the administration of a woolen cloth manufacturing company that was considered important to the war effort. It made cloth for Navy pea coats, among other things. When there was a local threat of sabotage he received a permit to carry a handgun.

I was at a boys' summer camp, probably in 1942, when my father came to visit me. This time he came alone, usually Mother came also. We took a walk in the woods and he told me that he was going to go to war. I don't recall if he said that he would become an officer in the Army Air Corps.

In earlier months he had been active in some sort of home guard activity. I think it was called the Motor Corps. We had a small metal sign attached to the front bumper of the car, and also to the front of his motorcycle. Both vehicles had large first aid kits. Both my parents had first aid training and were qualified to teach others. I recall they sometimes wore armbands, and my father sometimes wore a metal helmet and carried a club as he rode around on his motorcycle. My mother continued in the Motor Corps after my father left for the war.

We equipped each window in the house with a blackout screen made of wallboard and fitted very tightly. Not long after my father left, my mother and I went to live nearby with her parents. Food and gasoline were rationed, and we had books of coupons. When my father was stationed at Fort Devens in Massachusetts he would sometimes come home for a weekend's leave. His gasoline was also rationed, and I recall his telling of some deal to get extra coupons so that he could buy the gas to drive home.

I had an uncle, later to become a leader in the Maine government, who was also stationed close enough to come home, usually by train. The whole family would go to the train station, either to greet him or to see him off when he left. He was fluent in languages, and when he went up through Italy with Patton's tanks, he served as an interpreter for his unit.

As the months passed we became more and more conscious of the war. My wife recalled that, as a seven year old, when she first learned about the fighting, she asked her mother whether or not the war would reach them by Christmas. As time passed we understood her answer better as more and more small flags were displayed in house windows; each flag with one or more stars, each star representing a member of the family who was in the military.

My friends and I had decks of cards, called spotter cards, with silhouettes of aircraft, both American and enemy planes, so that we could identify any plane that flew over. We studied these judiciously. Every new package of margarine was sealed in a plastic bag containing a capsule of orange dye. The margarine was white and we had to squeeze the bag, break the capsule, and then kneed the bag to distribute the dye evenly until the margarine resembled butter.

My father was in the intelligence service and was stationed in Iceland. Being a good intelligence officer, he told us almost nothing about what he did. The only story I recall was when a German was picked up after he came ashore from a submarine. He was held in the local prison while being interrogated. My father, who could speak German, volunteered to dress up as another German captive, to be put into the cell with the first man, and to attempt to befriend him and possibly learn something of military importance from this friendship. That's all my father ever told us.

Following graduation from Philips Exeter Academy, Frank earned his BA from Amherst College and Master's degrees from both Yale and Bowdoin. He married the late Lois McGee; they had a son and a daughter. Frank's lifetime career has been as a teacher of mathematics at Philips Exeter Academy. He became involved in the early stages of the creation of RiverWoods, serving on its Board of Trustees until 2003. Frank is a master color photographer, and also participates in choral singing. In what is left of his spare time Frank likes to canoe on white water, or else go cross-country skiing in the white woods.

Joys And Sorrows

Betty Ivanowsky

DURING WW II, I worked as a nurse for the Hartford Visiting Nurse Association (VNA) in a district with a Public Housing Project. In order for a family to qualify for a unit in the project a member of the family had to be in the service or a worker in one of the many factories producing war materials. The residents were mostly young people who worked in one of the defense plants. They came from outside New England or from farms in northern New England. The wages were good but the hours long. Most of the factories operated twenty-four hours a day with twelve-hour shifts.

The men were seldom home except to sleep. Care of their children and household chores were the responsibility of their young wives. It was a lonesome time for these women until they made new friends and learned the ways of their new neighborhood. The wives of the men away from home and in the service had an exceptionally hard time.

The VNA made home visits to newborns and invalids. We gave moral and practical assistance to these young mothers. We ran a Well Child Health Clinic twice a week in our district. Once a month a doctor visited our district. Because of the gas shortage the VNA purchased some bikes for the nurses to use instead of cars. I used a bike. This was a time before most women wore slacks, so we had girls' bikes with a basket for our little black bags.

My father was an air raid warden during the war. He would go out into a very dark neighborhood with no streetlights to be sure no lights were showing from the windows of the houses. Everyone had blackout shades that were heavier than regular window covers. Connecticut was a vulnerable area for attack because Colt Fire-arms, Pratt and Whitney Aircraft Engines, and Sikorsky Helicopter factories were located there.

By the year 1943 the war had been going on for several years. People were tired of travel restrictions, gas stamps, food stamps, shoe stamps, and blackouts, etc. It was also a year of great sadness and loss in my family, but also of great joy.

My brother, Lt. Roger Norton Starks, was stationed on a subma-rine operating out of a base in Key West, Florida. On June 13, 1943, our minister came to tell us that he had had a call from my sister-in-law saying my brother's sub with a crew of forty had been sunk. There were five survivors, but my brother was not one of them. My brother was second in command of the sub. The captain's wife was not at the base, so my sister-in-law, pregnant and grieving, stayed on to help the other young wives, making arrangements for their transportation home. Finally, she came to Connecticut to see our family and collect her things. Then she headed for her home in California to have her baby.

My other brother was in the South Pacific on the carrier *Chanan-go*. He flew as a gunner on a torpedo bomber. When he returned from the South Pacific he stopped in Pasadena to see his widowed sister-in-law and his new niece, Elaine.

My fiancé and I had set an August 14, 1943, date for our wed-ding. I had selected a gown, attendants, flowers for the church, and a friend to sing. There was to be a reception in the church hall. No one was in the mood for a celebration, but our parents encour-aged us to go ahead. The flowers went to the church, the organist played our requests, and we omitted the soloist. There were twenty-four guests, no attendants, and two ushers. My dad in a white suit walked me down the aisle and gave me away. The groom was also in a white suit. I had returned my wedding gown but did find a long white dress and wore a short veil fastened to my mother's wedding tiara. We returned to my house after the ceremony for wedding cake, fruit punch, and a pleasant time. My uncle had put pebbles in our hubcaps. We left for Lake George making a very loud rattling noise and leaving a group of laughing people behind.

At this time there was a ban on pleasure driving. We were allowed to drive only to and from work with exceptions for emergencies. We applied to the local Office of Price Administration and received a permit to go on our honeymoon. It was a great time to be on the road as there was little traffic.

Born and raised in Hartford, Connecticut, Betty graduated from the school of nursing at Simmons College. After the war, she did volunteer work with the Red Cross as a nursing instructor and helped with blood drives. She also did work with the Girl Scouts. She and her husband retired to a home in Walden, Vermont, and after his death Betty moved to Exeter.

Memories

ALICE KINTNER

IN JUNE OF 1941, my father, an Army Reserve officer who had been on the front lines in France during World War I, closed his law office to go on active duty in the US Army. On December 7, 1941, my mother had not yet left their home in Ohio to join him in Louisiana where he was on maneuvers with General Eisenhower. So it was that Dad was working alone in his office late on Sunday night of Pearl Harbor. It wasn't until about eleven o'clock when he returned to his barracks that he first heard the news. He, who was one of the first to see that war was coming and to take personal action, was one of the last to hear when it did arrive.

We heard of the Japanese attack on Pearl Harbor about 5 p.m. on Sunday afternoon, December 7. On Monday morning, as part of my training at the Prince School of Retailing, a graduate program at Simmons College in Boston, I was working as a floor manager in the toy department at Halle's Department Store in Cleveland, Ohio.

Not a man of military age was in the store that morning. They were all signing up for the military and to go to war! This was before President Roosevelt had a chance to address the nation or Congress to declare war, which it did that afternoon. The event galvanized the country.

In 1942 I was living with my parents in Arlington, Virginia, just a few miles from Ft. Meyers where we had privileges to go to the movies—first run movies—for seven cents. Several rows ahead of us and maybe twenty feet away sat General George Marshall, alone.

It was well known General Marshall had cancelled all engagements in Washington for the duration of the war. Apparently, his only recreation when he wasn't running the war or advising the President was seeing the movies whether the film was good or bad.

Born and raised in northeastern Ohio, Alice graduated from Mount Union College in Alliance, Ohio. She did graduate work at Simmons College, and earned a Master's degree in Education at the University of Pittsburgh. Alice taught high school English at public schools in Pennsylvania, Maine, and Virginia, and later at The Madeira School outside Washington, DC. In retirement Alice and her husband Ed lived in Vermont and later moved to Exeter, New Hampshire.

Cardboard Wedding Shoes!

Jean Latchis
As told to Alice Kintner

MY FIANCÉ was stationed at Mitchell Field on Long Island. When he had leave, I would meet him at Penn Station in New York City. He was a pilot and loved flying. We wanted to wait until the war ended to get married, but as the war had not ended by 1944, we decided not to wait to get married.

Three pairs of shoes a year were all that people were allowed to buy under rationing. While I wanted a nice pair of shoes for my wedding, I did not want to use my allotment for a pair of shoes I probably would wear only once. Fortunately, I found a pair of shoes that were made of cardboard with a satin top, and they did not count as one of the three pairs I was allowed to purchase.

We moved to Long Beach, California, where my father-in-law found us an apartment. We ate many of our meals at the Officer's Club, as I was not a very good cook. My husband flew new planes to the troops in the Pacific Theater, and returned to California with old planes.

Born in New York, New York, Jean graduated from Beaver College with an AB in Economics. She was married in 1944 and raised two children. She was active in civic organizations in several places: Dublin, New Hampshire; Northfield, Massachusetts; and Brattleboro, Vermont. She also had time for gardening, swimming, and tennis. Jean died in 2011.

Cape Cod 1941–1945

HELEN LAUENSTEIN

IT WAS A Sunday afternoon and our church choir had traveled to the local radio station to sing. As we were leaving we were ushered over to read messages coming in on a telegraph machine… Japanese planes were bombing Pearl Harbor! None of us believed it to be real, only something the station had cooked up to demonstrate their machine. By Monday afternoon we knew it was real, as the strong, but emotional, voice of President Roosevelt resonated throughout our school auditorium.

Our family lived in Orleans, Massachusetts, on the lower Cape which was the location of a French cable station where messages traveled by underwater cable between Orleans and Brest, France. A contingent of black soldiers arrived to patrol the cable station. My mother issued orders for me to deliver food and hot coffee to them in the cold weather. Several people did not think this was an appropriate activity, but my mother was undaunted. (It was my first encounter with black people and racism.)

Orleans is surrounded by the Atlantic on one side and Cape Cod Bay on the other. The Atlantic Ocean along our coast was home to German submarines, sighted close to shore on a number of occasions, causing steps to be taken to protect our shores. My father and his twin brother, having served in World War I, volunteered in the Massachusetts State Guard, created to stand guard over the state.

Convoys of army trucks loaded with soldiers often came by our home headed for a camp in Wellfleet, further out on the Cape. An offshore lobsterman, good friend of my father, rescued a boatload of survivors from their torpedoed ship right off Orleans. He refused to inhibit his fishing, though often reporting submarines close by during these years. Shortly before the end of the war a large hospital ship was torpedoed off shore. The Cape and the beaches were shut off as many bodies washed ashore.

Listening posts were set up to look for possible enemy planes and on many Sunday afternoons our family volunteered to staff one such post in East Dennis. People were warned to close window shades at night and to watch for possible aliens coming ashore along our coastline. People with German sounding names were suspect and rumors abounded. I think I was too young to be afraid, but the war definitely impacted life on Cape Cod during these years.

Helen was born in Boston, Massachusetts, and graduated from Tufts University with a degree in Biochemistry in 1949. That same year she married Navy veteran, Milt Lauenstein. They lived in several Midwestern states before returning to New England, where she owned a travel agency and raised four children. Helen was active in numerous civic and social groups in Gloucester, Massachusetts, and has continued those endeavors as a resident at RiverWoods.

Spies In Maine?

CONNIE BROWN LOVELL

Caution on the Home Front

ONE OF THE furthest-out islands from Mt. Desert Island in Maine is Great Cranberry Isle. During the war many summer homes were closed on account of transportation difficulties. As my father was walking along the shore path one day, he met a man who, when asked about a path to the beach, said it was not a good way to get there because it was swampy and dangerous with quicksand. This was not the case as my father walked down the thickly wooded pathway, finding no quicksand, but rather a spring with a cup near it, and not far off a notched stick with a piece of paper stuck on it. Out of curiosity he picked up the paper and found it was the weather report section torn out of yesterday's Boston newspaper. It seemed to have been put there for some special purpose. Could it have been information for a submarine crew that could easily get ashore at night for fresh water and information? My father kept the paper and reported what he had seen to the Coast Guard at Southwest Harbor, the nearest town.

We were very aware of the need for precautions here at home. We knew of the many towers along the New England coast where volunteers were regularly on watch for enemy boats and planes. These were dedicated folks who memorized silhouettes of aircraft and spent hours keeping vigil. Homes were required to have black shades to keep lights from glowing at night and aiding unfriendly navigators.

In the current time when we are seeing increased security at airports and office buildings, it is interesting to remember that this is not the first time we Americans have had to guard lives, as well as freedom, on our own soil.

Spies Ahoy!

In July 1944 our five brothers were either in the service or working in war plants. Only our parents and we three sisters traveled from our home in Rhode Island to our usual vacation spot on Echo Lake, Mount Desert Island in Maine.

One morning the three of us were paddling up the lake and came to a small island. We noticed a cabin on the island. It seemed deserted so we landed and cautiously approached the cabin, looking through the window. The door was open to this small one-room building.

Strewn on a small table were papers with Japanese writing and the shipping section of the New York Times from the previous day. It wasn't hard to imagine what might be going on. Someone had been there recently and had left in a hurry. They couldn't have competed with the dash we made to get back to our parents!

My father reported our finding to the Coast Guard and later to the FBI. We never heard anything about the cabin, but I like to think we girls had a part in the war effort.

Connie married Ray Lovell shortly after the war. They had three sons and a daughter. Equipped with her Bachelor of Science in Nutrition and Child Development from the University of Rhode Island, Connie pursued a career in kindergarten and elementary school teaching wherever, among several Eastern cities, Ray was posted. She was an enthusiastic home maker (she helped build two houses) and community builder wherever she lived: Cub Scout den mother, Girl Scout leader, Sunday school teacher. Among other activities, Connie remains a leader of the RiverWoods Needle Workers.

Twins In Blue

RUTH MANGHUE
(on the left)

IN THE SUMMER of 1942 my twin sister and I, both teachers, were traveling to Kansas City, Missouri, to visit our older sister. As was our custom, we were dressed alike in blue dresses. On the train we met a group of Navy men who were heading to the Great Lakes Naval Training Center and we all had a four-hour wait in Chicago. We decided to go to Marshall Field department store and so we followed along with the Navy men in uniform. On the trolley they did not have to pay any fare and when we boarded and tried to pay, the conductor also waved us through, thinking because we were both in blue we must be part of the Navy group.

I bought a key chain at Marshall Field and we returned to the train station. Again the trolley car conductor would not let us pay, thinking we were part of the Navy contingent. We continued on to Kansas City, and I still have my key chain.

Ruth earned a BS in Education in the portentous year 1941, and plunged at once into secondary school teaching in several towns in eastern Massachusetts. Starting in the mid-50's she taught at Lasell Junior College in Newton, Massachusetts, for fifteen years, and earned a Master's from Teachers College, Columbia University, along the way. In the later years of Ruth's career she was Professor of Business Education at Salem State College. Ruth's work happily allowed her time to see the world. She has visited every continent except Antarctica.

War Work On The Home Front

PHEBE PERRY MIXTER

AFTER GRADUATING from Vassar College in 1942 I returned home to Cincinnati, Ohio, where I became fully involved in the war effort—working at the Baldwin Piano Company.

James Mixter had begun his career after college at Baldwin and had worked his way up to be in charge of personnel. He was unable to serve in the military because of previous, serious mastoid problems. With the conversion of Baldwin, from making pianos to making sections of airplane wings for training airplanes, Jim was in need of people to work in the factory—a great many of whom were women.

Because of my college math major and the fact that I could do some mechanical drawing I was hired as a draftsman, and spent the next two years employed on the home front. I was in charge of the Charts and Schedules and had to keep all the details updated every day. Because I dealt with all departments I was constantly on the run throughout the five-story building to keep the executives and department heads apprised of where we stood on each section of airplane wing that we manufactured.

Jim Mixter and I were married in 1944. The war ended in 1945 and we stayed in Cincinnati for the next thirty-five years, moving to New Hampshire permanently in 1979. Baldwin went back to making pianos and Jim remained with them for a total of forty years.

A native of Cincinnati, Phebe graduated from Vassar having majored in mathematics and architecture. She went to work in her home town for the Baldwin Piano Company, where she met her late husband, Jim. They had three children. Phebe found time for civic associations and hobbies of flower arranging, needlepoint, knitting, and fishing. Phebe died in 2010.

Wartime Efforts

Marian Smith Sharpe

The World's Fastest Plane

I WAS RECENTLY awakened in the night with 'Pratt Whitney Twin Wasp Engine' on my mind. I lay awake, these sixty-one years later, recalling the source of those unlikely words.

In 1943 I left high school typing 80-85 words per minute on an L.C. Smith manual typewriter. This skill, noted on an application, was viewed with favor by potential employers.

In 1944 I made application for employment to the Guggenheim Aeronautics Laboratory at the California Institute of Technology in Pasadena, California. After an intensive interview that included close questioning as to my loyalty to the United States, I was hired. I was told my employment qualified as a top secret 'war job' and that I was 'frozen' to the job for the duration of the war. My pay was fifty cents an hour.

My office space was a small makeshift arrangement with a tall stool for reaching the typewriter that sat on a high drafting table. At one end of the room was something called a film-reading machine and at the other end a window—which reassured me that I wasn't in a closet after all. Two men from Lockheed locked the door and explained the need for secrecy. Under the brick Guggenheim building was a wind tunnel currently testing what would be the fastest plane in the world. Instruments recorded the testing and those configurations were first computed, then plotted, and the final results given to me for typing. I soon came to understand that I would be working alone in a locked room, perched on a stool while laboring over a totally unfamiliar keyboard that included Greek and algebraic symbols. So much for the 80-85 words per minute.

It was a year or so later that the top-secret plane during my tenure was, indeed, identified as the world's fastest airplane (350 mph) with Lockheed's Pratt Whitney Twin Wasp engine—the P-38.

Bataan Survivors

In 1945 I moved to San Francisco where I boarded with a delightful Irish couple on Hemway Terrace. Their son was in the Army in Germany and they were willing to rent his bedroom for the duration of his tour of duty.

I was newly employed at I. Magnin & Co. as a model and stockroom girl in the elegant French Room on the 3rd floor. The room was always fragrant with fresh flowers in crystal bowls. From time to time I was called upon to model a garment for a customer but was otherwise confined to stockroom duties.

Chatter on the morning bus to work further confirmed the radio news at breakfast—a Navy ship was underway carrying survivors of the 1942 Bataan Death March. The ship was expected to arrive at noon in San Francisco; the soldiers would be transferred to city buses for travel along Market Street enroute to the Army's Letterman General Hospital at the Presidio. Volunteers were needed to help at the hospital. At noon I left my employment, with no plan to return, and joined the crowd of well wishers who were both welcoming and subdued in keeping with the tenor of the soldiers' ill health, culture shock, and travel fatigue.

Some seventy-six thousand soldiers, many close to death, were forced to walk sixty-six miles in the hottest season of the year with no shade, little food, and almost no water. If, for any reason, the soldier stopped marching, he risked being killed by bayonet or rifle. The butt of a rifle fractured skulls and Japanese tanks would run over men who fell. As many as eleven thousand men died along the way marching to their ultimate destination, a prison camp where they were held prisoner for three years. One soldier said, "To be on this march was what it must feel like to come to the end of civilization."

Hundreds of well-wishers lined the Golden Gate Bridge and beneath the bridge a fleet of fireboats lay ready to surround the ship with a spectacular water display of welcome.

San Francisco's mayor was making arrangements for the city's official welcome that included the striking of a special silver medallion, a gift to the survivors from the City of San Francisco. Lunch at the elegant Palace Hotel would fete the soldiers and their families. Attending the occasion would be high-ranking officers paying tribute to their fellow soldiers.

The first available city bus was quickly filled with eager volunteers responding to the urgent radio requests. We arrived at Letterman Army Hospital to the heart-breaking sight of soldiers in soiled, torn clothing, sitting on the floor of a very long corridor. Doctors were assessing their condition as best they could to determine who among them required immediate attention, and those well enough to board an airplane or a hospital train for medical care near their home. Many of the survivors arrived ill with diseases indigenous to the tropical Philippines; wet beriberi, dengue fever, yellow jaundice, scurvy, dry beriberi—an assortment of illnesses for which Letterman had no effective medications.

We volunteers were given notebooks and pencils along with instructions to remove the soiled packet on a chain from around the soldier's neck and record the information found there: name, serial number, blood type, DOB, religious preference, home address, phone number. Along with the soldiers we were also on the floor writing in our notebooks or on our knees reaching for, or returning, the canvas packets. These many years later I am reminded that in the 1940s women left home wearing skirts and nylons, likely purchased with a stamp or two from their War Ration book. ("Rosie the Riveter" was a notable exception.) Given the mores of the day we were not dressed to conduct business on the floor.

In time the corridors thinned out and those who were well enough to travel were sent to their homes for follow-up care. A number of volunteers returned to their regular employment while others made application for employment at Letterman. My stenographic skills were acceptable and I, too, became an employee.

Letterman Army Hospital was a busy destination for the Army wounded and sick from the South Pacific and other venues. As the men began recovery they were often in the corridors becoming acquainted with other patients and exchanging stories of their experiences in the war. Two fellows, each with a crutch and one leg, raced down the corridors daily and into the clerical offices with much whooping and hollering. Even the doctors stepped aside when they saw the two of them coming. It was some weeks later when one of the amputees said he was eager to see Abbott & Costello's new movie, *The Naughty Nineties,* and asked if I might like to go with him.

With the doctor's permission, we boarded a bus and went into the city. It was a pleasant enough evening but I was uneasy as my date navigated his way onto the bus, off the bus, up and down the theater slopes and later, in the dark on a poorly lighted, uneven sidewalk in the hospital area. He, of course, managed every challenge perfectly with his one leg and one crutch.

Towards the end of the war, a small stockade was built to house the German and Italian prisoners. Their labor was important for operating the hospital and the extensive park and gardens of the Presidio. We were told in no uncertain terms to ignore the POW's whistles, advances, and in one case, the sentimental love songs in a perfect imitation of Bing Crosby's crooning. It was difficult to hide our amusement at the antics on the park grounds.

The statistics for Letterman are staggering. In 1945 alone, the hospital received seventy-three thousand patients. In 1995 the hospital and Research Institute were deactivated. Neither architecturally significant nor up to seismic standards, it was removed to make room for the Letterman Digital Arts Center that today, along with five hundred historic buildings, occupies the 1,480 acres.

As part of a military reduction program, in 1989 Congress voted to end the Presidio role as an active military installation. It was transferred to the National Park Service, thereby ending 219 years of military use.

Marian was born in Chicago but spent most of her early adult years in California. She was employed by the California Institute of Technology-Pasadena; Letterman Hospital, San Francisco; and the University of California-Berkeley. She was married to Robert Sharpe, a Sacramento lawyer, in 1959 and had two sons. When she was widowed she moved east to be near her sons, first to Ridgefield, Connecticut, and more recently to Exeter, New Hampshire. As a writer, she has created Japanese haiku poetry. Marian has an extensive collection of "coal plate cover" rubbings from her many trips to London.

VJ Day Moment

KATHERINE HOBSON SOUTHWORTH

O<sup>N AUGUST 14, 1945, I was nine years old and living, during the
war years, in Denver, Colorado. The War had been very influ-
ential in many areas of my life. Because I was concerned, and anxious to understand what was going on, I became an avid reader of
newspapers. My mother's two brothers were in the service, serving
on ships overseas. The incentive to find out what was happening in
the world propelled me to skills beyond the usual reading or geog-
raphy challenges of the early school grades.

It was a warm and sunshiny August day when I set forth for the 5
& 10 on Colfax. My quest was a small Mickey Mouse toy that I had
seen in the store, and badly wanted. Problem number one was lack
of funds. But, not to be deterred by such an inconvenient situation
I arrived on the scene and discovered there were two of my wanted
items left on the shelf. Without a lot of lingering or thought, I simply lifted one off the shelf and walked toward the exit. I pushed
open the door, stepped into the sunshine, and took a deep breath.
I was terrified as the realization struck home—I had just stolen
something. My heart was pounding, I felt sick. I thought I had better head for home.

At that very moment, in the sunshine of a Colorado day, every
siren, church bell, automobile horn went off, rang, and blared. The
noise built, got louder. It seemed as if the sound reverberated off
the buildings and off the mountains. I was frozen in place! How
could they have discovered my theft so quickly? And organized police to come for me? I took off like a shot—down the alley, into the
back door of the house, up to my room. Safe. Heart pounding.

As the news came through to me—the War was over. The celebrating had begun in those moments when I had come out of the store.

In time my father determined something big was troubling me. I spilled the story of my crime to him. He was kind in offering to accompany me back to the store to return my stolen item to the manager. I was sure I could not do it. But I did do it and was so thankful that my time in criminal activity was brief.

Then I could be truly thankful that the War was over, and my uncles would come home again, and I didn't need to read the papers quite so thoroughly. Back to being an ordinary nine-year-old with just a memory of that wayward moment.

Born in Boston, Massachusetts, Katherine grew up on the coast of New Hampshire. After college and marriage to Robert Southworth, she lived in New York City where they raised three children and Katherine was involved in the educational arena as Assistant Director of the Episcopal School. Retirement brought them back to New Hampshire where Katherine served in local government and as an EMT on the volunteer ambulance service in North Hampton.

A Foxhole To Play In

Jack Taylor

I REMEMBER MY Dad coming home for lunch and bringing the morning newspaper. He would sit on the couch with Bill, 5, and me, 4, on either side to read the comics to us. I can still see the 6-inch-high letters of a headline one day that prompted Dad to call to Mom in the kitchen, "He's done it again!" That must have been one of Hitler's invasions in 1938. Frequently, we listened to the news with Lowell Thomas. I remember listening to news bulletins about the attack on Pearl Harbor.

Rationing of food and gas was handled by the teachers at the schools in Leominster, Massachusetts. I guess we students had a day off when people in the neighborhood came to the school to sign up for ration books of stamps.

Defense stamps and bonds were promoted to the students. I think I bought a 10-cent stamp every week. We pasted them into special booklets. Sixth graders went around to the various classrooms and handled the collection of orders and cash. Later they delivered the stamps.

My third-grade teacher was the aunt of my classmate John. We went home for lunch, and every afternoon she would ask John if there had been a letter from his older brother, her other nephew. That was 1942-43, so he was in North Africa. He did survive the war.

We saved aluminum foil and flattened tin cans and toothpaste tubes. I remember seeing a large pile of flattened cans beside a railroad siding. I hope they were used eventually. We felt good about saving them.

Even boys were urged to knit squares for afghans. My trapezoids must have been a challenge to the volunteer who tried to assemble the final afghans.

Early in the War, soldiers from nearby Ft. Devens staged a day of maneuvers in Leominster. I suppose they were learning about tactics to be used in the towns of Europe. Part of my family's small woods overlooked a key intersection, so one of the army teams stationed a soldier there in a foxhole. My brother and I hung out there that afternoon and watched the sentry observe the Army vehicles going by. Of course they didn't refill the hole, so we had it to play in later.

I delivered newspapers during part of the war. At age ten, I don't think I read the headlines I was delivering. Victory Gardens were important, and my family had some areas suitable for others to garden. I learned enough about gardening to plant one for our family. Labor was in short supply, so even my neighbor in his 80's worked at a nearby woodworking factory.

My brother has reminded me of the Airplane Spotter's Guide to enemy airplanes. There was a paper silhouette you placed in a little cardboard telescope. The idea was to compare the silhouette with an airplane in the sky and then report somewhere.

VE Day was a big relief. Then came the news of the atomic bombs. My schoolteacher mother was able to explain what an atom is. Finally there was VJ Day. Lots of people gathered in the town square to celebrate.

Born in Leominster, Massachusetts, Jack graduated from Worcester Polytechnic Institute and earned a PhD in physics at MIT in 1961. He then served as a lieutenant at the Army Signal Corps Laboratories, doing research on detecting nuclear tests. He taught at Drexel Institute of Technology and Otterbein College, and programmed computers at Boeing and Microsoft. After retiring from the software industry Jack, with his wife Nancy, moved to Exeter.

Childhood Memories of World War II

Nancy A. Taylor

DURING WW II my father was an air raid warden in our town of Melrose, Massachusetts. This meant that when the siren went off in the middle of the night, he had to go across the street from our house, climb up the rocky hill to the highest place, and look for enemy planes. Meanwhile, my mother would get my brother and me up and take us into my grandmother's bedroom where we would wait until the all clear signal. I can remember asking my mother what my father would do if he did see a German plane, but I have no memory of her answer.

We had dark shades on all the windows in our house that were kept down as soon as we turned on the lights. I also remember my father putting some tape on part of the headlights on the car. It was a treat to ride in the car as gas rationing meant that pleasure rides were not frequent. Weekly grocery trips and sometimes a ride to church were the usual trips in the car. In good weather we would walk the mile or so to church.

During school if the air raid siren blew, the class walked down single file to the basement, and sat against the wall. For a first and second grader, this was a scary experience as we all wanted to be with our families.

Mixing the yellow capsule into the white "oleo" to make it yellow was a fun activity. I loved squeezing the package and watching it turn yellow. Occasionally, my mother would hear that there was butter available in the dairy and egg store in downtown Melrose, so we would walk there and stand in line to purchase the butter.

We had a victory garden like most people. My mother and grandmother would can the vegetables. We would save the fat from cooking, and crush the empty cans of fruits and vegetables.

My uncle was in the Navy, so my grandmother placed one of the banners with a blue star on it in one of the windows. I remember asking her if we could get one with a gold star on it because I thought they were prettier. She told me the gold star meant that the person was killed in the war, so I no longer wanted a gold star banner. My uncle must have been on a ship some place around England or Wales as he met a young widow with a daughter my age. My grandmother corresponded with her, and I became a pen pal with the daughter. We would send CARE packages to them, as meat was scarce.

Buying war stamps in school was a big event. There was a contest to see which of the classrooms sold the most stamps. There was a special flag that was hung in the school if the school sold a certain amount of stamps, but I do not remember the amount. I do know how upset my second grade teacher was when once our school did not meet the goal. She told us we had to do more jobs around the house to earn money so we could buy more stamps the next week.

As a child I had very narrow feet, and because shoes were sometimes in short supply during the war, buying a new pair was usually an all day project. My mother and I would start at the store where my last pair had been bought, but most of the time it was necessary to try several stores until a pair was found that fit me.

On VE day the older boys in the neighborhood hung Hitler in effigy from the lamppost by our house. Lots of people were outside their houses having fun. Everyone was happy. The newspapers had pictures of people being released from the concentration camps. I found these scary and very sad.

Born in Massachusetts, Nancy graduated from Keuka College. She taught various elementary grades in New York, Kansas, and Colorado. Later she received her Master's from Governors State University, Illinois, and started and directed a Child Life Program for the Pediatrics Unit at a community hospital. After twenty years in Washington State, Nancy and her husband Jack moved to Exeter.

Growing Up During World War II

BARBARA TRULSON

A S A FOURTH GRADER I had heard some rumblings about war in Europe. It didn't mean much to me, and little did I guess that this war would later have an impact on my family.

Months later Dad was recalled to the Navy as a lieutenant commander. His assignment was to the USS *Philadelphia*, a light cruiser. At the time his ship was in the Pacific and was traveling back and forth from California to Pearl Harbor. When it came to the US, Mom and some of the other Navy wives would travel to the ports in order to be with their husbands. One time there was a rumor circulating that the ship was coming in to a Pacific port, so many of the wives, including Mom, thought they would surprise the men when the ship arrived. Imagine the surprise, and waste of time and money, when the ship passed through the Panama Canal and on to Boston. Dad came home to see us kids, but he was pretty irate that Mom had wasted that time they could have had together.

Not long after that Pearl Harbor was bombed by the Japanese and with the devastation left we were very glad that the USS *Philadelphia* was now in the Atlantic, and would be there through the rest of the war.

Just in case it ever became necessary, we had air raid drills and blackouts. These weren't very scary, because I knew they were only practice drills and never did become a necessity.

While I was in grade school we were chauffeured back and forth from home to school. We thought this was pretty nice, but it wasn't until years later that we learned that Mom had received some threatening calls about something happening to us if she didn't reveal some information, which she didn't have. There were also times when Mom would hear that the *Philadelphia* had been sunk. She would have to suffer with this information until she received a letter from Dad dated later than the supposed sinking. The wait was usually about a month. Because this happened so often the ship was nicknamed "the Galloping Ghost of the Sicilian Coast."

One day I was sitting on the stone wall of an iris garden where a wedding was taking place—watching as an uninvited guest. My brother came to me and said that Mom wanted me home immediately. I rushed home thinking all along the way that something terrible had happened to Dad and that probably he had been killed.

At the end of the war he returned to Concord with his Navy career behind him, and as a Rear Admiral. Perhaps growing up with a Navy father was tough, but I believe it made me strong.

Born and raised in Concord, New Hampshire, Barbara moved to Iowa after graduating from Colby-Sawyer College and the University of New Hampshire. Other moves took her to Ohio, Maryland, and New York where she worked as a free-lance commercial artist specializing in the design of needlepoint canvases and taught art to handicapped children. Eight of her panels depicting the Old and New Testaments of the Bible hang in the Narthex of the Community Church in Chappaqua, New York. For the last twenty-five years she has lived in Hopkinton, New Hampshire.

War Changes A Women's College

JANET WATSON

I WAS A STUDENT at Smith College in the fall of 1941. Just as for the men, life changed drastically for college girls on December 7th. We had a dance on Saturday the sixth. My date had brought a carload of his Dartmouth classmates, and I arranged dates for his friends. Among them was Win Watson, my future husband. All had a good time. The guys stayed with friends at Amherst College.

On Sunday, there were various social activities, but we all eventually met at Rahar's Bar so the guys could arrange for the rides back to Dartmouth. As we walked in, we noticed how quiet the patrons were. Then we were told of the bombing at Pearl Harbor, and began to feel the sadness and fear of the others.

On Monday many of the guys enlisted! The College was closed that day. That was the first of many changes. Later, Smith helped the war effort by being a training location for a WAVES program. We students were proud of them.

I graduated in 1943 and married Win. We were stationed in Florida where he was in the Army Air Corps.

Born in Chicago, Illinois, Janet moved to California and graduated from Beverly Hills High School. She earned a BA degree in literature at Smith College. Living in Connecticut for many years, and wintering in Florida, she balanced family and civic responsibilities with interests in golf and bridge.

Lend Lease

MARILYN LINDBERG WENTWORTH

A N ECONOMIC stimulus came to my small, mostly Swedish Minnesota hometown, (population 1500, including the patients in the Epileptic Hospital), when the woolen mill received a contract to knit wool socks for the Lend Lease Program.* Previously, the business revolved around the sale of practical rough wool winter clothing, plus selling the service of carding wool out of old clothing to provide wool batting for making winter quilts. The town was still in the depths of the Great Depression.

For the first time, many town women went to work outside the home, knitting socks on machines. It was piecework. The pay was 2 cents a pair, no pay for a machine-caused second, and the women had to pay the mill 2 cents for every operator-caused second. My uncle was very popular with the ladies at the mill because he was responsible for keeping the machines running. No socks = no pay.

After the United States entered the war, a number of defense plants were built around the Twin Cities (Minneapolis and St. Paul) providing more work opportunities. However, government rules required the written consent of the woolen mill owner before one could leave employment at the mill for other government work.

With our entry into the war, many products including food, gas, and tires, were rationed. My mother would swap food stamps with a sister living in Minneapolis. She would give blue stamps (canned goods) in exchange for white stamps (sugar). Sugar was needed for canning the lugs and bushels of fresh fruit which mother canned each summer. Since most of our vegetables came from our large gardens and were consumed fresh, home canned, or preserved in our root cellar, we had little use for the blue stamps required to buy commercially canned vegetables.

A black market and subterfuges commonly arose wherever there were shortages. My best friend's father ran a cattle feed lot in town. As we were leaving for an out-of-town high school football game, he warned us if we stopped for a snack after the game not to buy hamburgers. He said horsemeat and diseased meat were sometimes being sold.

Because my father was working in the defense industry, he qualified for added gas stamps. Car tires were more difficult to obtain and required inspection and special status. Old tires would have to be presented at an inspection station to receive a certificate stating they were unsafe to drive. The tire would then be presented, with the attached certificate, at a tire store and exchanged in order to buy a new tire. The shortage resulted in ingenuity in obtaining the most mileage from the inner tubes and tires. The damaged inner tubes were repaired with heavily glued patches. 'Boots' made from old tires were placed on the inside of a damaged tire to cover holes or cuts.

* Lend Lease was Congressional legislation which enabled President Franklin Roosevelt to sell, transfer, exchange, or loan supplies to the United Kingdom, Soviet Union, China, and France to help them defend themselves. It was passed on March 11, 1941, before the United States entered the war against Japan and the Axis powers.

Born in Isanti County, Minnesota, Marilyn attended the University of Minnesota where she met her future husband, Bob Wentworth. She taught school in Minnesota, Virginia, and Illinois before they began a family of three children. While living in Madison, New Jersey, she served in elected and appointed local government positions. After working on Wall Street for several years, she entered graduate school at age fifty, earning an MS degree in Bio/Nutrition and becoming a Registered Dietitian, followed by teaching college-level nutrition courses. She and Bob lived in Manchester, Vermont, before moving to Exeter.

Minnesota — 1943

ROBERT F. WENTWORTH

THE BOY WAS 13 years old in 1943 and deeply involved in the Boy Scouts. He lived in Rochester, Minnesota, a town of 14,000 persons already famous for the Mayo Clinic, but far from any military operations, except for that mystery building going up in the next block, where the Clinic was to perform "War Work" for the government.

The War, however, was vivid in his imagination. Older boys were leaving home at age 17 for service. His scoutmaster, Mr. Fiksdal, having taught the Boy first aid, rope climbing, and Morse code by flashlight, was being inducted into the Army. Intriguing and aloof older girls in town, attending the Mayo Hospital Nursing Schools, were visited on weekends by army trainees from Wisconsin's Camp McCoy. These young men came on the train Saturdays with overnight passes to return by Sunday night curfew at camp. The town had an airport with a rotating 360-degree beacon light atop the Clinic at about 900 feet. It was kept dark then except for important flights bringing Clinic patients and doctors. The bells in the same tower sounded 9 p.m. curfew for youngsters in town.

The Boy had duties for the War Effort. At the Piggly Wiggly grocery store, where he worked stocking shelves, one of his tasks was to flatten, tie, and stack cardboard for war re-use as pulp. On Saturdays he rode the flatbed of a truck collecting saved and flattened tin cans from the downtown restaurants, hotels, and rooming houses. Then DUTY came in a big assignment!

The Mayo Clinic had plans for a medical detachment as part of the Home Guard. The plans included Air Raid Drill preparations for possible attack. Town residents wondered if that was deemed likely because of the Mayo Clinic mystery building under construction.

Trained and eager, the Boy was assigned as a messenger for a medical doctor who lived in his neighborhood, which had access to the Mayo steam tunnels and underground walkways to hospitals and hotels. During air raid drills the doctor had a helmet and black bag. His wife, a trained nurse, wore a cap and blue cape. Both had trained in Boston and had accents that, to the Boy, sounded definitely English, perhaps from London where Edward R. Murrow reported on air raids.

Well, there was no air raid in rural southern Minnesota, but there was a Boy ready with pencil, spiral notebook, and Boy Scout flashlight.

Years later, Mr. Fiksdal returned from his hike all the way to Berlin and opened a flower store across from St. Mary's Hospital. The Boy used his knowledge of Morse code as an Officer of the Deck and Navigator serving on a US Navy destroyer in the Korean War. In due time, it was revealed that the Mayo Clinic mystery building housed research on drugs for the war wounded and a centrifuge to design flight gear for pilots undergoing "G stress blackouts" (due to gravitational forces).

Robert was born in Rochester, Minnesota, and is a graduate of the University of Minnesota. His full time working career, following his service in the Navy, was with American Telephone and Telegraph Company subsidiaries and Headquarters in New York City as a financial and planning executive. Mid-career education included a Senior Management program at Dartmouth College. In semi-retirement he served as an Independent Trustee and Board Chair of the Audit Committee of the First Investors Funds Family in New York City.

An FBI Adventure

John Witherspoon

PRIOR TO THE outbreak of World War II, J. Edgar Hoover and the Federal Bureau of Investigation (FBI) had established a reputation as the world's leading crime prevention organization. It was apparent that the war would give it further opportunities—like catching spies and saboteurs.

Mr. Hoover, as a way of preventing the horde of applicants for the Bureau, claimed to require a law or an accounting degree, although the draft forced him to accept men who were otherwise qualified. I had a law degree and a wife who was not anxious to see me march off overseas, and with the urging of two friends who were already FBI agents; I applied and was accepted by the Bureau.

The stories we were told about the capture of desperate criminals were exciting but, as it turned out, not all of us had such experiences. My most exciting adventure in my four and a half years as an agent took place in Schenectady where I was what was known as the resident agent and responsible for investigating all federal crimes in that area.

A young lady had reported to the FBI that she had been attacked and transported over the Pennsylvania border for immoral purposes by a young man whom she named, and she described the automobile in which the crime had occurred. The sister of the alleged kidnapper lived in Schenectady and it was my job to interview her to see if she could tell me where the suspect was. I went to her house and as I approached I saw, in front of the house, a car that exactly fit the description of the subject's car. Trained detective that I was, it occurred to me that the subject might be in that very house.

My training had also taught me never to arrest anyone by myself. I had developed good relations with the Schenectady police and I went to their headquarters, described the situation and recruited a police detective to back me up. Together we went back to the sister's house.

The sister, who looked like a good housewife, answered my knock. When I identified my companion and myself as law enforcement officers and asked for the whereabouts of the subject, the sister said she didn't know. In my best detective manner I pointed out that the subject's car was parked in front of the house and this made me suspect that the subject might be right there. She absorbed this information, hesitated momentarily, and motioned us into the house. She took us through the house to the kitchen and nodded toward the stairs, which led down into the cellar.

You could not see down into the cellar because after four steps down there was a landing and the stairs turned at a right angle. It was apparent that someone would have to lead the way down those stairs into the presence of the kidnapper, and it was my case, and that someone was obviously I. I loosened my jacket so I could get at my revolver, and backed all the way by the Schenectady detective, started down the stairs.

We reached the bottom of the stairs without incident, and faced an empty cellar. The subject's name was very similar to that of a prominent singer of the time and in my firmest voice I said I was the FBI and instructed the singer to come out. From behind the furnace appeared a handsome young man who was obviously more scared than I was.

We had no trouble taking him to the police station and getting his side of the story. He said that he and the young lady had dated, had intimate relations, and that she had gone to Scranton, Pennsylvania, with him willingly. They spent two or three nights there, got into an argument and she left for home. Her accusation was an attempt to get even with him.

My job done, I left the young man to the tender mercies of the Schenectady police who, I later found out, had taken the subject to court where the judge dismissed the case, telling the young man to go back to Baltimore to his wife and child.

I went about my business after submitting my report to Washington, happy in the knowledge that my exciting adventure would give Mr. Hoover one more statistic of FBI success.

Born in Wilkinsburg, Pennsylvania, John was educated at Choate and Harvard in history and literature, receiving his LLB in 1940. A widower, he worked at the Governor Dummer Academy as Director of Admissions and at the Anna Jacques Hospital in Newburyport, Massachusetts. He served on the Rowley, Massachusetts, Planning Board.

Living Abroad

The War From Down-Under

Nancy W. Alcock-Hood

WHEN AUSTRALIA joined with Great Britain and France in declaring war on Germany on September 3, 1939, I was nearing the end of my second of five years in High School in Launceston, Tasmania. When the war ended with the surrender of Japan on August 14, 1945, it was my third year of University at the University of Tasmania in Hobart. During this entire period there was food rationing, petrol rationing, and many items such as automobile tyres almost non-replaceable. Unforgettable times were events such as regular drills of students in school to proceed to trenches, which had been dug in the adjacent Royal Park, in preparation in case of air raids.

Boys my own age enlisted early in the Royal Australian Army Corps, the Royal Australian Air Force, or the Royal Australian Navy. Many units were sent to Europe, North Africa, and initially to other overseas locations.

My eldest brother who had been active in the Light Horse Regiment in Tasmania—analogous to a branch of the Army Reserve—joined the Royal Australian Air Force (RAAF) in August 1940 and was posted to Air Training Schools in Victoria and South Australia. He trained as a bomber pilot on Lockheed Hudson aircraft and was attached to Squadron 13. About the same time my sister, the second oldest of my siblings, joined the Women's Auxiliary Air Force and was also posted to Victoria.

We were very much aware of the war in Europe. Our main source of news was a battery-operated radio, our rural area had no electricity up to that time. In January 1941 Australian Army Regiments, together with British, won the battle in Tobruk, North Africa. We were informed of the Battle of Britain and the Dam Busters air raids by a British Squadron on three major German dams. German air raids on English Cathedrals were particularly disturbing. Destruction of Coventry Cathedral on 14 November 1940 and some 4,000 homes in the vicinity really hit home. Australians contributed CARE packages especially to British families in England throughout the entire war.

On 19 November 1941 we were shocked to hear that HMAS *Sydney*, a light cruiser, had been sunk in the Indian Ocean off the West Australian coast, with loss of all of the 645 hands. The German auxiliary cruiser, *Kormoran*, and the *Sydney* were engaged in battle and the circumstances remain controversial.

At least seventy crewmembers of the *Kormoran* were lost. The survivors were taken prisoner and were subsequently able to give some details of the sinking of the *Sydney*. The resting place of the *Sydney* was not located until 2008. Among the Australians who were lost, one was a close relative. All 645 who drowned are remembered at the Australian War Memorial in Canberra.

The sinking of HMAS *Sydney* was soon followed by Pearl Harbor, 7 December 1941. The United States and Britain declared war on Japan. In the meantime, my brother had been commissioned to Darwin, in the Northern Territory. He was a bomber pilot flying a Lockheed Hudson aircraft, attached to Squadron 13. His service number was 408056, which has been foremost in my memory to this day. Although he corresponded regularly with members of the family, we were not aware of his activities and the fact that he was in Darwin at the time of bombings. On 1 October 1942, he flew on a reconnaissance mission over the Timor Sea. His plane failed to return, and he with the crewmembers was reported missing. No evidence of their plight has been reported.

Just a month later, 6 November 1942, my second oldest brother who had been in the Army reserve, joined the RAAF and was subsequently posted to New Guinea, where he served as ground crew until discharge on 4 April 1946.

The indeterminate fate of my brother and his crew weighed heavily on my mother. Even until her death in 1980 she examined photographs of groups of Australians published in newspapers, hoping to identify him. Several members of his squadron wrote to her during the months that followed his ill-fated flight. It was assumed that his plane was shot down and the Air Force ultimately pronounced his death.

Many American servicemen spent leave in Tasmania and I remember the streets being overrun with Americans in white sailor's outfits or khaki uniforms. Some conflicts occurred since Australia had a policy by which no colored immigrants were permitted. It was only later that I was aware that the African Americans were assigned to outlying areas and not big cities.

It was considered that Australians were somewhat complacent, especially during the early years of the war. In view of the lack of reporting of events for security reasons this is understandable. In retrospect we were unaware that there had been sixty-four bombing raids on Darwin from 19 February 1942. There had been more than one raid on Leamonth and Broome in Western Australia, and Horne Island and Townsville in Queensland. Submarines were active in the vicinity of Sydney and a number of Australian ships had been sunk or attacked.

It is not surprising that during the jubilations expressed around the world on VE Day, Australians were demoralized. It was two months later that the first atomic bomb was dropped on Hiroshima. Shocking as this was, it gave hope of the impending end of the Pacific war, which occurred on 14 August in Australia. Then was the time for very rowdy celebrations.

Nancy earned her Bachelor of Science in her native Tasmania, and her PhD from the University of London in 1960. After two years back in Australia as a Research Fellow, she joined the Sloan-Kettering Cancer Center in New York as a research associate, remaining there for 20 years. She then accepted a Professorship at the University of Texas Medical Branch in Galveston, Texas. She still serves there as an Ad-

junct Professor, returning to Galveston periodically. She has won numerous honors and awards, including Fellow of the New York Academy of Medicine and Distinguished Scientist of the Association for Women in Science. In 2007 Nancy married RiverWoods fellow resident Dr. Henry Hood. Together they have enjoyed traveling, including a few returns to Tasmania.

Leaving Home

CONSTANCE BAKSYS

I WAS BORN and raised in Lithuania, the southernmost of the Baltic countries, bordered by Germany, Russia, and the Baltic Sea, which became a crossroads of combat during the Second World War. I had finished my studies of history and literature at this time. I chose not to teach because of the political implications and therefore danger not only to myself but also to my family.

The war in Europe started in 1939; Hitler's armies occupied one country after another. In the fall of 1939 the Russian Red Army established military bases in Lithuania, and in June of 1940 invaded and occupied the country because Russia needed an ice-free harbor. The American Congress never recognized the Russian takeover of the Baltic countries and their loss of sovereignty. However, our lives were changed immediately.

The Russian Communist occupiers took control of every aspect of life, nationalizing all industry, commerce, agriculture, and education. Food products, grain silos, and agricultural produce were seized to supply the Red Army. Ration cards for food were distributed to Lithuanians only when they voted in predetermined elections, in which voters were given a list of Communist candidates. An armed soldier inspected the ballot before it was placed in the box, and then stamped the voter's identification papers, thus allowing the individual to obtain a ration card. Rationing was established for living space as well. A prescribed square footage was allowed per person, and if that amount was exceeded, then Russians or others would be brought in to share the quarters.

In schools, indoctrination into the Communist ideology and the idolization of Stalin were mandatory. History books were rewritten and the study of Russian was required. Civilians, students, and children were arrested and placed in prisons as political enemies. A fifteen-year-old boy, with whose family we were well acquainted, threw a picture of Stalin through a school window. He was sent to prison and despite his mother's entreaties, was never returned to her. People suddenly disappeared during the night, and entire families went missing.

Massive deportations to Siberia started one year after the Soviet occupation. June 13, 1941, was a night of horror in the Baltics, which we remember even today. From one in the morning till three a.m., Soviet trucks went door-to-door waking people with any civic, political, or educational background, forcing them to dress immediately, and then taking them to rail stations. Tens of thousands were taken. Men—fathers, brothers, husbands—were separated from their families and put in separate livestock cars which were nailed shut for the duration of the two week trip to Siberia. Women and children, as well as women taken from hospitals with their newborn infants, were also taken in livestock cars with standing room only. When people asked where they were being taken, the response was, "You will see."

In Siberia women and children were placed to labor in state farms; men were sent further north to gulags or hard labor camps. During the day they harvested lumber and at night some of them endured torture. This was the fate of my brother, who was separated from his wife and four-year-old daughter. After these massive deportations commenced, people were afraid to sleep in their own homes and spent the nights changing locations, even sleeping in fields. As Lithuanians were forcibly removed, Russians took over their homes and possessions.

On June 22, 1941, only a week after that "Night of Horror", the Soviets were planning to seize people as they left church services. The Germans, however, launched a surprise *blitzkrieg*, bombing Russian planes, tanks, and installations, and invading Lithuania. The Soviet plans were found and disclosed, as they made a hasty retreat to Russia. I found that my parents' names had been on the list of those next to go.

We lived for three years under German occupation. At this time the persecution of the Jews began. My mother, who had recently been widowed, sheltered and hid a young Jewish boy. It was at great peril to herself and her children, as all would be arrested and sent to concentration camps if found out. We were warned by a Lithuanian police officer that our house was about to be searched, and my mother found another shelter for him. This boy survived and eventually made his way to Israel. As an adult he found my mother, to thank her and let her know he had planted a tree in Israel in gratitude for her kindness and courage.

When America entered the war and the Germans started to retreat, we were in the path of two fronts. Daily we heard the sound of gunfire and bombs exploding, and it was not uncommon to see an aerial dogfight overhead. Immediately upon nightfall we darkened all lights and shut the windows with black shades, as was mandatory. To see the targets for bombing, the Russians would illuminate the skies with floodlights attached to parachutes.

On October 13, 1944, we received orders from the Germans to leave our homes and leave Lithuania. Those of us who were fortunate enough to catch the last train crossing the border arrived in Vienna. Those who were traveling by vehicles were subjected to gunfire from Russian planes as the Russians reinvaded Lithuania. On our first night in Vienna, we slept on the floor of the train station. Continuous daytime air raid alarms sounded as Allied planes flew out. But we were happy to see them, feeling that the Americans were our liberators and we would soon be able to return to Lithuania. Night bombing continued in Vienna; we dressed for bed in our winter coats knowing that several times during the night we would be required to rise immediately and seek out a bomb shelter. As the Russians approached Austria, Allied planes dropped leaflets urging residents not to fear the Russians but to welcome them. However, we knew that being Lithuanian refugees, if we were captured by the Russian army we would be sent directly to labor camps. After great bureaucratic hurdles we were able to flee to the Bavarian Alps.

The war ended while we were in the Bavarian Alps. Germany was divided into four zones, Russian, French, English, and American. The United Nations (UN) founded camps for refugees and displaced persons (DP), the difference being that displaced persons had been forced to leave their homes and country. Being already in Bavaria, we traveled to nearby Munich, which was within the American zone. Once established in the DP camp for Baltic nations, the United Nations Relief and Rehabilitation Administration program employed me.

A memorable day was when General Eisenhower visited us. We greeted him with a welcoming reception and reiterated our desire to return to Lithuania. As a result of the Yalta Treaty forged by Roosevelt, Churchill, and Stalin, Lithuania, a previously independent country, was given as a war appeasement to the USSR. For us, returning to a Communist Russian-occupied Lithuania would mean automatic deportation to Siberia. Eisenhower replied that he could not start another war now, but that we would not be forgotten. This was a strong blow to our hopes of returning home. Soon after, the UN initiated emigration proceedings. We felt very dismayed that we were so close to our true homes and yet would have to cross an ocean to find another home. Because we were in the American Zone, our choices were Australia, South America, or North America.

Epilogue
After approximately three years of submitting applications, written and verbal, as well as health and ideological screenings, we were allowed to emigrate to the United States. With $10 given by Catholic Charities, we left in debt to the US for the $800 passage. The day I arrived, after a tumultuous eleven-day ocean passage, I sought and found employment paying minimum wage. Language was a barrier, which prevented me from finding work that would utilize my education. We were happy and relieved to be on US shores after the terror of war, but to quote Maria von Trapp, "*A refugee has lost his*

country, his friends, his earthly belongings. He is a stranger, he feels misunderstood…He is a full-grown tree in the dangerous process of being transplanted, with the chance of not being able to take root in a new soil…." As in Austria and Bavaria, we found many generous, caring, and welcoming people in the US who helped us start our new lives. That year we applied for US citizenship and five years later we obtained it—a citizenship of which I am very proud. We were glad to have become a part of this country. God bless America, land that I love, still the best country.

Born in Lithuania, Constance attended its University. Her education helped her in finding employment in a postwar world. She met her Lithuanian husband, Casimir, at the DP camp where he was the resident leader. A relative sponsored the family's emigration, (husband, mother, and youngest brother). She and her husband found work the day after arrival, but not in their field. Citizenship was required for accountants. Her husband worked for the Ford Co. and she with Faberge. They retired to Florida and after the death of her husband Constance moved to Exeter to be near her two daughters.

Seeking Safety

SHEILA HULL

SEPTEMBER 1940—the war had been going on for a year and for the last few months I had spent many nights under the dining table, which is where you went if you didn't have an air raid shelter in your back yard. In the first year the Germans were concentrating on the northeast coast where the coal and shipping were.

The British government was sending children overseas to get them out of danger. At this point everyone thought the war would be over in six months. Much to my mother's chagrin my father decided it would be a good idea to get me to a safer place. The choices were Canada, United States, or Australia. He thought the war might move to the East so Australia was no good. The United States was full of foreigners so I could not possibly go there—so Canada it was.

So many ships were sunk in crossing that the plan was halted. Suddenly we got a telegram saying I was to go to Glasgow in two days. No time to think what was happening to me, at the age of fourteen, I was on my way. Some of the ships in my convoy were sunk so the plan was ended after I got to Canada. Sailing up the St. Lawrence River to Montreal in mid-September I thought I had entered a new world and indeed I had. The colours were so beautiful I will never forget my first glimpse of Canada.

My new home was in Hamilton, Ontario, with a couple that had an eleven-year-old adopted daughter. To me it was a very strange sleeping arrangement; the wife slept with the daughter in one room, the husband on a couch in another, and I had a room to myself. I was very unhappy and wanted to go home. My Dad spoke to me over a radio program and persuaded me to stay until spring when the crossing would be better.

High school was a real change. In England boys and girls had separate schools and never the twain would meet. Here there were football games and dances—what fun. School was a place to have fun and do some studying. Most families had a phone and cars and the houses were centrally heated, an exciting world for me.

The couple I was living with was grossly overweight and went on an orange juice diet every weekend. Of course this didn't do much good because they gorged all week but it was very hard on me. I was so hungry one night that I sneaked downstairs and stole a piece of bread. They accused me of stealing money so in tears I went to the Children's Aid Society (they were in charge of my welfare) and explained I didn't steal money, only a piece of bread.

They acted quickly and changed me to another home where there were two daughters, one my age and the other two years younger. What a joy. They were so good to me until I graduated from high school and wanted to go to college. Why, they said, would a female go to college? She is only going to get married. So off I went again. I moved to the YWCA and worked my way through the local college. Summer vacations were long, from the beginning of May till mid-September. The first summer I worked at a factory that made Sten guns for the army. I learned to run a turret lathe machine and by working thirteen-hour shifts, six days a week I was able to make enough to almost pay my way for a year.

While in school I worked weekends in various stores to keep the bank account positive. The next summer I tested sand for molds in a steel foundry. I can still remember what a beautiful sight it was when the molten steel was poured into the sand molds. Needless to say in these jobs I met a very different type of person. I learned to be very tolerant.

My college years went by fast. I had promised my parents that I would go home for a year when college was finished. This was not easy because by this time I was engaged to a Canadian. But I went home, shivering through the winter with only a coal fireplace for heat. I had a hard time getting a job because the British did not think much of a Canadian degree, but finally got a job at the University of Durham (England) in a chemistry lab. The year finally ended and I went back to Canada to marry a guy I had dated from the age of fifteen. I felt very fortunate that I had been able to go to college and had fallen in love with Canada and later the United States where there are lots of foreigners like myself.

After the war Sheila moved to Hamilton, Ontario, where she finished secondary school and earned an MS degree in 1946 at McMaster University. After moving to the US she married Bob Hull in 1973; they had four children. Sheila taught computer programming and later, math and science at Exeter Junior High. She was a docent at the University of New Hampshire Art Department, and also volunteered as a teacher of swimming to handicapped individuals. Sadly, Sheila died in a car accident in 2010.

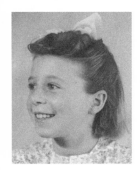

Antwerp Sirens

IRENE HYLAND
As told to Margo Harvey

WHEEEE-OOOOH-WHEEEE-OOOOH-WHEEEE-OOOOH...THE SIRENS. That is the first thing I remember when I think of my childhood. I was ten years old when the war began in the spring of 1940 when the Germans invaded my country, Belgium. People were fleeing, mostly south to France, but the Germans caught up with them and took Paris two weeks later. My parents and I hid in the cellar of our home in a suburb of Antwerp. My father was an architect. He had foreseen that the Germans were going to come. He reinforced the cellar and stocked it with water and all kinds of food on shelves that he built. He did a good job. We mostly lived and slept down there during the bombardments and the occupation. My father was called to serve in the Belgian Army, but he came home after five days because he couldn't find his unit!

I think I was lucky to be ten years old, because I was old enough to remember and to understand at least partly what was happening, and young enough to feel safe with my parents. I was the only child in my family. Every day I walked to school. There were school busses and streetcars, and many kids rode bicycles, but I chose to walk. It was a French speaking school. French is my first language and I also speak Flemish, of course.

There were Jewish kids in school, who had to wear yellow stars on their sleeve. One by one, they stopped coming; we never knew what happened to them. Later I went to a different, private French school. That school actually looked for kids in the Jewish quarter and sneaked them out, brought them into the school and hid them, taking away their yellow stars. Every day we were given milk to drink and an orange to eat, which we were not allowed to take home to share with our parents. People like us who were fairly well off could buy food "under the table", i.e., in the black market, but poorer people often went hungry. The Germans took almost all the food.

During the occupation there wasn't much work for my father in architecture, so he rented a big piece of property, built seven tennis courts on it and created a tennis club, which he managed. We were a big tennis family. At the courts my father gave private tennis lessons that many people were happy to get, and pay for. Every Saturday night there would be a dance at the Tennis Club, where people would dance to records of English and American dance tunes. But one night some Nazi soldiers came in and smashed all the records—they wanted us to dance to German tunes!

Toward the end of the war the bombs were falling from Allied planes, in the fight to retake Europe from the Nazis. Just outside of Antwerp was the huge Gevaert film factory that made all kinds of film, photo and x-ray and art films and so on. The Germans had taken the factory to use for their own military purposes, and the Allies wanted to destroy it. An Allied bombing raid came in one night to bomb the factory, but they missed their target and destroyed a whole suburb. Two thousand people died that night. There was a rumor that the American pilots were drunk, but that probably wasn't true. There were the most enormous black headlines in the paper the next day—I shall never forget that. Among those killed was a dear friend of mine, a girl a little older who had gone to help the injured. They bombed, and she died.

We were very lucky that our house was not looted and not much damaged during the war. My father had buried our good things— the silver and jewelry—in a box that he buried in a secret place. All the windows were boarded up with wood on the outside, like most everyone else's. The only damage we found inside was a hole in a very beautiful portrait of my great-grandmother as a young woman, a painting life-size and about one hundred fifty years old. The hole had apparently been torn by a piece of shrapnel that we found on the floor. It's amazing that it penetrated the wood and the glass of the window with such force. I kept the piece of shrapnel for many years. I am very sorry that I lost it. The painting is now with my daughter in Belgium. We shall never have the hole repaired; we want it there as a reminder of what happened.

I don't remember much about the end of the war. If there were big celebrations in town, my father probably wouldn't let me go. I was only fourteen, which was still a child in Belgium. What I remember most is the sirens–wheeee-ooooh-wheeee-ooooh–I shall always have that sound in my ears.

Irene was born in Antwerp, Belgium, where she attended the College of Maria Jose. She worked as secretary to a diamond merchant for a number of years before becoming a certified tennis teacher and opening her own tennis school. She has three daughters from a previous marriage. Irene met Kerwin, her present husband, when he was in Belgium on a Fulbright Grant. They married nineteen years later, and lived in Rhode Island until her husband's retirement when they moved to Exeter.

From The Other Side

GISELA NITKA
As told to Margo Harvey

IN WORLD WAR I, I was just a kid: I was born in 1911. We lived in Berlin. I was one of six children, four brothers and two sisters. Our father was a physicist, he worked in a government research institute and I think he had something to do with instruments for submarines. I remember—this is ridiculous—he once came home with his fingernails all silver; he'd dipped them in quicksilver! That's all I remember, that's what children do remember. Oh, but I remember the face of my father when the war ended. That was something terrible.

My husband Heinz was also a physicist, *summa cum laude* from the University of Heidelberg, a fraternity brother and colleague of my father; he used to come to our house, and that's how we met. We were married in 1933. Heinz was working in image making, x-rays, and the like. We were horrified when the Nazi government came in. My father had a nervous breakdown, was in a sanatorium. But scientists are not politicians!

By the time the war started, we had three children and I was busy taking care of them, seeing that they got enough to eat. The rationing was very severe, we ate mostly potatoes and turnips and things like that; we were very lean living. Heinz was in the Air Force; he slept mostly at his office.

My brother got into the war and ended up in Siberia. The Russians neglected the camp; I think it was not evil intentions but just sloppiness. They were all starving. So my brother decided to walk out! He walked all the way across Russia back to Berlin; the only trouble was that he had no clothing but the uniform he was wearing, which gave him away. However, in Russia no one bothered him, but once he got to Germany, that was difficult. He found, or stole, something brown to wear. But when he got home, he was so starved that his mother didn't recognize him.

After the war ended we moved to England where Heinz already had a job. The English wanted the German scientists to work for them; they were all invited. It was really like a concentration camp, though it didn't look like one. Many of the projects the men worked on were German inventions, like synthetic rubber. In the end, Heinz was Director of Research and Development for what was originally a German company that was seized by the British. We lived for three years in England, then Heinz was offered a job in the United States and we moved here.

Gisela was born in Germany and grew up in Berlin. Although she wanted to go to medical school, her father gave preference for higher education to her four brothers. The war broke out when she was a young mother of three; during those years she cared also for a number of nieces and nephews from more threatened areas, struggling to feed them all on the potatoes, onions, and beets which were the only foods to be found outside of the costly black market. She became an expert dressmaker and tailor, making all the children's coats and other clothing. After the war, in England and the United States, she entertained lavishly for her prominent physicist husband, did fine embroidery, and volunteered in libraries. Gisela died in 2010.

Post War Service

The Marshall Plan – Paris

Bart Harvey

IN 1949 I WAS at the Littauer School at Harvard struggling to write a doctoral dissertation for a degree in Political Economy and Government. In the early spring an official from the American regional office in Paris of the European Recovery Program came to Harvard recruiting junior economists for work in that office. I had been one of five who worked the previous year on a student project to design such a program, and the prospect was attractive. As I recall our design bore considerable resemblance to what turned out to be the actual one. Fortunately, Margo, my wife, was up for it. We had two small children and a third due in May. So I signed up, but negotiated a September departure date in the foolish hope that I could finish the thesis during the summer. I never went back to it.

At the end of August I had a two-week orientation at the Economic Cooperation Administration (ECA) headquarters in Washington, DC. During my absence Margo sold the house, packed us up for the trip, arranged for shipment of our stuff to Paris, and gave the dog to the renters downstairs.

We departed from Boston at noon in a TWA Constellation, one of those lean, mean-looking four-motor propeller planes. We landed for refueling in Gander, Newfoundland, in a snowstorm. The plane had less than a dozen passengers, including the five Harveys, the youngest of whom was in a basket. The stewardesses, with nothing else to do, took very good care of us, plying us with, among other things, champagne. Our two-year old daughter, who had never had such good gingerale, celebrated briefly up and down the aisle, and then slept through the night. Fortunately we had strong tail winds and were able to skip the scheduled stop at Shannon.

We were met at the airport by a good friend, wife of a Littauer colleague, who had preceded us by several months and had found and rented us a house! It was a very French villa in a big garden in Ris Orangis, a suburban village south of Orly Airport.

I could commute by train or car for the 20-30 minute trip to Paris. Our office was in the Hotel Talleyrand on a corner of the Place de la Concorde. Most of the interior had been converted into offices by temporary walls, but the conference room and some of the directors' offices retained their eighteenth century splendor of carved and frescoed ceilings and walls. My assignment was as an assistant (read bag carrier, cable screener, report drafter, occasional sub-committee attendee) for the Director of the Program Division. The Program Division worked with the Committee of European Economic Cooperation (CEEC), the group established in response to the American call for Europeans to assemble their economic statistics, define their needs, and reach agreement on the amount and division of needed assistance.

It is often forgotten that the Soviets and East Europeans were included in Marshall's invitation. They came to the first meeting in Paris in the summer of 1947. When they saw the scope of information and collaboration required, the Russians pulled out and pulled the East Europeans with them.

For those that remained it was a pioneering effort. Never before had they been privy to each other's detailed figures on production, consumption, import, and export. Never before had they faced the problem of assessing their own and their neighbors' needs on the basis of commonly accepted economic criteria. Working with them meant coaxing and coaching, reporting progress and problems to ECA/Washington, and American urgings to the Europeans. We served as part of the chain of communication and compromise between the Europeans, who saw the US as naive and immensely wealthy, and the Europeans who wanted as much as they could get with as little modification of their traditional ways as possible, and the US Congress that was impatient and unclear as to the problems and wanted a reborn Europe at minimal cost.

The basic mechanism of the European Recovery Program was

quite simple and suited to the circumstances of the time. The critical shortage in the European economies was foreign exchange. They had plenty of human and institutional resources and lots of money, indeed too much in most cases. But their money was not convertible, i.e., no good for buying anything from another country. They had sold their gold during and right after the war, mostly to the US to buy survival. Without imported materials, parts, and replacement machines, their factories could produce few exports. What little foreign exchange they had was tightly controlled. A businessman could buy abroad only with an import license.

Our program fitted into the picture at that point. Following the discussions on needs in the countries and in Paris, ECA would sign an agreement with each country as to how many dollars it could have that year and what kinds and amounts of things they could be used for. Supply and transportation limitations were almost always acute considerations, not just financing. The country's Ministry of Finance and/or Trade would then issue import licenses with those allocations to country importers who would proceed to make regular commercial deals with the American exporter. The importer paid as usual, but his check instead of being converted into foreign exchange in the central bank to go to the exporter, was deposited in a special "counterpart" account. The exporter received as his payment a voucher with which his bank would credit his account and charge the ECA account at the Treasury.

It was an intriguing system in which neither the Europeans nor we ever saw a dollar, only the imports that the dollars bought and which the European users paid their own money for. Then there were the special counterpart accounts in the local currency. Five percent of these were siphoned off for US administrative expenses in the country, duly charged to our administrative appropriations.

The rest was used for investments within the country by agreement between the US Country Mission and whoever in the government had a say in such things. Uses varied greatly: the French had ambitious plans for expansion of coal and steel production that absorbed most of the counterpart there. The Italian Minister of Transport had simply gone ahead and rebuilt the rail system in 1946-7 regardless of his lack of money. Most of the counterpart there went to liquidate those debts. The British had imported heavily from India on credit during the war. Most of UK counterpart went to liquidate national debt, enabling them to repay the Indians. A problem in all countries was how to use these large sums without causing further inflation and yet still have something to show, since the principal evidence to local consumers of US aid was the sign on the counterpart-financed investments. The dockworkers and textile mills saw the ECA shield on arriving bales of cotton, but the European housewives paid hard cash for the resulting shirts and sheets, which bore no such sign.

The official languages of the Committee of European Economic Cooperation were French and English. Most of the Europeans could use either, but many were more comfortable in French, to my great discomfort, the flow being quite beyond my high school learning. Sometimes I could catch the drift, other times a more fluent colleague would clue me in. But it remained a struggle. Papers, fortunately, came out in both languages. Even when they didn't, I could struggle through written French at my own pace better than the oral one at the speaker's rate.

One of the more intriguing moments of the months in Paris was when a young member of the Turkish delegation asked if I would help him with editing a program presentation they had to make. As I was to discover in a later incarnation, Turkish is not an Indo-European language, and English is very difficult for Turks, and vice versa. It was quite a struggle, involving asking at numerous points just what were they trying say, but I think I helped them.

A happy occasion was our first, full-blown diplomatic dinner at the residence of the head of the Danish delegation. We were not used to cocktails before dinner, a different wine with each course at dinner, followed by cognac with coffee and whiskey and water later in the evening. However, we survived, and I don't think we disgraced ourselves. I became quite fond of the Norwegian and Danish delegates, and was constantly intrigued by the contrast in approach to problems between the pragmatic British and equally arrogant, principle-driven French. The Germans had a well-accepted observer group there, but their aid was a function of the military occupation and not part of CEEC or ECA business.

There was a lively crew of fellow juniors and not so juniors in the office who delighted in venturing forth, especially after a rather stiff official reception, in a group of fifteen or twenty to some favorite little hole-in-the-wall restaurant for dinner. This invariably took the rest of the evening. We thought the delay was because the chef sent his boy out to obtain the wherewithal to cook whatever we had chosen from the long, complex menu. The result was always delicious, the wine good, and the conversation better. We knew we were involved in a great and good enterprise, and morale was high. Indeed, to me the Marshall Plan, Truman's Point Four, and the Peace Corps rank as the three really fine American contributions in the twentieth century.

Bart returned from the Philippines to enroll at Harvard, where he earned a Master's in International Relations and a Master of Public Administration. Before completing his doctoral dissertation, he was tempted by a job offer with the Marshall Plan in Paris. With his wife Margo and four kids in tow, he served with the Economic Recovery Program there, in The Hague, and in Rome. After an interval in Washington, he was posted to Ankara, Turkey, and finally, as Director of the AID mission to Kabul, Afghanistan. Ensuing years were spent working with non-government agencies for economic development in the Third World. In retirement, Bart took up painting. Bart died in 2010.

Contributors

Adams, Brad
Alcock-Hood, Nancy W.
Alexander, Judd
Alling, Charles
Aplin, Peggy
Baksys, Constance
Bassett, Don
Bates, Gail O.
Bates, Robert H.
Berkowitz, Esther
Bingham, Robert Carol
Blumenthal, Mac
Boyle, Joe
Brown, Joan
Collier, Betty
Darlington, Joan
Dixon, George
Doyle, Lewis Kelvin
Dunseith, Herman
Ferguson, Bill
Fullerton, John H.
Gustavson, Bob
Gutmann, Frank
Hampton, Harry
Harvey, Bart
Hood MD, Henry
Hull, Sheila
Hyland, Kerwin
Hyland, Irene
Irwin, Carl
Ivanowsky, Betty
Jervis, Fred
Kintner, Alice
Kintner, Ed
Latchis, Jean
Lauenstein, Helen
Lauenstein, Milt

Lovell, Connie Brown
Manghue, Ruth
March, Richard P.
Martin, Spencer
McCarthy, Joe
Merritt, Dick
Mixter, Phebe Perry
Murray, John
Nickerson, Wes
Nitka, Gisela
Parrella, Lucy Grover
Prince, Allan
Remien, Arthur
Richardson, Stephen
Ritter, Jerry
Schaeberle, Bob
Scharff, Monty
Sharpe, Marian Smith
Shealor, Bob
Smallwood, Bill
Southworth, Katherine Hobson
Southworth, Robert A.
Spang, Bob
Spiers, Ron
Taylor, Jack
Taylor, Nancy
Tenny, Frank
Trulson, Barbara
Wade, Robert C.
Warlick, Louis
Warner, David
Watson, Janet
Wentworth, Marilyn Lindberg
Wentworth, Robert F.
Wicklein, John
Willits, Robin D.
Witherspoon, John
Woodward, Maddie

Index